50.00

ECONOMIC INTEGRATION IN NAFTA AND THE EU

Economic Integration in NAFTA and the EU

Deficient Institutionality

Edited by

Kirsten Appendini
Senior Officer
United Nations Food and Agriculture Organization
Rome, Italy

and

Sven Bislev
Associate Professor
Copenhagen Business School
Denmark

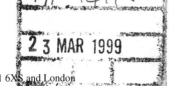

First published in Great Britain 1999 by
MACMILLAN PRESS LTD
Houndmills, Basingstoke, Hampshire RG21 6XS and London
Companies and representatives throughout the world

A catalogue record for this book is available from the British Library.

ISBN 0–333–73319–3

First published in the United States of America 1999 by
ST. MARTIN'S PRESS, INC.,
Scholarly and Reference Division,
175 Fifth Avenue, New York, N.Y. 10010

ISBN 0–312–21864–8

Library of Congress Cataloging-in-Publication Data
Economic integration in NAFTA and the EU : deficient institutionality
/ edited by Kirsten Appendini, Sven Bislev.
p.   cm.
Papers presented at a workshop held in March 1997 near Copenhagen.
Includes bibliographical references and index.
ISBN 0–312–21864–8 (cloth)
1. United States—Economic policy—1993——Congresses.   2. Canada–
–Economic policy—1991——Congresses.   3. Mexico—Economic
policy—1982——Congresses.   4. European Union countries—Economic
policy—Congresses.   5. North America—Economic integration–
–Congresses.   6. Europe—Economic integration—Congresses.
I. Appendini, Kirsten A. de.   II. Bislev, Sven.
HC106.82.E27   1999
337.1—dc21   98–38453
                                                                  CIP

This book is printed on paper suitable for recycling and made from fully managed and
sustained forest sources.

10   9   8   7   6   5   4   3   2   1
08   07   06   05   04   03   02   01   00   99

Printed and bound in Great Britain by Antony Rowe Ltd, Chippenham, Wiltshire

Contents

vi   *Contents*

Preface

This book is a product of a workshop on 'Unequal Integration', held near Copenhagen in March 1997, assembling a group of scholars from Mexico, USA, Denmark and Great Britain. This event grew out of the association between Kirsten Appendini, then still professor at El Colegio de Mexico, and the Department of Intercultural Communication and Management at the Copenhagen Business School. We felt that the international agendas of our departments were sufficiently interrelated to deserve a collaborative research effort. Both were engaged in research on internationalization, also in the form of regional integration. The other term defining the workshop, inequality – in and between states – is a growing problem in a world where the protective powers of the states dwindle with the oppressive ones.

Exploring the interface between inequality and integration is not a mainstream approach. Gathering a group of scholars concerned with those items took some searching among friends and colleagues, but the group finally put together turned out to be highly productive, both in terms of a good atmosphere at the workshop and in terms of good and timely papers. Only a selection, and a thoroughly edited one, of those papers have been included in the present volume. In the end, it turned out that the most promising perspective when discussing the interrelation between inequality and integration, is *economic institutions*. By implication, the analysis of the problems of both the North American Free Trade Agreement (NAFTA) and the European Union (EU) is most convincingly expressed as a critique of the institutions developed to implement the ideas of economic integration behind those projects. It also turned out that the papers on NAFTA were generally the more interesting ones, probably because NAFTA is still so new and less thoroughly analyzed than the EU. Therefore, a majority of the papers are on NAFTA.

The editors wish to express their gratitude to the participants of the workshop, also those whose papers we felt were outside the theme of our book. And we thank the Copenhagen Business School, both the President and the Department of Intercultural Communication and Management (DICM), for sponsoring and co-funding the workshop as well as the editing of the book. The workshop was supported by a grant from the Danish Social Science Research Council. Kevin McGovern, research assistant and assistant professor at the DICM, provided highly qualified editorial assistance. Jane Rossen provided efficient, friendly and reliable secretarial assistance.

Rome   KIRSTEN APPENDINI
Copenhagen   SVEN BISLEV

List of Abbreviations

APEC	Asia Pacific Economic Cooperation
ASEAN	Association of South-East Asian Nations
ASEM	Asia Europe Meetings
CEC	Commission of the European Communities
CECA	Canadian Environmental Law Association
CETES	Certificados de la Tesoreria
CJM	Coalition for Justice in the Maquiladoras
CNC	National Peasant Confederation
CTM	Confederación Mexicana de Trabajadores
CUFTA	Canada-US Free Trade Agreement
DICM	Department of Intercultural Communication and Management (Copenhagen Business School)
ENGO	Environmental Non-Government Organization
EU	European Union
ECJ	European Court of Justice
EFTA	European Free Trade Association
EZNL	Zapatista National Liberation Army
FAT	Frente Auténtico del Trabajo
FTA	Free Trade Agreement
FTAA	Free Trade Area of the Americas
GATT	General Agreement on Tariffs and Trade
GPT	General Preferential Tariff
GSP	Generalized System of Preferences
IATTC	Inter-American Tropical Tuna Commission
IBWC	International Boundary and Water Commission
IGC	Intergovernmental Conference
INEGI	Instituto Nacional de Estadistica Geografia e Informatica
IPR	Intellectual Property Rights
ISI	Import Substitution Industrialization
LAFTA	Latin American Free Trade Area
LCAB	Labour Conciliation and Arbitration Board
Mercosur	Mercado Comun del Sur
NAALC	North American Agreement on Labour Cooperation
NAEEC	North American Agreement on Environmental Cooperation
NAFTA	North American Free Trade Agreement
NAO	National Administration Office

NGO	Non-Governmental Organization
NIPA	National Income and Product Accounts
OAS	Organization of American States
ODA	Official Development Assistance
OECD	Organization for Economic Cooperation and Development
PAN	Partido Acción Nacional
PEAT	Programa Elemental de Asistencia Tecnica
PIF	Programa de Industrialización Fronteriza
PRI	Partido Revolucionario Institucional
PROCAMPO	Programa para del Campo
PROCEDE	Programa de Certificación de Derechos Ejidales y Titulación de Solares Urbanos
PROMOCAM	Programa de Modernización del Campo
PRONASOL	Programa Nacional de Solidaridad
SAA	Statement of Administrative Action
SEA	Single European Act
SHCP	Secretaria de Hacienda y Credito Publico
SMS	Standard Related Measure
SPS	Sanitary or Phytosanitary Measure
TEU	Treaty of European Union
TNC	Transnational Corporation
UAM	Universidad Autonoma Metropolitana
UE	United Electrical (worker's union)
UNORCA	Unión Nacional de Organizaciones Regionales Campesinos
WPSP	White Paper on Social Policy
WTO	World Trade Organization

Notes on the Contributors

Susana Borrás-Alomar is a political scientist and Assistant Professor in the social sciences department, Roskilde University. Her research interests are centred on the European Union as a political system and on industrial and innovation policies.

Kirsten Appendini was a Professor of Economics at the Colegio de Mexico, specializing in Mexican agriculture. She has recently joined the Division of Rural Development at the United Nations Food and Agriculture Organization in Rome.

Sven Bislev is a political scientist and Associate Professor in the department of intercultural communication and management at Copenhagen Business School. His research is on European welfare states, public–private sector relations, and regional integration.

Maria Elena Cardero is a Professor in the graduate studies department of the Economics Faculty at the Mexican National University. She teaches international economics and trade, and is now studying the effects of trade liberalization on female employment.

Etelberto Ortiz Cruz is an economist and Professor of Economics at the Universidad Autonoma Metropolitana-Xochimilco. Current research is on the theory of competition and structural change, basically in the Mexican economy.

Bodil Damgaard holds a position as researcher/Professor in the Latin American Faculty of Social Science (Facultad Latinoamericana de Ciencias Sociales, FLACSO-México). Labour and globalization are her main research topics.

Edmé Domínguez Reyes is a political scientist working at the Ibero-American Institute at the University of Gothenburg, Sweden. Her research is on Eastern Europe, women studies, and the regional consequences of NAFTA.

Raúl Garcia-Barrios is a researcher at the Centro de Investigacion y Docencia Economicos, in Mexico City, specializing in Mexican peasants and agriculture.

Ricardo Grinspun is Associate Professor of Economics and Director of the Centre for Research on Latin America and the Caribbean (CERLAC) at York University, Toronto. His research focuses on the interdisciplinary aspects of economic integration, regionalization and globalization.

Hans Krause Hansen is Assistant Professor of Spanish Language and Culture in the department of intercultural communication and management, Copenhagen Business School. His PhD was on Mexican corruption and discourse analysis.

Robert Kreklewich is a PhD candidate in social and political thought, York University, Toronto. His research is mainly on international labour standards and social dumping and comparative political economy of trade regimes.

Sima Motamen-Samarian is a Senior Lecturer in Economics and Finance at the University of Westminster. Her research is mainly on economies of emerging markets, and her current research is on NAFTA and its impact on the Mexican economy.

Morten Ougaard is Senior Associate Professor of International Politics and Economics in the department of intercultural communication and management, Copenhagen Business School. He has written on American foreign economic policy and international political economy.

Dorte Salskov-Iversen is Associate Professor of English Language and Culture in the department of intercultural communication and management, Copenhagen Business School. She has written on discourse analysis, British public sector reform, European integration, and labour market issues.

Blanca Torres is a Professor at the Centre for International Studies at El Colegio de Mexico. She has written several books and articles on US–Mexican relations.

Pekka Valtonen is researcher in the department of sociology and social psychology at the University of Tampere, Finland. He has specialized on the structural changes in the Mexican agrarian sector.

1 Introduction

Sven Bislev

This is a book on the problems of *constructing institutions* to handle the processes of economic integration in Northern America and Western Europe. The term *'deficient institutionality'* as the sub-title signals that our papers share a critical attitude to the results of institutional construction; the schemes for economic integration build institutions that influence market behaviour, but generally fail to adequately address the socio-political issues.

Institution-wise, the two integration projects are very different: The European Community is very much a creature of Europe in the 1960s; its purpose is political (security), its form is legalistic (a Treaty, with a Court to uphold it) and the states are the main actors in the institutional set-up. By contrast, the North American Free Trade Agreement (NAFTA) is a late 1980s' project: an exclusively economic purpose, and a minimalist, litigational co-ordination mechanism where initiatives are left to private actors.

European integration is a synoptic and holistic effort: the ambition has been to handle as many of the effects and preconditions of economic integration as possible. North American integration is anarchic and atomistic: economics is a science, and economic gains are objective. Everything else will have to adapt to the changes flowing from economic progress. Nonetheless, both are examples of macroscopic social engineering – the change-oriented tinkering with structures, institutions and trajectories that encompass whole societies and millions of peoples' lives.

'Societal engineering' on this scale involves several problems: instruments that are blunt and extremely complex; future scenarios which are vulnerable to a large number of unpredictable factors; immovable social structures and historical trajectories that form behaviour, shape expectations and limit opportunities. The European and North American projects both suffer from unpredictable futures and contradictory structures, when trying to change the economic situation. But they have chosen different instruments and different strategies of institutionalization, as illustrated above; accordingly, they are confronting dissimilar symptoms of their deficient institutionalities.

The present volume contains a number of critical analyses of both the aims of the integration projects, the instruments chosen, and the influence of history and culture. NAFTA is criticized for being under-institutionalized, ignoring the social and political problems created by a massive market opening. It is also criticized for being biased towards the interests and forms of the larger, dominant participant. The EU may be over-institutionalized in the sense that it influences almost everything, and produces binding regulations in a vast number of areas; but at the same time it has an underdeveloped political institutionality, being unable to implement and monitor its multitudinous initiatives. And in a number of areas, economic integration efforts have proven themselves inconsistent and insufficient.

This introduction proceeds by relating the two integration projects to theories of integration – both economic and political. After that, the papers in the volume are briefly presented.

ECONOMIC INTEGRATION AND INSTITUTION-BUILDING

In both economic and political theories of integration, the problem of institutional development seems to have been underevaluated. Institutions for the formation of integrated markets, or for the building of political communities, have been assumed to either spontaneously arise or to be a legal–technical problem of passing suitable laws and regulations.

In economic theory, institutions have been important as definitions of the action-world in which economic agents operate. Two different perspectives have been applied, however – 'classical' institutionalism and 'new' institutionalism. In the classical version, institutions are socially-given, and they constitute the frameworks for the individuals' actions. In the 'new' version, institutions are still frameworks for action, but they are conventions dependent upon the individuals' consent (Hodgson, 1994).

Most theorization about economic integration operates, explicitly or implicitly, in the neo-institutionalist universe: institutions follow the pattern of individual preferences as evidenced in the processes of exchange. If new trends emerge, institutions will adapt. The basic theorem of economic integration theories is the theory of comparative advantage, developed into theories about the international division of labour. Such theories assume that specialization and division of labour entail cost-reductions because production processes will move to locations where costs are lower (because of lower factor prices, more efficient technologies and so on). Combined with the assumption of advantages of scale coming from the growth of markets, consumers should be able to reap increased benefits from larger supplies at lower prices. There may be delays and imbalances in the process towards rational allocations and equilibriae. But if institutions are in the way of rationality and optimality, they should either be reenginered by professionals, or one may assume that demands for better institutions will bring them about.

Economists have analysed the distribution of actual or potential consumer benefits among different groups – regional distribution, social distribution, or distribution among factors of production – but the existence of a positive sum of benefits has seldom been doubted. Some economic analysis outside the mainstream questions those assumptions, explicitly or implicitly: in cases of radical *inequality* it is entirely possible that integration means exploitation. That is not only a tenet of 'structuralist' or Marxist analysis: also in classical-institutional terms the argument is possible that if a country with a weak development of institutions and infrastructure is integrated with a country whose market institutions are strong and efficient, the weak country may lose out altogether, and the assumption of net positive benefit becomes entirely theoretical.

As witnessed by some of the papers in this volume, this is quite obvious in the Mexican peasant sector and in Mexican agriculture more generally: Mexican peasants were caught up in a web of state agencies both for marketing their outputs as well as for buying their inputs, and private markets of many main crops were interlinked with state agencies. When the state withdraws, peasants and farmers in many regions face imperfect and segmented markets.

These problems are compounded by politico-institutional factors: Mexican peasants are 'liberated' from a corporate state, in the process losing their identity as members of the local community that was reconstructed by agrarian reform, often on the basis of 'traditional' communities (Chapters 3 and 5, this volume). The institutions supporting their livelihood disappear – both the institutions for agricultural support, and the integrated politico-administrative structures. Though former institutions were far from efficient, not to say just or fair, and there was much to be gained from reforming them, there was also much to be lost by abolishing them. In their place, a liberal-democratic public sector, complete with political and administrative components, is supposed to appear. But it doesn't: the construction of a democracy, the institution of civil rights and effective political processes, the formation of a professional public bureaucracy is a slow and painful process. Contrary to neo-institutionalist perceptions, the supply of market institutions is not something that occurs via market mechanisms. If for no other reason, then because market mechanisms do not begin to exist without those institutions. And market institutions are part of the political collectivity whose transformation is a matter both of bargaining and interpretation – of the negotiation of interests and the transformation of cultures.

Manufacturers face a similar situation. Mexican industry has been resting on a system of protection, subsidy, corporatist labour relations and special privileges. A very inefficient system in terms of creating internationally-competitive businesses, but a system that fulfilled a number of functions in the context of Mexican society. Opening up for North American investment and abolishing subsidy and protection means discarding large chunks of the inefficient, bloated, public and semi-public sector. But it also means scrapping several necessary public functions and removing the conditions of existence for many firms. Access to American markets is a potential gold-mine – but so think all the others, and the resulting cut-throat competition makes the gigantic American consumer and producer markets some of the most difficult in the world to operate in. The skills and resources needed for the exploitation of the huge US and Canadian markets are not available in any great measure in Mexican business life.

Also for Canadian business, the exposure to American competition is a threat as much as an opportunity precisely because of the institutional form given to the NAFTA agreement. Under the agreement, any protection of industrial and service markets is illegal – meaning that many Canadian traditions of public provision are becoming outlawed, undermining the traditional co-operation between the public and private sectors in Canada. And the way to challenge such market protection is through private litigation – a US national businesses sport.

For the larger enterprises as for the small, often family-based enterprises, economic problems are compounded by political and social factors: in Mexico, the gradual elimination of protected jobs means the termination of traditional forms of social protection. The construction of new forms is a huge job for a frail and overloaded politico-administrative system. The decline of the dominant party and the monopolistic trade unions eliminates the traditional source of influence – however inefficient and corrupt – for workers' interests. The cuts in the public sector discard both bloated public corporations and necessary public services. And in the first instance, the new shortage of funds has increased corruption instead of diminishing it.

In the US, despite the exceptions and special clauses written into and onto NAFTA, US workers feel the effect of free trade without social protection: in those few sectors where a significant outsourcing to Mexico happens, a lack of social protection is felt. And in other areas, an increased inflow of illegals from the starving Mexican countryside may be the result of an agreement that sanctifies free trade and neglects its social and political effects.

The European integration project is running much according to the famous progression sketched by Bela Balassa (1975) – from free trade area to economic union, through a progression of stages where political and economic factors demand more integration to reap an increasing amount of economic benefits. But the birth of the European Community took place in a context where due consideration was given to political and social factors. Only in the 1980s, after the development of integration had been stifled for a while (by accumulated differences of interests and an exhaustion of the first integrationist resources), did neo-liberalism take hold of EC thinking.

Building on national traditions of rather extensive regulation, however, it is often claimed that there is no lack of economic regulation and social protection in Europe. The European Union, however, is a strange creature: it is assuming state and supra-state functions, and in many ways dominating the legislative, regulative and economic policy agenda. But it is still politically ineffectual, tiny in terms of fiscal strength, and with a less than minimal administrative apparatus. EU policies are regularly flaunted by national governments when it is in their national interest to do so (Greece on Turkey and Macedonia, France on nuclear testing, Germany on Yugoslavia) or when large sums of money are involved (British beef, French and German industrial subsidies). Fiscally seen, the EU spends only 2 per cent of the members' GNP, and regulates directly (through price fixing for farming and fishing products) another couple of per cent. And, administratively, the 'bureaucrats in Brussels' number only around 0.02 per cent of the total labour force in the countries included – as against the 10–30 per cent found in the member states. The result is that European policies are open to national circumvention, to fraud, and to inefficient implementation.

This demonstrates the huge problems involved in transforming existing institutions from constructions that care for national needs and interests, into adequate frameworks for free trade and factor movements. The national institutions are not technically neutral arrangements functioning according to an anonymous logic; they are invested with national culture – values and concepts – and build on national historical trajectories that reflect the accumulated substance of centuries of political conflict and compromise. To 'neutralize' or 'Europeanize' the nationally-specific logic, and to give over the right of initiative and decision to a supranational community, is a task exhibiting the extreme complexities of national governance and involving all the most conflict-prone cleavages of the national polity.

POLITICAL INTEGRATION AND INSTITUTION-BUILDING

Just as for theories of economic integration, the European Union has been the model also of theories of political integration (Haas, 1961), and several mechanisms have been suggested for its development:

- *'Federalism'*, one of the integration-theoretical schools, sees 'European' integration as driven by *political ideas and ambitions*, with community-building efforts on a supranational scale. That is not really a 'mechanism', but (unlike the ones to follow) federalist theory suggests a model for the development of governmental institutions.
- So-called *'functionalism'* suggests that a *logic of macro-societal development* leads to integration, via the need for co-operation in the performance of public functions. When the scale of production grows, and technology and trade become internationalized, some policy areas are better served by international co-operation.
- *'Neo-functionalism'* adds a third mechanism, that of *élite formation, socialization and integration*: as functional needs arise, the ones to address them are the élites that participate in international co-operation and that have become accustomed to and engaged in the development of such.
- A fourth school, *'transactionalism'*, sees the *increase in international contacts* as the source of integration – the means of transport and communication making it possible for still more people to develop still more positive feelings towards other peoples.
- Finally, in *'intergovernmentalism'*, *rational, interest-based bargaining* is the supposed mechanism: governments bargain over their interests and reach compromises that reflect their resources, perspectives and strategies.

European integration has been driven by all these forces: a federalist
movement during and right after the Second World War, a functional
need to co-ordinate the production of iron and coal, the formation of a
Europeanized élite, the growth of transactions among European countries, and countless hours of scheming and arguing over the accommodation of national interests. As a consequence, no theory can
explain the process of European integration – much less the institutional form of integration. The EU has elements of a federal structure,
but is emphatically not a federal state (it has, for example, no constitution). But neither is it a mere technical shell around functional co-
operation – all the European treaties express themselves on values and
ideas and political goals in the co-operative effort.

European integration has been institutionalized as a highly original
mixture of state structures and intergovernmental organization – and
developed in the direction of state-ness. From the outset, the European Court of Justice (ECJ) could be interpreted as equivalent to an
international arbitration court; but it has developed in the direction of
a supra-Supreme Court with direct jurisdiction over EU citizens
(Stone, 1996). The European Assembly, a get-to-know-each-other
sort of body, developed into a directly elected parliament. The High
Authority/European Commission, planned as a functionally limited
body to attend to the specific areas of concrete co-operation arrangements, developed into a Central Administration, busy with the planning of policy developments in practically every field imaginable. And
on top of the specialized Councils of Ministers, a European Council
has developed embodying the will to find political solutions and
advance integration.

Still, the state character of the Union is far from complete. It lacks a
constitution, a set of binding principles or a consistent ideology – as
distinct from the more declaratory and separate sets of principles in
the Treaties. From the large repertoire among European states, the
Union has not been able to choose one model of institutionalizing
government (Page, 1995; Schmitter, 1996a & b; Caporaso, 1996).
Despite the advanced development in the fields of agriculture and
trade, a common policy in the social field has tended towards a lowest
common denominator (Streeck, 1996). Positive integration has proven
hard to achieve given the national agendas of the governments per-
forming the top-level decision-making in the Council (Scharpf, 1996).
Corporatism remains embryonic and fragile, meaning that workers'
interests are weakly present in Bruxelles, compared to the armies of
business lobbyists (Schmitter and Streeck, 1992; Andersen and

Eliassen, 1993; 1996). Environmental and consumer concerns are hard
pressed to compete with the better represented and more efficiently
institutionalized interests of agriculture, industry and business.

Besides being an unfinished democracy (because of the lack of
balance in interest representation and the weakly institutionalized
political-communicative rights), the EU is also sometimes pictured as
a potentially dissolving entity – the centrifugal forces unleashed by the
partial taming of the nation-state are making themselves felt in frequent assertions of regional autonomy. Nothing dramatic has hap-
pened yet, but there is a definite trend towards stronger national
autonomy in several member nations (Marks, 1996; Amin and Tomaney, 1995). And the present conception of the community is too weak,
institutionally and ideologically, to provide a new formula for the
cohabitation of state and region.

Those Eurocentric theories of political integration (Hurrell, 1995
pp. 332ff; Archer, 1992 p. 99) provide little guidance towards understanding **North American integration**. NAFTA, firstly, is not built
upon any federalist ideology or movement. Despite federalism being
an American invention, it has not been extended to the regionalist
project in North America. Functionalism is also redundant, because no
functional co-operation schemes were or are particular to the NAFTA
participants (as different from only two of them, or other groupings of
American states). Thus, the idea of neo-functional élite integration is
irrelevant. Transactionalist and interdependence theories are more
relevant – the level of transactions is high in the border regions
between the southern US and Mexico (Lowenthal, 1987; Lowenthal
and Burgess (eds), 1993). Also in the north, US–Canadian linkages are
tight along the border, involving many of the crucial American industries.

Hurrell (1995, p. 358) and Inglehart, Nevitte and Basanez (1996, pp.
151ff, 166) suggest a division of labour between the two broad groups
of political integration theories: theories of national interests and
rational bargaining may explain how nations are thrown together in
the first place. Theories about the development of functional co-
operation, of mutual links, identities and understandings may then
take over and explain from there the dynamics of integrational evolution. Such an eclectic stage theory has the advantage of exploiting all
the theoretical possibilities, but in the case of NAFTA it may be overly
permissive: it still remains to be seen how far functionalist logic and
the formation of common values and identities will reach in the development of integration. Inglehart, Nevitte and Basanez (1996) find

some 'value convergence' (that is, increasingly similar responses to value-oriented survey questions) between the US, Canada and Mexico, and argue that it will lead to more integrative attitudes. But whether it does, and whether policies will be shaped by those attitudes, are still open questions.

Previous analyses of the development of North American integration tend to see it in the light of (especially US) foreign policy objectives and rationales – applying the approach of intergovernmentalism or neo-realism. Surely, the background of NAFTA was the convergence of economic policy and international trade strategies that took place among the three governments in the 1980s (Barry, 1995). But while such theories adequately describe a lot of limited and short-term processes, the larger picture of societal structures and cultures evades them. And they provide little room for non-governmental players, a factor of considerable importance in both the establishment and the running of the EU (Pierson, 1996) as well as the NAFTA. The perspectives suggested or implied in our papers (see below) are, for example, to see the three participating countries in terms of their economic structures and resources; their negotiating abilities; their differences in national and cultural backgrounds; and their situations in the world political and economic systems.

THE PAPERS

After this Introduction, Part I addresses the fundamental problems of economic institutions in a situation of market-based internationalization: three papers discuss the construction of regional projects, analyzing the deficiencies and biases of their institutions. Grinspun and Kreklewich, from whom we have borrowed the sub-title of the book, suggest in Chapter 2 the term 'deficient institutionality' for the organization of NAFTA, and characterize NAFTA as a set of economic institutions which have proved efficient when it comes to preserving a neo-liberal, export-oriented economic model, protecting the interests of large firms, but sadly deficient with regard to sustaining social progress. Garcia-Barrios, in Chapter 3, discusses the significance of economic institutions on a micro level: the market-oriented reforms of Mexican peasant agriculture were implemented by professionals that saw themselves as operating under an objective behavioural logic, which did not need to be adapted to concrete historical circumstances. The results were that markets did not – and do not – function, and that the integration of Mexico into NAFTA has produced rural dissolution, misery and poverty. Conceptions of justice and efficiency, essential parts of any moral order and necessary building blocks of institutions, are different as between traditional local communities and modern states. If the newly created institutions are incompatible with the ones that regulate local communities, social dissolution is bound to follow.

Ougaard's Chapter 4 deals with the general trend towards institutionalizing international economic integration, both globally and regionally. Both the NAFTA and the EU are situated in a growing web of such integration schemes being both partners in international co-operation and instances of the trend towards regional integration. Ougaard argues that instead of building neo-mercantilist regional fortresses, both schemes follow the norm of 'open regionalism', furthering the aim of liberal economic relations on a global level. NAFTA, however, hesitates to go beyond liberalism: the social side-effects of economic liberalization are not addressed. The EU may be the only model of a regional integration scheme which attempts to deal with those issues – and also an instance of the inherent difficulties in doing that.

Part II contains five papers discussing the political institutions necessary to establish the economic integration projects. The first three papers are on NAFTA: Hansen and Appendini, in Chapter 5, analyse the social and political insertion of Mexican peasants in the liberal reform process. The post-1917 PRI (Partido Revolucionario Institucional) state was closely connected, symbolically and politically, to communal property in agriculture, *ejido*, and all that it implied. The present process of liberalization purports to construct a new social and cultural identity – the rational and free-market-oriented peasant. But identity construction on the symbolic level must fit lived experience to make sense and take root in the social fabric. Otherwise, separate universes of meaning in the different social spheres – government, markets, politics, production and morality – fail to connect, disabling the development of societal integration. In this area, too, NAFTA plays the role of strengthening the liberalized elements, and because of the way NAFTA is construed, of preventing institutional innovation that might ease the transformation between the old and the new.

In Chapter 6, Damgaard Pedersen investigates the labour unions in the free-zone (*maquiladora*) Mexican electronics industry, and the attempts at establishing cross-border co-operation with US unions. Trade liberalization has exposed Mexican workers to direct competition with US capital, and in the process the traditional protection of

Mexican workers has been removed. The institutions peculiar to the PRI state, of one-party state-led corporatism, were neither efficient nor democratic. But when they do not exist, as in the maquiladoras, workers are vulnerable to harsh management tactics. Some US unions, feeling the competition from low-wage production in Mexico, have taken a few initiatives to start trade union co-operation, but found it difficult to locate suitable partners.

Environmental problems – pollution and resource exploitation – constitute another transboundary issue. A special side agreement to NAFTA, the North American Agreement on Environmental Co-operation (NAEEC), was entered into on US insistence to establish procedures for the handling of environmental problems. In Chapter 7, Torres looks at this agreement, focusing on Mexico's unwillingness towards including environmental provisions in the co-operation. For Mexico, the costs of establishing and applying strict environmental standards may appear prohibitively high, given the structural differences between a third-world economy and two of the world's most advanced economies. And the possibility of using environmental standards to protect US producer interests is very open. The positive effects of the NAEEC have been agenda-setting: new or strengthened contacts between environmentally interested organizations in the three nations, and extra publicity around the problematic spots.

Two papers focus on the EU: A solemn pledge to improve the standard of living of Europe's less privileged strata and regions constitutes an integrated part of the EU's political project. Bislev and Salskov-Iversen, in Chapter 8, explore the EU Commission's efforts to strike a balance between market enhancement and social solidarity, which brings it close to advocating a welfare state despite the peculiar absence of such commitments in the institutional history of the EU. The contradictory nature of the situation is found reflected in the wording of Commission documents regarding the 'social dimension'.

In Chapter 9, Borrás-Alomar discusses the process of modernization in the European periphery, specifically Spain, in its relation with the European integration process. The formation of a democratic identity and construction of democratic institutions in Spain have been deeply influenced by its insertion in the European Communities. The developmental gulf between North and South in Europe is less than that between Mexico and its northern neighbours. Besides, the EU has attacked the problem with an array of 'cohesion' and 'structural' policies, enabling a positive interaction of integration and convergence, different from the hegemonic situation in NAFTA.

The four papers in Part III deal with US hegemony in North American integration – its sources, mechanisms and consequences. For many years the USA did not experience any necessity of building alliances with its immediate neighbours. It was a global player with a multilateral approach to foreign economic policy, and in relation to its neighbours it was safer to rely upon hegemony than on any formalized scheme that entailed concessionary accommodations to good neighbourliness. The increased contacts with Canada and Mexico, and the liberalization efforts in both countries (most dramatic in Mexico), however, made formalized relations relevant (Barry, 1995; Inglehart, Nevitte and Basanez, 1996). In Chapter 10, Dominguez looks at the different identities of the three nations involved in NAFTA. Those identities are developed through quite distinct historical trajectories, often in opposition to each other, and considerable barriers exist to the formation of a common regional identity. Identity-forming processes may be initiated from above (through NAFTA institutions) or from below (through civil society), but the questions of distribution and power involved in the integration project question the possibility of successful integration.

Valtonen, in Chapter 11, sketches the overall predicament of the neighbours of the USA, analyzing their possibilities of establishing alternative relations to balance the overwhelming power of the US. In Chapter 12, Cardero examines the asymmetric nature of the NAFTA agreement. The way integration and liberalization are defined corresponds to the interests of the stronger partners – the USA and the large corporations. Both in questions of trade liberalization, of regulation of competition, and of the protection of property rights, more concessions are given to US interests than to the other participants. Ortiz Cruz and Motamen-Samadian, in Chapter 13, show how a new dualistic structure is developing in the Mexican economy. The liberal policies introduced before NAFTA did not overcome the structural problems of import dependence in the modern sectors and isolation of the traditional ones. The traditional direct subsidization of domestic production was replaced by exchange rate manipulations. The result was that productivity did not grow quickly enough in the modern sectors, and financial liberalization only added to the risks associated with international exposure in an unstable situation. Worst of all, however, a dualism is continuing to develop even inside the modern sector: between an internationally-integrated part that is unstable and does not generate employment; and a domestically-oriented part which generates employment but is not developing international competitiveness. NAFTA integration did little to change that situation: instead of overcoming dualism, it may have deepened the problem.

The two different integration projects with their divergent histories, structures and ideologies are difficult to compare. An all too obvious temptation is to take qualities that the analyst feels are missing in his 'own' project, and to ascribe them to the 'other' project. That temptation is not always resisted: critical NAFTA researchers have been overly optimistic about the significance of EU articles on the social dimension and subsidiarity. EU economists, on their side, have seen the simplicity of NAFTA's institutional framework as a smart solution to the burdensome bureaucracy of Brussels. In all analyses of supranational integration, moreover, there is a difficult choice of perspective – between national agendas and international ones. Is the neo-liberal agenda of NAFTA an expression of US hegemony, or is it a reflection of a global trend reflected through the structures of the three participating nations? Is the European Union governed from 'Brussels', or is it a power game between nation-states? Those perspectives occupy the minds of many researchers looking at the regional integration projects. The present volume tries to add some additional flesh to the bones of 'integration theory'. Whether such a theoretical creature really exists or not is a matter of contention, but there is an undisputed need for a wide range of further analyses of international integration.

References

Amin, A. and Tomaney, J. (eds) (1995) *Behind the Myth of European Union* (London: Routledge).
Andersen, S.S. and Eliassen, K.A. (eds) (1993) *Making Policy in Europe* (London: Sage).
Andersen, S.S. and Eliassen, K.A. (eds) (1996) *The European Union: How Democratic Is It?* (London: Sage).
Archer, C. (1992) *International Organizations* (London: Routledge).
Balassa, B. (1975) *European Economic Integration* (Amsterdam: North-Holland).
Barry, D. (1995) 'The Road to NAFTA', in D. Barry (ed.) *Toward A North American Community?* (Boulder: Westview Press), pp. 3–14.
Caporaso, J. (1996) 'The European Union and Models of State', *Journal of Common Market Studies*, vol. 34, no. 1, March 96, pp. 29–52.
Haas, E.B. (1961) 'International Integration. The European and the Universal Process', *International Organization* vol. XV, no. 4 (Autumn 1961), pp. 93–130.
Hayward, J. and Page, G. (eds) *Governing the New Europe* (Cambridge: Polity Press).

Hodgson, G. (1994) 'The Return of Institutional Economics', in N. Smelser and R. Swedberg (eds), *Economic Sociology* (London: Sage), pp. 58–76.
Hurrell, A. (1995) 'Explaining the Resurgence of Regionalism in World Politics', *Review of International Studies*, vol. 21, pp. 331–58.
Inglehart, R., Nevitte N. and Basanez, M. (1996) *The North American Trajectory* (N.Y.: Aldine de Gruyter).
Lowenthal, A.F. and Burgess, R. (eds) (1993) *The California – Mexico Connection* (Stanford University Press).
Marks, G. (1996) 'Competencies, Cracks and Conflicts: Regional Mobilization in the European Union', in Marks *et al.*, *op. cit.*
Marks, G. Schmitter, P. Schapf, W. and Streck, W. (1996) *Governance in the European Union* (London: Sage).
Page, G. (1995) 'Patterns and Diversity in European State Development', in J. Hayward and Page (eds), *op. cit.*
Pierson, P. (1996) 'The Path to European Integration', *Comparative Political Studies*, vol. 29(2), April, pp. 123–63.
Scharpf, W. (1996) 'Negative and Positive Integration in the Political Economy of European Welfare States', in Marks *et al.*, *op. cit.*
Schmitter, P.C. (1996a) 'Examining the Present Euro-Polity with the Help of Past Theories', in Marks *et al.*, *op. cit.*
Schmitter, P.C. (1996b) 'Imagining the Future of the Euro-Polity with the Help of New Concepts', in G. Marks *et al.*, *op. cit.*
Schmitter, P.C. and Streeck, W. (1991) 'From National Corporatism to Transnational Pluralism: Organized interests in the Single European Market', in *Politics and Society*, vol. 19, no. 2, June 1991, pp. 133–64.
Stone, A. (1996) 'Constructing a Supranational Constitution: Dispute Resolution and Governance in the European Community' Working Paper, *European University Institute*, 1996.
Streeck, W. (1996) 'Neo-Voluntarism: A New European Social Policy Regime?', in G. Marks *et al.*, *op. cit.*

Part I
Economic Institutions and Internationalization

2 Institutions, Power Relations and Unequal Integration in the Americas: NAFTA as Deficient Institutionality

Ricardo Grinspun and Robert Kreklewich[1]

INTRODUCTION

At the Summit of the Americas in Miami, December 1994, the heads of 34 nations in the western hemisphere, led by President Clinton, committed themselves to establishing a Free Trade Area of the Americas (FTAA) by the year 2005. They reconvened in Santiago, Chile, in early 1998 to formally launch the FTAA negotiations. According to the documents signed by the leaders, this massive integration effort will herald a new era of equity, growth and sustainable development. Whether it will actually do so may be questioned by looking at the experience of NAFTA, which has led the integration process in the Americas and has been seen as a model for integration.

Can one reconcile current efforts towards economic integration with the goals of human sustainable development (UNDP, 1992)? If so, how? One must first move beyond narrow economic analysis to reconceptualize what trade agreements are, and what they mean, from a more critical perspective; that is, one that does not isolate economic variables from the larger societal context, one that does not ignore the distribution of power, wealth and income alongside efficiency gains, comparative advantage and economies of scale, and which envisions alternative models of economics and society to those put forth by proponents of neoliberalism.

An ample body of research already exists promoting the benefits, as well as cautioning about the challenges, of growing economic

17

integration in the western hemisphere (Hufbauer and Schott, 1994). It is largely a 'functional' analysis – functional for neoliberal-minded governments, business lobbyists, and the intellectual representatives of other dominant groups. It structures policy-making in a way that addresses their narrow interests. The debate on economic and trade-related costs and benefits of hemispheric integration obscures other crucial aspects of integration, such as its institutional form and its distributional and social impacts. Ultimately, it is the latter which determine whether integration is sustainable, either socially or environmentally.

The institutionality of the North American Free Trade Agreement (NAFTA) is seriously deficient. This conclusion assumes a broad, critical meaning to 'institutionality', as explained below. We argue that NAFTA will detrimentally impact on social indicators throughout North America. It poses serious questions relating to the region's economic, social and environmental sustainability as integration proceeds. Moreover, the models used in NAFTA have global relevance. The model applied in the World Trade Organization (WTO) for intellectual property rights is, for example, similar in its thrust to the one in NAFTA.

Let us be clear: we do not question the potential benefits of international trade or economic integration. Integration of subregional, regional and continental economies is proceeding quite rapidly, concomitant with a broader process of globalization wrought by a complex matrix of developments at the level of world order, the nation-state and production (Cox, 1987). The primary issue is *how* to integrate or, more specifically, what form of institutionality are we putting in place to achieve integration. We cannot answer the latter without critically inquiring as to *how* these processes are shaped at the local, national and global scales. In particular, we are deeply concerned about integration serving, and being shaped by, dominant groups for their narrow interests, rather than being democratically-instituted and amenable to the broader human needs of current and future generations.

We must look forward in our thinking. In the case of Latin America one cannot go back to protected, closed economies. Rather, we need to mobilize social forces in local, national and international arenas to question – and change – the institutionality of integration currently in place. To assist in this critical effort we provide a conceptual taxonomy of the institutionality of integration. It focuses on critical aspects of the institutional form of integration to better deconstruct the issues raised above. More importantly, it challenges us to think about alternative ways to integrate domestic economies and design international linkages.

We proceed as follows. We first focus on the institutionality of integration and address the salient aspects of its institutional form; we then canvass the deficient institutionality of NAFTA and its resulting implications. In subsequent sections we review a key area of institutionality that is having a global impact, as in the case of intellectual property rights.

THE INSTITUTIONALITY OF INTEGRATION

Definitions

The focus of this paper is institutions, and particularly the institutional frameworks in which recent trade agreements such as NAFTA and the new WTO are embedded. A dictionary of sociology defines *institution* as 'an established order comprising rule-bound and standardized behaviour patterns'. The same source defines *institutionalization* as 'the process, as well as the outcome of the process, in which social activities become regularized and routinized as stable, social-structural features' (Jary and Jary, 1991, p. 239). For our purposes, we will define *institutionality* as a set of related institutions that define a larger established order. The reason we focus on institutions is clear: it is this established order that ultimately impacts on people's lives, rather than the written word of trade agreements or the lofty promises of those who advocate for them. 'In the last analysis', as one report so aptly put it, 'it is institutions that provide people with opportunities, identity and security' (UNRISD, 1995, p. 2).

A process of *integration* 'brings together' two or more social units, thus strengthening the economic and social links, communication and exchange between them. This integration can be formalized through *agreements* among countries (generally among governments of particular countries, provinces and states), or can happen through informal mechanisms (through the actions of various social actors in those countries). In what follows we focus on *formal integration agreements*, which can take various forms: formal trade agreements such as NAFTA, formal treaties such as the Maastricht Treaty in the European Union, or formal declarations by summits of heads of state such as the declarations of Central American presidents.

We propose a conceptual taxonomy of integration. From our perspective, the most salient aspects of the institutional form (or institutional framework) of integration, embodied in any actual agreement, are the following:

1. *Scope and coverage*: here we refer to the scope and coverage of agreements that regulate the process of integration. Which aspects of integration does the agreement deal with? Which aspects does it *not* deal with? What areas of integration will be institutionalized by the agreement, and which are not? How comprehensive are the linkages between countries or regions in each area that is covered?
2. *Regulatory framework*: this is a broad category that includes the organizational structures and the substantive content of mechanisms and regulations put in place to implement and support an integration agreement. Regulatory frameworks typically include a complex matrix of five components:

   - *organizational structures*: the creation of new structures, or changes to existing organizational structures (for example, the establishment of the North American Environmental Commission in the NAFTA supplemental agreement on the environment).
   - *political and economic arrangements*: these are arrangements put in place as part of the agreement, but which are often not spelled out in the legal text itself (for example, the commitment by the Government of Canada to implement changes to the legislation regulating generic pharmaceutical drugs as part of the Canada–US Free Trade Agreement; the commitment of the Mexican government to make constitutional changes in various areas as a result of NAFTA) (Dillon, 1993).
   - *regulations and rules*: establishment of, or changes in, regulations and rules at the local, national and international levels in a variety of areas (market access, rules of origin, investment, sanitary and phytosanitary, technical standards, labour migration, intellectual property, competition policy, social programs, and so on). These rules and regulations dictate what is and what is not allowed in the new regime.
   - *enforcement mechanisms*: these are mechanisms to enforce the regulations and rules (for example, juridical norms and tribunals, dispute settlement mechanisms, political and economic pressures, 'technical' committees, coercive measures by

superpowers, 'structural adjustment' programmes by Bretton Woods institutions).

- *implementation mechanisms*: these are mechanisms that have to do with the coming into place of the new agreement. They initiate and introduce the new organizational structures, rules and regulations (for example, ratification, harmonization of domestic legislation, timetables, grand parenting clauses, transitional measures, and so forth).

3. *Agency and power relations*: agency refers to newly-created or existing local, national and international actors, formally given (or informally subsuming) roles in shaping, implementing and having ongoing access to the new regulatory framework (and thus, who stand to gain from such a framework). Power relations refers to the relationship among such actors within existing social relations of power, and the effect of the agreement on such relations of power, particularly from the vantage point of groups marginalized from the above processes.

This conceptual taxonomy of integration differs substantively from the commonplace reference to the institutionality of integration. When mainstream experts discuss the institutionality of trade agreements, they refer only to a subset of the regulatory framework as defined above. In particular, they will avoid discussing either agency and power relations, or will not delve, in general, into aspects of the coverage and regulatory framework that impinge on social and environmental impacts. Rather, they focus attention to those particular economic outcomes that are important for their constituent audiences. Thus, they will discuss issues such as customs union versus free trade area, 'positive versus negative' listing, trade creation or diversion, job gains or losses, or the negotiating sequence that leads different sub-regional groupings to come together to form a larger group. Without diminishing the importance of these issues, the need to accelerate social progress and sustainable development both in the northern and southern parts of the hemisphere entails a much broader perspective on the institutionality of integration (Grinspun and Cameron, 1993).

The taxonomy presented above is useful because it can be applied to any specific case. Here we further probe how this taxonomy can be applied to critically 'read' the institutional framework of a given agreement:

1. *Scope and coverage*: one can distinguish between areas of focal, marginal and no coverage. Is the coverage of particular areas of activity deep, comprehensive and absent of exceptions? This is the focal area of the agreement. Or, in contrast, is the coverage shallow, partial, restricted, declaratory, exhortatory and full of exceptions? This is an area of marginal treatment. And, of course, there are areas not covered by the agreement. Moreover, regarding the breadth of coverage: if the agreement has many focal areas, it is a broad agreement; and if it concentrates in a few focal areas, it is a narrow agreement.

2. *Regulatory framework*: the nature of a regulatory framework may be coercive, accommodative or non existent. Areas of focal coverage typically require a coercive regulatory framework. Such a framework has powerful organizational structures; binding political and economic arrangements, regulations and rules, as well as enforcement and implementation mechanisms; strong penalties for non-compliance; and rigid timetables for implementation, with little sensitivity to the domestic or local impact of the new regulatory framework. Its stipulations expressly supersede those in other agreements.

    Areas of marginal coverage often coexist with an accommodative regulatory framework. It has substantive terms that are declaratory, exhortatory, voluntary, lacking in meaningful action, or ridden with cumbersome or prolonged enforcement procedures (that is, no real enforcement mechanisms); weak organizational structures; flexible timetables for implementation and strong sensitivity to the domestic or local political impact of implementation; and stipulations that generally are superseded by other agreements.

    Areas not covered by the agreement do not have a formal regulatory framework. However, the emphasis is on the word *formal*. The result of actions by governments and market players in a deregulated context can create an *informal* regulatory framework that is as powerful and significant as a coercive regulatory framework. Such is the case, for example, of governments promoting exports in a context devoid of labour and environmental regulations. This creates an informal regulatory framework that promotes 'downward harmonization' of labour and environmental standards. An informal institutionality can also 'take over' areas of marginal coverage that have an accommodative regulatory framework (see item above).

3. *Agency and power relations*: when analysing a specific agreement, is the aim of the agreement to preserve, consolidate or alter existing social relations of power? If so, in favour of which social group(s)? Which social groups participated in the shaping and implementing of the agreement? Who has access or standing to procedures to enforce regulations and penalties? Which social groups were excluded or not consulted or will be marginalized as a result of the agreement's impact?

THE NARROW AND DEFICIENT INSTITUTIONALITY OF NAFTA

There is little doubt that western hemispheric integration will take institutional forms that resemble, or at least be significantly modelled after, NAFTA (Hufbauer and Schott, 1994). One reason is that the United States played a central role in shaping the NAFTA according to its hegemonic needs, and its intent is to play a similar role in the FTAA. Using the conceptual taxonomy developed above, we suggest that the most salient aspects of the institutional framework of NAFTA are as follows:

1. *Scope and coverage*: focal areas concentrated on key corporate issues, particularly market access and investment and promotion of privatization and structural adjustment, as well as strategic areas for the United States, such as energy, financial services and intel-lectual property. Marginal coverage of labour standards, labour rights, as well as environmental and social concerns. No coverage of key bilateral and trilateral issues such as drug trade, human rights and security, corruption and governability, illegal migration and political and democratic process. Thus, NAFTA has deep coverage in only a few limited areas: overall, the agreement has a very narrow scope; many key areas of limited interest to large corporate capital are under-covered or without a formal cover.

2. *Regulatory framework*: NAFTA promulgates a very sophisticated, complex and powerful regulatory framework in the areas of focal coverage. Briefly put, this includes: binding enforcement mechan-isms for trade disputes; a strong regime of investment rights, 'national treatment' rules, and intellectual property rights; expert tribunals that are undemocratic and biased towards the defence of corporate interests; and clear rules of origin. Left undefined was a

uniform code of subsidies; its absence means minimal restraint on the US ability to pursue aggressive unilateral trade actions.

The sum total of these regulations, political and economic arrangements, enforcement and implementation mechanisms, and organizational structures, is a powerful regime that protects large transnational capital, enhances US hegemony in the region, and functions as a strong conditioning framework to promote neoliberal restructuring in each country (Grinspun and Kreklewich, 1994; Ranney, 1993). In contrast, very weak regimes for labour and environmental enforcement and non-existent regimes for structural adjustment leaves minimal or no framework for socially sustainable, equitable integration. The absence of a formal institutionality creates the conditions for an informal institutionality of a negative character. One sees pressures for the downgrading of the environment as an element of international competition (Daly, 1993) and downwards harmonization of social and labour standards in North America (Grinspun, 1993).

3. *Agency and power relations*: NAFTA consolidates US hegemony in North America and preserves asymmetries of power relations among the three countries. It accentuates power imbalances between transnational capital and small domestic producers – a predictable outcome given the dominant role political and corporate élites played in shaping the agreement. The agreement consolidates neoliberal restructuring in Mexico and constituent groups with vested interests in such restructuring. It also enhances the role of trade experts and consultants, business lobbyists and technocrats. Finally, it restructures relations between state and civil society in such a way that it constrains interventions on behalf of marginalized social groups.

An institutional framework that is abundantly coercive and developed in areas that are crucial for transnational capital and US hegemony, yet, on the other hand, so bereft when it comes to protecting the interests of marginalized groups, is transparently a 'deficient institutionality'. Building the institutions of hemispheric integration on this faulty foundation will not be conducive to human sustainable development. Rather, the ongoing effort to expand and formalize this type of institutionality is contributing to acute political, economic and social tensions across the hemisphere.

In particular, the institutionality of economic integration is reinforcing a neoliberal, export-oriented economic model; a model that is

having worrying consequences for Latin American countries – growing
social costs (Devlin, 1993); growing inequalities (Altimir, 1994); rising
poverty (Feres and León, 1990); a greater degree of structural hetero-
geneity, social fragmentation and marginalization, which are barriers
to genuine democratization and social cohesion (Bano, 1993); and a
lack of sustainability of the process of change (Pastor and Wise, 1994).

The premise of this work is that there is an urgent need to reconceptualize the coverage and scope of western hemispheric integration,
re-orient its regulatory framework, and expand the range of social
groups that participate in it.

COMPARING WITH THE EUROPEAN UNION

A comparison with other integration efforts can be enlightening. In
particular we look at salient aspects of the institutional framework in
the European Union (EU). The *scope and coverage* of the EU is
broader, with a range of focal areas beyond those of immediate interest to transnational and large corporate capital, including: migration;
labour mobility; social policy; labour standards and social dumping;
agriculture and supply management; structural adjustment assistance
for low-standard and under-developed southern European countries.
More marginal, but still significant coverage of political and democratic processes (for example the European Parliament); juridical
processes (for example the European Court of Justice); as well as
expanding coverage to nascent areas pertaining to co-ordination of
fiscal policies, monetary union and foreign affairs.

In terms of its *regulatory framework*, the EU – in the aftermath of the
Single European Act (SEA) and the Maastricht Treaty – has moved
closer in the direction of a federalism of European states (though this
creates tensions with the principle of subsidiarity). The Maastricht
Treaty also initiated processes to address social and democratic deficits
in the aftermath of regional liberalization and the promulgation of a
European-wide market in the SEA. Legislative and executive authority
is centralized in the European Commission and Council of Ministers.[2]
There is a strong role for the European Court of Justice (ECJ) to
enforce compliance of member states with EU obligations; relatively
broad standing to the ECJ is available (in contrast to most expert
tribunals of NAFTA), depending on the subject matter at hand. The
European Parliament's traditional consultative and advisory role has
been expanded by the Maastricht Treaty to include greater legislative

powers via the principle of co-operation in select matters (mainly social policy and research) and co-decision procedures which increase Parliament's scope to propose amendments to both the Commission and Council (for example in areas such as environmental protection, education, public health, consumer protection and free movement of workers). The legal status of the Social Charter remains uncertain: legally enforceable rights and obligations or declaratory, general constitutional norms to supplement interpretation of EU directives and regulations? There has been limited success thus far in implementing directives pursuant to the Charter – weak or non-existent regimes for EU-wide collective bargaining, minimum wages, or right-to-strike – but these may yet evolve from the limited, though important, steps taken in the Works Council Directive to promulgate companywide, consultative and information-sharing mechanisms between management and employees' representatives in larger-sized, transnational corporations in Europe.

As regards *agency and power relations*, there is an accentuation of power between transnational, large, corporate capital and small domestic producers and labour (established or not), but this is less acute than in the North American context. Also a contrast is that market liberalization is proceeding with limited, though important, steps taken to preserve the concept of a social market across Europe, and by extending linkages for civil society supranationally and promulgating countervailing forces to the strict logic of market forces.[3] Possibilities are now emerging for an institutionalization of a genuine 'social dialogue' between major social partners at the European level, with impetus from the Social Chapter of the Maastricht Treaty. This treaty may yet bring forth new dynamics in labour and social policy (Bercusson, 1994). Restructuring state and civil society may progressively ensure an upwards harmonization in environmental, labour and social standards and regulations, instead of the reverse – a persistent concern in North America. A dilemma of over-regulation and excessive bureaucratic centralization in Brussels continues, resulting in a lack of accountability in EU decision-making.

Thus, the European Union presents a more balanced institutionality, deficient perhaps of the over-institutionalization of the bureaucracy in Brussels. The social and democratic deficits left in the wake of the ambitious liberalization project unleashed by the SEA are being seriously addressed, although the efficacy of their success remains questionable. One cannot expect otherwise given the massive institutionality required to promulgate a genuine federalism of European states. In summary, European policy-makers, in the context of the European Union, have recognized that economic integration requires a complex institutionality which covers fiscal, labour, social, environmental, migrational, political and other themes (Dominguez and Hettne, 1994; Bazen and Benhayoun, 1992). That, in itself, is a significant improvement over the paucity of vision that underlies the institutionality of NAFTA.

AN EXAMPLE: INTELLECTUAL PROPERTY RIGHTS

As alluded to earlier, intellectual property rights (IPRs) represent one of the 'new' focal areas of coverage in the NAFTA and the integrated trade regime being pursued globally through the WTO. This is not surprising, since IPRs are vital to the new global economy whose core is in knowledge-based industries (bio-technology, computer engineering, software design, telecommunications, pharmaceuticals, data processing).

The conventional wisdom is that IPRs are 'technical issues' that are better left to the 'experts' to resolve – a misleading, manipulative belief. In reality, IPRs beg complex issues of power: defining what is 'knowledge' or 'innovation'; drawing the line between what should remain in the public domain and what can be commodified and privatized; and deciding who has the right to appropriate the benefits of knowledge and for how long. Paradoxically, a very protectionist new regime for IPR – whose main objective is to constrain the free flow of information – is sought through the medium of 'free trade agreements' such as WTO and NAFTA (Dillon, 1993; McDougall, 1996).

IPRs were, for the first time, a focal part of a trade agreement in the Uruguay Round on GATT negotiations. Annex 1C Agreement on trade-related aspects of Intellectual Property Rights set a detailed regulatory framework including minimum standards of protection with respect to copyright, trademarks, patents, lay-out designs of integrated circuits, and undisclosed information. World Trade Organization (WTO) members must incorporate these minimal standards within their national laws and adopt free trade principles of national treatment and most-favoured nation in these areas. Member states must also create enforcement mechanisms for IPR violations and provide for effective dispute settlement.

The scope and coverage of NAFTA is such that it both widens and deepens the scope of IPR protection. Chapter 17 of NAFTA extends

IPR protection into several new areas, including sound recordings and satellite signals. Article 1709(12) stipulates that NAFTA signatories 'shall provide a term of protection for patents of at least 20 years from the date of filing or 17 years from the date of grant'. The overall intent of Chapter 17 is to cast a very wide net with a strong enforcement mechanism.

The new regulatory framework for IPR being created through the WTO, the NAFTA and other means, represents an ambitious attempt to harmonize IPR regimes on a global basis. This is a far-reaching effort to establish a coercive regulatory framework both nationally and internationally, done with the full backing of the United States. A key element of the enforcement mechanism in the Americas and elsewhere is the application of US bilateral and multilateral power to coerce enforcement. Transnational corporations (TNCs) are applying lobbying efforts in many countries as part of a broad and concerted enforcement campaign. The agency and power relations underlying this institutional framework for IPR are transparent. The IPR regime addresses narrow, commercial concerns articulated by trade consultants and industry lobbyists, manufacturers' associations, corporate lawyers and government experts, with very little input from broadly-based community, consumer and social groups whose members' lives will be significantly impacted by these regimes, particularly in developing countries. Those who will suffer the consequences of this regime are indigenous peoples expropriated from their traditional knowledge (Posey, 1990); peasants who lose control over seeds and their means of reproduction; citizens who will have less access to health care, education and culture in an IPR regime that promotes privatization and tiering of basic services.

The main rationale for increased IPR protection is that it provides strong incentives for research and development. The evidence in support of this proposition is questionable and fails to consider other serious social side effects. Transnational corporation investment decisions respond to a complex set of push and pull factors (proximity to markets, infrastructure, political stability, and labour force characteristics). It is uncertain how any one factor will affect the investment decision calculus. From a developing country perspective, increased IPR protection can stifle creativity and knowledge development which might otherwise further biodiversity (Shiva, 1993). IPR protection also may act as a barrier to scientific research, particularly in areas of biotechnology where patent rights extend to both the products and processes of research. The patenting of processes discourages their use in research except by powerful states and commercial enterprises. Patents are also often taken out merely to be shelved to prevent the development of competing technologies in many industries.

In the case of NAFTA, one might reasonably expect that the new 20-year extension of monopoly rights over patented medicines will stimulate investment by pharmaceutical companies and spur new biotechnologies and drugs. But there are also serious social costs for this added protection: a likely increase in the prices of medicines, which adds to mounting health-care costs; a deterioration of access to health care services for those in traditional sectors and impoverished groups, most of whom lack health-care insurance; and job losses in the generic drug industry. These costs are borne by those generally least able to afford them. In the absence of further institutionality (for example strong watchdog agencies to ensure that pharmaceutical companies live up to their investment commitments and to monitor drug price increases), NAFTA's IPR regime will affect the health and welfare of individuals in an uneven and unfair manner.

A more likely explanation for the corporate campaign to secure more stringent IPRs is the desire to raise the profitability of capital worldwide, particularly of capital in knowledge-intensive industries. Given that the large majority of patents, trademarks and copyrights are held by a small number of corporations in the North, such a stringent regime means increased flows of royalties and other payments, and thus higher profitability and more concentration of wealth in the hands of these corporations. In particular, such a regime represents a powerful mechanism to sustain the transfer of resources from the South to the North (now that the 'debt crisis' has become less effective in securing that continued transfer). It also impedes the development of new competition for western corporate capital from southern or eastern firms freely 'borrowing' western technology (for example in the way South Korean and Japanese firms have done). Thus, from a global political economy perspective, this new regime constitutes a major effort to promote concentration of wealth in one extreme, and marginalization and impoverishment in the other. This effort, though, is couched for public consumption in much more appealing rationale.

A second – appealing but doubtful – rationale of IPR protection is that it will facilitate the transfer of technology to developing countries. Enterprises have greater incentive to do so because of stronger guarantees against wrongful expropriation. This rationale fails to recognize that the primary need of developing countries is to develop their own indigenous technological capacity and intensive industries which have backward and forward linkages with the local economy. Technology transfer must be more than a passive process of merely paying for and adopting existing technologies of developed countries. There is evidence to suggest that to the extent IPRs encourage a transfer of technology, it is on terms unfavourable to developing countries. Patents may block the free flow of knowledge from the formal sector of the North to the formal sector of the South. On the other hand, IPR regimes give little or no protection to, or undervalue, the informal sector of the South and the free flow of knowledge from that sector to the formal sector of the North (Shiva, 1993; Crucible Group, 1994).

This raises serious issues of inequity and rightful ownership. Regions near the equator (for example the Amazon rain forest) possess the bulk of the world's biodiversity and genetic material. The overwhelming number of the world's most powerful transnational corporations are headquartered in the North. Most repositories of genetic knowledge and innovation remain in the public domain in the South (for example peasant farmers and indigenous tribes). Indigenous peoples, rural peasants and local co-operatives generally lack a conception of private property and freely share their knowledge without compensation to those who would patent it for exploitation. This asymmetric exchange of bio-technologies has subsidized US agricultural output for wheat, rice and beans (Shiva, 1993).

IPR regimes, either by design or effect, displace developing country farmers as competitors with transnational corporations. The peasant farmer unwittingly becomes a free supplier of raw materials to transnational corporations, and is then forced to purchase patented seeds and hybrids back at monopolistic prices. This enforced dependency is a direct consequence of legal systems which draw an arbitrary distinction between what cannot be patented (the genetic material in nature – and knowledge of it) and what can be (seed and hybrids derived from such material).

The new global regime for IPRs has all the characteristics of a deficient institutionality. It includes powerful protection for those who hold most of the patents, trademarks and copyrights (that is, a small group of powerful corporations in the North). Almost everyone else is left unprotected: indigenous peoples who would like to maintain control over their traditional knowledge but do not have access to the requisite economic and legal resources to acquire IPR protection (Crucible Group, 1994); peasants who want control over their means of production; or citizens who want access to health care technology in the form of public services. This deficient institutionality is not surprising. It is part of a broader institutionality – in NAFTA and the WTO – oriented to protect the interests of very narrow but powerful economic interests.

Identifying a deficient institutionality enables one to conceive, propose and pursue alternative institutional forms that sponsor broad human, sustainable development. In the case of IPRs, the alternative to the deficient *formal* institutionality promoted through NAFTA and the WTO is not the *informal* institutionality implied by the absence of regulations and/or enforcement of IPRs (that is, generalized piracy and absence of protection). Such informal institutionality – particularly piracy – functions as poorly-organized, quasi-anarchic, defensive protests against onerous demands emanating from an unfair IPR regime. It is not an adequate institutional solution. An appropriate institutionality is an enforceable regime that recognizes multiples social needs. This regime would find a better balance between the interests of producers and consumers of IPR; between North and South and the latter's developmental needs; and between the creators of new knowledge and the holders of traditional knowledge (Raghavan, 1990).

CONCLUSION

This work is part of an ongoing effort to shift the discussion from 'whether to integrate?' to 'how to integrate?' The focus is on the institutional framework of regional integration. We have proposed a simple conceptual taxonomy of integration that focuses attention on the scope and coverage of the integration agreement, the regulatory framework that it imposes, the social actors that shape it, and the power relations that underlie it.

NAFTA is an example of deficient institutionality. Its institutional framework addresses narrow economic interests and is not conducive to human sustainable development. Whether one studies its overall impact or concentrates on specific areas of coverage, such as intellectual property rights in this work, or agriculture, North–South relations, labour and social aspects in other works, there is powerful evidence for this conclusion. Moreover, as the more balanced institutionality of the European Union demonstrates, these areas can be addressed without jeopardizing the integration project.

There is no doubt that the proposed Free Trade Area of the Americas will contribute to a new system of relations in the western hemisphere. We must now address the institutional forms of hemispheric integration so that we can achieve an equitable distribution of benefits, avoid or minimize unnecessary social and environmental costs and ultimately make this hemispheric integration a sustainable process. In order to achieve these goals, we need to redefine the institutionality of integration. This will happen only by incorporating new actors and changing the power relations *vis-à-vis* dominant actors. Civil organizations must find new means of empowering themselves to become more involved and influential social actors. We remain hopeful that the peoples of the Americas can and will develop an agenda and alternative vision of hemispheric integration that responds to their needs and aspirations.

Notes

1. The authors acknowledge the editorial feedback provided by Kirsten Appendini and Sven Bislev.
2. The Commission is a supranational institution with a large bureaucracy of 15 000 staff members across 24 Directorates-General, Services or Groups.
3. For example, the Works Council Directive, the Social Charter and the Social Chapter of Maastricht, and the expanded role of the European Parliament; also structural adjustment assistance.

References

Altimir, O. (1994) 'Income Distribution and Poverty Through Crisis and Adjustment', *CEPAL Review*, vol. 52.

Bano, R. (1993) 'Socioeconomic Structure and Collective Behaviour', *CEPAL Review*, vol. 50.

Bazen, S. and Benhayoun, G. (1992) 'Low Pay and Wage Regulation in the European Community', *British Journal of Industrial Relations*, vol. 30(4), pp. 623–38.

Bercusson, B. (1994) 'Social Policy at the Crossroads: European Labour Law after Maastricht', in R. Dehousse (ed.), *Europe After Maastricht: An Ever Closer Union?* (Munchen: Law Books in Europe).

Cox, R. (1987) *Production, Power and World Order* (New York: Columbia Press).

Crucible Group (1994) 'People, Plants and Patents: The Impact of Intellectual Property on Biodiversity, Conservation, Trade and Rural Society' (Ottawa: International Development Research Centre (IDRC)).

Daly, H. (1993) 'The Perils of Free Trade: Economists Routinely Ignore its Hidden Costs to the Environment and Community', *Scientific American*, November, pp. 50–7.

Devlin, R. (1993) 'Privatizations and Social Welfare', *CEPAL Review*, vol. 49.

Dillon, J. (1993) 'Intellectual Property Rights in NAFTA: Implications for Health Care and Industrial Policy in Ontario' (Toronto: Ecumenical Coalition for Economic Justice).

Dominguez, E. and Hettne, B. (1994) 'Regionalism: The Cases of Europe and North America Compared', paper presented to *48th International Congress of Americanists*, Stockholm-Uppsala.

Feres, J.C. and León, A. (1990) 'The Magnitude of Poverty in Latin America', *CEPAL Review*, no. 41.

Grinspun, R. (1993) 'NAFTA and Neoconservative Transformation: The Impact on Canada and Mexico', *Review of Radical Political Economics*, vol. 25(4), pp. 14–29.

Grinspun, R. and Cameron M.A. (eds) (1993) *The Political Economy of North American Free Trade* (New York: St Martin's Press).

Grinspun, R. and Kreklewich, R. (1994) 'Consolidating the Neoliberal State: Free Trade as a Conditioning Framework', *Studies in Political Economy*, vol. 43, pp. 33–61.

Jary, D. and Jary, J. (1991) *HarperCollins Dictionary of Sociology* (New York: HarperCollins).

Hufbauer, G.C. and Schott, J.J. (1994) *Western Hemisphere Economic Integration* (Washington: Institutite for International Economics).

McDougall, C.L. (1996) *Intellectual Property Rights and the Biodiversity Convention: The Impact of GATT* (London: Friends of the Earth).

Pastor, Jr., M. and Wise, C. (1994) 'The Origins and Sustainability of Mexico's Free Trade Policy', *International Organization*, vol. 48(3), pp. 459–89.

Posey, D. (1990) 'Intellectual Property Rights and Just Compensation for Indigenous Knowledge', *Anthropology Today*, vol. 6(4), pp. 13–16.

Raghavan, C. (1990) *Recolonization: GATT, the Uruguay Round and the Third World* (London: Zed Books).

Ranney, D. (1993) 'NAFTA and the New Transnational Corporate Agenda', *Review of Radical Political Economics*, vol. 25(4), pp. 1–13.

Shiva, V. (1993) 'Biodiversity and Intellectual Property Rights', in R. Nader *et al.* (eds), *The Case Against Free Trade* (San Francisco: Earth Island Press).

United Nations Development Programme (1992) *Human Development Report 1992* (New York: Oxford University Press).

United Nations Research Institute for Social Development (1995) 'States of Disarray: The Social Effects of Globalization', *UNRISD Social Development News*, no. 12, Spring/Summer.

3 Free Trade and Local Institutions: The Case of Mexican Peasants

Raúl Garcia-Barrios

INTRODUCTION

Economic integration policies striving for more economic co-operation, efficiency and productivity have sometimes unintended and undesirable effects. Under a wide range of circumstances and by means of diverse trans-locational dynamics, market-oriented integration policies may account for local institutional deficiencies and failures, and be accompanied with more social fragmentation, marginalization, inefficiency and differentiation, and hence with an increased feeling of injustice. As such, it may be a cause, and not only a consequence, of local and global problems. Furthermore, in some cases the lack of ideas and instruments to successfully confront problems at the global level may be a problem itself on account of the loss of institutions at the local and trans-local level.

My purpose in this chapter is to explore the causes and consequences of the most misfortuned agricultural integration policy of Mexican peasant agriculture. Mexican peasant agriculture was directly affected by a programme of structural reforms initiated by the government in the late 1980s, which were part of a larger policy package of market-oriented reforms intended to stimulate investments and economic growth by reducing state intervention in the economy and increasing market forces. Changes included the redesign of property rights, the removal of many government controls, and the insertion of the agricultural sector in the international division of labour (NAFTA).

The effects of the reforms on Mexican peasant agriculture, which I briefly describe in the following section, were not those envisioned by their architects. The reforms not only produced a major profitability crisis, decreased households' income, and exacerbated migration in the peasant sector, but muddled the rural institutional setting. Instead of

34

finding themselves face to face with the market, most peasant groups may now be rather confronting a non-market economic and political re-institutionalization of the rural economy, that could be creating local exploitative relations and further inefficiency in rural areas. Recent data at the community level suggest that the method of usury of capital and land expropriation and concentration may be extending throughout Mexican rural areas. The evolution of exploitative relations in the rural milieu clearly shows the shortcomings of the governmental integration policy to create efficiency and compensate the short-term negative consequences of the reforms.

The architects of the reforms would not forecast these results. The main question I address here is: why? To give a plausible answer that may be relevant to equivalent problems in other countries and sectors, I first explore the limits to the ethics of efficiency that was behind the Mexican government's economic deregulating practices and rhetorics. I will argue that, given the particular conditions of peasant life that prevailed in rural areas, it was utopian to apply an integration policy based on deregulation and the attempt to circumvent the people's concepts of local justice. To define local justice, I will follow Charles Taylor in distinguishing it from 'absolute' justice – of which economic efficiency, as is usually understood by neoclassical and neo-institutional economic theorists and practitioners, is a major constituent. For our purposes, absolute justice may be defined as

> the ideal of the hyper-Kantian agent, capable of living by rules which utterly leave out of account his or her own advantage, and which thus could be agreed by everyone, since they are not designed for anyone's good in particular. This could be the kind of person who really could say that he of she considered his of her talents and capacities as community assets, at the service of all indiscriminately.

Local justice, on the other hand, has an Aristotelian and historically contextualized nature. It may be defined as an ideal set of procedures of distribution historically established according to criteria of desert, goods internal to the production practices, and basic needs, which are defined by mutual recognition and indebtedness in the pursuit of the common good. Plain individuals, as we will see, tend to think and act both in terms of local and global justice, albeit many times in contradictory and frustrated ways. Empowered economists, on the other hand, like to think about themselves and other policy-makers as Kantian agents. This faulted perspective has major policy implications, since the institutions, economists design to acquire 'absolute' justice may render situations that are unfair from the local perspective, and may provoke behavioural responses of moral individuals that cause inefficiency and economic stagnation. Consequently, they may not maximize the probability of reaching 'absolute' economic efficiency.

I will therefore argue that because of the incoherent ethical discourse underlying most economic analysis, policy-makers experienced a kind of model mis-specification. The logical consequences were several unintended and undesirable effects which contributed, despite the good-will and intelligence of most economists, to exploitation and poverty, for the sake of efficiency and development. The last part of the chapter briefly explores some causes of such flawed ethics. I will argue that part of the explanation lies in a modern structure of moral utterance that grants a privilege to a most particular blend of moralistic-technocratic conceptions of social action and political power. Such ethical structure, however, is not the right tool for the job. If the purpose of integration is mutual interest and co-operation, the international institutions of development cannot go on considering neither the design of the integration processes nor the practice of the maximization of efficiency as neutral or detachable from the individual and collective objectives and the potential behavioural conflicts they give rise to when confronted in daily life. We must face these objectives and conflicts in order to understand them and design institutions suitable to the cultural and ideological diversity of the world we live in, and also to the reality of human conduct.

THE REFORMS: ANTECEDENTS AND UNINTENDED CONSEQUENCES

By the early to mid-1980s, Mexican agriculture was submerged in a deep crisis which had arisen both from structural conditions of economic disarticulation and public policies which for a long period supported the coexistence of a costly agriculture with non-agricultural growth. The traditional Mexican public policy of agricultural development involved a complex set of contradictory and inconsistent actions and continuous vacillation, that maintained a relatively static agricultural and agrarian structure which could (partially and unevenly) service the 'social contract', but was clearly incapable of coping with the increasing demand for cheap agricultural products. Constraints on output prices and indirect taxation through overvaluation of the exchange rate (fluctuating around the 30 per cent range) were offset by a rather high level of state presence in the provision of foodstuffs, agricultural inputs and the marketing of products at heavily subsidized prices and, therefore, a rather low level of presence of private service operators (including economic organization by producers themselves). Governmental presence was pervasive in irrigation development, seed supply, and so on. Such massive public expenditure, however, was provided together with subsidies, a macroeconomic environment which meant a constant attraction of non-agricultural uses of private resources, a persistent overvaluation of the exchange rate, and a political system characterized by paternalistic corporativism, strong governmental failure and biases in public service provision.

Fiscal and political restrictions on government intervention imposed a pattern of public services provision unevenly distributed among different sectors and regions of the country (Robles and Garcia-Barrios, 1994). In some regions, a 'modern subsidized' peasant economic environment was created within a governmental strategy of promoting the productivity of basic crops (at the beginning, the aim was a low-price foodstuff self-sufficiency; later, it was a tool for reducing the load on the trade balance). The producers enjoyed special public support and infrastructure for the production, gathering and marketing of grains. Moreover, they received strong subsidies to production via the guaranteed price system, access to cheap credit, technical assistance and subsidized inputs, and so forth. Consequently, this policy involved the development of local and regional markets, and the drastic reduction of transaction costs for family units. In this environment, producers applied 'green revolution' technologies to produce with low costs a hybrid corn that covered most national demand (the rest was low-quality forage corn imported from the USA).

Most peasants, however, operated in a semi-modern economic environment where foodstuff supply was publicly supported and welfare programmes applied, so peasants could benefit from consumer subsidies provided by the state. Agricultural production and commercialization, however, did not receive proper support from the government (characteristically, the largest subsidies to production were provided through fertilizer prices), so peasants usually faced high transaction costs in the input, credit and product markets, and shadow price bands. As a consequence, they preferred to adopt subsistence strategies of agricultural production. Although precarious, communication services and transport for humans and products were usually available, and a large part of the population had become semi-proletarianized.

The agricultural and rural policy that induced this structure was extraordinarily costly in economic terms and created deep contradictions and problems, both at the macro- and the micro social and economic levels. Obviously, the purpose (or, at least, the hope) of the rural areas' reformers was to encourage deep changes that would lead to competitive investment in production and services. The main features of the new policy were a strong commitment to an open and integrated economy, a sharp decline in input subsidies, a renewed priority to public investment in agriculture, and a commitment to rural welfare. Withdrawal of the state from marketing services for both products and inputs was aimed to induce the entry of the private sector or producers' organizations. The price guarantee programme was eliminated from all primary commodities except corn and beans, there was a massive scaling-down of input subsidies, and interest controls were eliminated. There was a massive withdrawal of parastatals, but public investment in the agricultural sector as a whole experienced a large increase, made possible after the debt overhang had been reduced: external support by the Brady Plan, IMF–World Bank financial transfers, and the one-shot capital transfers through re-privatization of the banks and the sale of public enterprises made that possible, though only in the short term.

Other reforms were aimed at creating spaces for the promotion of new institutions and forms of organization aimed at achieving economies of scale in production and marketing, improving access to information, and developing market power. If properly used, such reforms could constitute a social resource for rural development. For example, with a properly negotiated power balance, contractual associations such as the rental of land could become important forms of access to land and capital, providing 'income ladders' for vertical mobility. Such association forms would indeed allow the atomization of land use and capital access in spite of the observed concentration of land and capital ownership.

Looking at the actual consequences of the reforms, however, it seems that the expectations of a (quasi) spontaneous take-off were mostly illusory. Using a nationwide sample, De Janvry, Gordillo and Sadoulet (1997) studied the immediate impact (1990–94) of the reforms on the *ejido* agricultural sector of the country. There was a drastic decrease in access and an increase in the service cost of production inputs, a significant technological disruption, a virtual abandonment of the sector in terms of technical assistance across all farm sizes, a drastic increase in the rates of migration and semi-proletaria-nization, an increasing return to self-consumption and to cattle raising.

Additionally, there was an increase in transaction costs in the marketing of products, inputs and credit. The main effect expected from the reforms was an increase of investments in rural areas at the productive level, as well as in commercialization services. Only in the latter of these two areas of investment has there been a clear increase, but in an atmosphere of lessening the local competition and isolating service suppliers, which reflects the rise in transaction costs in these activities and the lack of complementary investments from the state. Rural areas have experienced the emergence and proliferation of two pre-revolutionary phenomena: market cornering and usury, both prohibited by the Constitution. For many years, the Mexican people considered public provision of foodstuff and the marketing of products at heavily subsidized prices among the most relevant consequences of the 1910 revolution, since among their many purposes they intended to regulate the market and reduce the presence of this kind of private services. The official abandonment of these activities with the reforms and the eradication of the restrictions in the use of land as collateral in credit transactions have made it possible for these highly exploitative activities to re-emerge in rural areas.

Table 3.1 below shows the dominant nominal rates of interest of the last years in the informal credit markets and in the transactions among family members and friends in four communities in three different regions of the country. The family interest rates shown in the table may reflect some sort of kinship subsidy, but we believe that they also reflect the real local financial costs more accurately than the rates that the lenders charge. A particular case, that of Paso del Muerto validates this hypothesis. This community made up of *mestizos* (mixed race) has a long history of internal coherence and community solidarity in their struggle for their land. In this community, the money lenders charge the same rates as family members; this makes rates much lower than the prevailing rates in other communities of the region (for example the indigenous community of Cheranatzicurin).

The consequences of usury and market cornering include a dynamic of permanent indebtedess and the operation of the method of usury, of land expropriation and concentration (Bhaduri, 1983). Both processes have evolved in Mexico, increasing poverty and migration in the rural areas.

In the most favourable areas, a reconstruction of the marketing system did in fact occur. In some 'modern subsidized' poles[1] with a

Table 3.1   Nominal interest rates

Community	Creditor	
	Moneylenders	Family and friends
Francisco Villa, La Frailesca, Chiapas (1995)	180% (up to 230)	120%
San Juan y San Augustin Edo de Mexico (1994)	240%	—
Paso del Muerte Michoacan (1996)	120%	120%
Cheranatzicurin	360%	50–120%

surplus production of corn, the de-capitalization seems to have been smaller than in other areas of the country. Despite their high vulnerability to the reduction of public production and marketing subsidies, and despite the relative rigidity of their agricultural technology, the productive and marketing infrastructure previously established prevented the peasant producers of these areas from suffering the drastic exposition to new transactional costs that affected the rest of the country more severely. However, this did not prevent important productive, environmental and institutional changes from occurring in these areas. These changes have created an acute feeling of uncertainty about the kind of the new social order, and especially of the new role of corn agriculture. For example, the La Frailesca region, in Chiapas, has been the setting for sharp protests and resistance movements against the wearing away of the price of corn.

In most regions, however, the reforms shifted the position of smallholders and minifundistas originally situated in the 'modern subsidized' and 'semi-modern' environments to more precarious situations. Given the strong concentration of bargaining power and rent-seeking privileges associated with large-scale ownership of land or capital, and weakness of legal structures and government failure, the potential organizational benefits of the reforms were easily lost.

WHY DID THINGS GO WRONG? THE LIMITS OF THE ETHICS OF EFFICIENCY

Many Mexicans expected the reforms to deepen injustice in rural areas. The reformers, however, could not agree with these expectations: they were convinced that the reforms were necessary and fair, and most still feel no reason to change their fundamental convictions. Most interestingly, it has been very difficult to construct and maintain a coherent opposition philosophical perspective that may support a political and economic alternative.

Clearly, the reformers sustain their actions in a modernist political philosophy. Together with most educated people, they believe that the variety and heterogeneity of human goods is such that its search cannot be rationally and democratically guided by any unique moral principle. However, they argue that this search can be reconciled by co-operative mechanisms that identify the right option in any choice and make possible an efficient allocation of resources irrespective of any notion of community good. They believe this notion of 'absolute' justice is the only one with a rational basis, and that it is a precondition for the use of any other notion of justice. They believe the reforms established the conditions for such kinds of neutral mechanisms, since they were specifically constructed to remove external constraints to the spontaneous build-up of efficient economic institutions and co-operative organizations. Hence, they would return the agricultural sector to a 'normal path of evolution' driven by individuals' private and unrestricted interests in profitable co-operation. Therefore, their consequences had to be optimal institutional rearrangements that minimize transaction costs, make the most of economies of scale, and permit a more efficient reassignment of resources, risks and information in rural areas.

The monopolistic power of traders and usurers could be interpreted as a natural consequence of both the structure of transaction costs and the existence of scale economies in the extraordinarily imperfect rural markets. As such, reforms would represent a welfare improvement for everybody. Furthermore, the gains in allocative efficiency would generate neat efficiency gains that would be accumulated in the short term in other parts of society, and then transferred to compensate the direct welfare losses of the poorest. To guarantee this result, they designed their policies and compensatory mechanisms taking into account the liberal rights to subsistence and property. As usual, these rights were legitimized in terms of the minimal conditions necessary to protect the individual, and the acquirement of allocative efficiency and investment capacity.

All these beliefs and expectations neglect the real process of institutional development. The reformers did not recognize or understand the sources and dynamics of the institutional context of Mexican rural life, and the motivational structures they determine in agricultural production. Furthermore, the reformers neglected many of the requirements of a normal life and the criteria of 'local justice', particularly those related to the cultural patterns, productive routines, normative principles and historical traditions of the people. This has been a source of inefficiency, stagnation, and major social and political unrest in the countryside.

Removing constraints to economic activity is not enough. Interest-driven competitive economic and institutional activity depends on individuals having the virtues and resources to achieve the goods internal to significant social and productive practices, including those that correspond to integrating whole human individual and communal lives. Economic policies, together with their socio-psychological and cultural consequences, may contribute to disarticulate such practices and virtues, and disrupt the social organization determining co-operation, efficiency and resistance. In Mexico, years of systematic manipulation and discrimination against the rural poor generated a widespread institutional disarray, which explains the low productive capacity of most peasant agriculture, the great instability and uncertainty of rural market transactions (that is usually in the labour, credit and product markets), and the reduction of opportunities to establish and maintain viable and stable non-market transactions (including relationships with the state) that could enhance fair local co-operation and circumvent market failures. The institutional setting favoured those forms of economic and political investment that enhance dependency and conflict, market power and high and increasing transaction costs. Furthermore, it also reduces systemically the capacity of the poor to reorganize endogenously in the face of new challenges; that is, to invest material and social resources to build up or alter contracts and associations to sustain desirable efficient production, resource management, and technological change. The peasants' institutional deficiency is 'reorganizing-restricted'.[2]

Reorganizing-restricted institutional deficiency in poor local communities is one of the most characteristic (and tragic) structural phenomena of modern rural life in Mexico. Its most immediate economic expressions are labour surplus, semi-proletarianization, high mobility, and detachment from the land and the social community. It also affects the economic position of the peasantry *vis-à-vis* other national sectors, shaping the particular nature of their economic relationships and exchanges. On account of the institutional and cultural biases that exist in the country, a large amount of attributes of the indigenous or *campesino* production lose their quality, or simply are not perceived and valorized, when they enter the flow of national goods and services. Bonfil (1989) captured this situation when he described the existence within Mexico of a denied campesino and indigenous civilization: *El Mexico Profundo* (Deep Mexico). One of the consequences of this denial, the productive logic of self-supply and self-sufficiency, can be interpreted as a symptom of the truncation of the productive and organizational development energies within the indigenous civilizations. This energy loss covers many indigenous productive practices and technologies. It is therefore a substantial source of static and dynamic inefficiency. There are several factors external to the communities that explain such a situation, such as public ignorance, discrimination and disdain for the indigenous culture, market information deficiencies (for example adverse selection) and cheap-foodstuff governmental policies. However, reorganizing-restricted institutional deficiency is also relevant, as it prevents most poor producers from negotiating with the state the terms of agricultural and subsidies policies, as well as fighting cultural blindness, paternalism, and the anti-peasant biases of governmental administrations. It also stops them from collectively financing the informational and transactional mechanisms that would be required to build operational markets. Consequently, peasants' institutional deficiency is also at the roots of the faults in the exchange of information between the peasant groups and the rest of the nation.

Its consequences also dig deep into the socio-political arena. In Mexico, the post-revolutionary modern state promised to provide indigenous societies with a wider, national, identity. Most national governments, however, failed to supply the economic and social support and stimulus necessary to cultivate in the rural areas the crucial components and virtues of such an identity. Instead, state intervention was characterized by a strong grip over the allocation of public expenditure and investment, the access to institutional credit and productive resources, and the definition of new technological, institutional and political options. In many cases, the governments permitted or even favoured the emergence of regional 'transactional oligarchies' and 'political bosses'. In most communities, this form of intervention of the state accelerated political deterioration.

For many years, indigenous and peasant societies had suffered from socio-pathological depression, a loss of communitarian self-esteem, and a lack of confidence in their capacity to govern themselves which provided the perfect social psychological environment for the further development of strong manipulative-paternalistic but severely inefficient local and regional governments and oligopolistic market structures. Even though important remnants do exist, the mechanisms to create internal consensus, to negotiate with external private agents or the government, and to mobilize collective labour have weakened or fallen into disuse. Patterns, routines, norms and traditions are in a grave state of disorder, and individuals have lost their collective capability to imagine and construct productive projects based on a coherent conception of a common good life. Peasant agricultural practices, together with the goods internal to them and the virtues necessary to acquire such goods, have been radically marginalized and their significance deeply obscured, therefore obscuring their significance in terms of the whole life of individuals and the lives of communities. Hence, the potentiality that plain peasants have for developing out of their experience of practices an understanding of themselves and their cultural roots has continuously been frustrated.

But, although incapable of supporting a coherent concept of a good life on which to support agricultural development, rural norms and traditions still have a strong grip on the Mexican people's particular sense of social justice. They were constructed in a long history of social unrest, resistance and revolution, and as such have contributed to shape a special set of moral references defining the legitimate means of satisfaction of the basic needs of the population. On their account, Mexican people have never come to terms with the liberal 'solipsistic' conceptualization of the basic needs. There is, instead, a widespread sense that human satisfaction depends in several ways on our performance in social relationships. Therefore, the Mexican laws and social customs clearly recognize a people's right to public health, social protection, identification, understanding, creation, recreation, participation and so on, and the popular demands on the state as a major provider of the means of satisfaction of the basic needs have continued to proliferate in the country.

Most importantly, the struggle for means to satisfy people's basic needs has been traditionally attached to the struggle for the land and the maintainance of the revolutionary agrarian reform. Powerful sociopolitical local and regional identities were constructed around such resistance. In some cases this struggle provided the resources to (re-) activate/construct/invent rural political institutions. I have recently conducted studies of the consequences of the reforms in several communities in the country that suggest that perhaps the single most important factor allowing the poor peasantry to take advantage of the opportunities of the market-oriented policies may be a long history of communal internal coherence, solidarity, participation, administrative know-how and political awareness developed in their continuous struggle for their land. This, however, has created a major political and economic paradox within the liberal reforms, which have as a basic tenet the need to affirm property rights and completely end the struggle for land in the rural areas. The result has been a major political protest and the upsurge of two guerrilla movements.

The norms and traditions of Mexico's rural revolution continue to be powerful factors regulating the behaviour of peasants; they provide the framework that defines legitimate ways of satisfying fundamental needs. Based on this framework of 'local justice', individuals make judgements not only about the efficiency of resource allocation, but also the virtue (or rather the virtues) of both the procedures and the resulting distribution. Those judgments have psychological consequences in individuals, and produce culturally-determined emotional reactions that influence the efficiency of economic processes and institutions.

Economic agents whose rights are violated may experience moral and psychological suffering, and consequently the costs of stimulating the actions needed by established standards will increase. Costly contracts and institutions, such as efficiency wages or supervision mechanisms, have to be established to provide sufficient 'incentives'. Moral suffering may also generate direct resistance as soon as a maximum tolerance level is reached, depending on individuals' moral will and on their punishment capacity. Individuals will attempt to reduce their exploiters' benefits, even when this involves additional costs or risks that reduce their welfare even more.

Both kinds of emotional responses will provoke contractual inefficiency, productive investment deterrence, and economic stagnation. Governmental and private actions such as withdrawal from the provision of public goods, the end of agrarian distribution, usury or market cornering, are understood and lived as direct violations to these rights, and are therefore sources of such problems.

The utopian nature of Mexican liberal reforms is now evident: in the design of institutions there is no way of separating the means from the objectives, or circumventing the moral evaluation based on locally-defined concepts of justice and rights. So the variables established by efficiency, distribution, justice and participation conditions in an economic relationship are all closely related. As a result, given unjust initial structural conditions, deregulation will not be enough to attain efficiency. Instead, liberal reforms may trigger 'new' forms of investment that are exploitative and inefficient. In Mexico, four factors contributed and will go on contributing to this process unless the Mexican population takes immediate action:

- the conditions of reorganizing-restricted institutional insufficiency in Mexican rural zones;
- the frailty of the economic and social infrastructure created by the Mexican government during the years of its control;
- the financial and social power of the transactional oligarchies; and
- the methods with which the Mexican government has intended to create the necessary conditions for the integration of Mexican rural zones into the international division of labour.

ON THE SOURCES OF TECHNOCRATIC OPTIMISM

Between 1989 and 1992, the years in which the reforms were carried out (in spite of all the considerable protests in the rural zones of Mexico), optimism prevailed among the reformers. On several occasions the secretary of agriculture in charge of the reforms, who was an extremely intelligent and educated man, stated publicly that he had never set foot in the rural areas. Such a statement shows a very special kind of ignorance because it goes hand in hand with a deep self-confidence. What was the source of such self-confidence?

In this chapter I have argued about the existence of a normative tangle and logical contradictions in the economic behaviour of the men and women of Mexican rural areas. On the one hand there are no rational guidelines to live a full common life, on the other hand there is a need to collectively define and respect individual, social and communitarian human rights. On account of this, the rural life projects whose definition necessarily requires debating Mexican national goals (for example sustainable development) are under suspicion, and most educated individuals find a more or less coherent meaning in just two kinds of moral life projects. The first is a professional life (as scientists, artists, businessmen, workers, military men and so on) dedicated to the efficient creation and/or production of goods and services of social utility – without questioning the meaning of this utility – or to the creation of efficient and neutral institutions aimed at assigning private or public goods to the conflictive goals of social life (for example the markets, as ideal as possible, the educational institutions, the hospitals, the armies, and so forth). The second is a life dedicated to the defense of autonomies and rights.

The reforms in the Mexican countryside were carried out by professionals, supposedly experts in institutional design, who worked under the following assumptions: there was no point in defining new national 'goals or objectives' for poor rural inhabitants (for instance self-sufficiency in food supply, production of cheap nourishment, defense of indigenous culture or biodiversity, proletarianization), because this would originate an unending debate between the conflicting groups. Neither was it important to provide resources specifically directed to make traditional practices flourish. It was simply enough to set up exchange and process mechanisms that were neutral to the debate of objectives and would maximize economic efficiency, which is the cardinal virtue and main provision of justice in economic institutions. This is the definition of modernity.

With this aim in mind, it was not necessary to know the countryside, it was merely enough to deregulate it and create new conditions in which the neutral mechanisms of competition and the market could operate. If for any reason there was any need of intervention (for example to compensate those who were affected, to safeguard their rights or to regulate the powers of monopoly), they had the knowledge and the right tools to do it ideally. With these actions they were sure of the best conditions to attract new investments that would in turn generate economic growth. Only this mechanism was realistic and complied with all the intellectual, efficiency and moral requirements of our times, so there was no other better alternative. That was essentially the moralistic-technocratic point of view of the reformers and the basis of their self confidence.

For these professionals, struggling in favour of the acknowledgment or the defense of the rights would be problematic. One of the causes is that the social identities, existential meanings and human needs that necessarily underlie the definition of such rights are complex dynamic processes that can be understood in terms of particular relationships with other changing identities, and the individual and collective agents can usually embody simultaneously several interacting identities. Another difficulty is that their definition is not exempt of valorative contents, and therefore the rights are also the subject of the never-ending social debate of modernity. Consequently, the rights are concepts that are full of problems and contradictions. Most of them lack consensus which creates the conditions for an infinite number of normative conflicts to arise among the different social and cultural groups. However, eager to protect the potential of individual and communitarian autonomy, many of us are ready to recognize rights whose application domain by far exceeds the mere subsistence. At present, the governments, the NGOs and millions of independent individuals of all the world's societies assign substantial efforts and resources to the identification and protection of individuals and cultural groups whose identity and autonomy are under threat, or at least seem to be so.

Most policy-makers have found a pragmatic way out of such a moral mess through the rhetorical separation of efficiency, distribution and 'local justice'. In this chapter we have seen the illusory nature of this kind of ethics of efficiency; but the generalized belief in separability has provided 'social engineers' with a privileged social position to practice the professional virtues of 'legitimate' power and institutional design. Their admiration of the mechanisms of the self-regulated market has a narcissistic and self-protective aspect, but also a decisive influence upon the development of the technocratic and moralistic attitude and character of the so-called 'decision-makers'.

However, the policies which have emerged from the moral-technocratic arguments are powerful enough to have the support of the world community. Today, the international order is notable for a greater interdependence among countries for the production of goods and services and the hyper-mobility of capital. The links between exchange rates and trade, interest rates and economic activity, between monetary and fiscal policies, have become increasingly uncertain, thus increasing the uncertainty of nations when facing the possibility of a catastrophe. Because of this possibility, international economic organizations hold the power to generate believable threats to compel a nation to change its constituent social function: instead of generating domestic policies to meet the local and complex interests of the people, states impose the logic of self-regulated markets pleading that it is the only legitimate way to maximize efficiency and well-being.

In Mexico, for many years the fear, uncertainty and moral powerlessness of the people led us to maintain moral-technocratic governments which were ready to defend the latter concept of national interest to the end. The governments believed that the demands of those not in favour of this definition of national interests are either a product of ignorance and irrationality, or they are the illegitimate attempts of power groups which are only following their own personal, selfish interests (which justifies the ruthless and many times undemocratic use of force against them).

Mexico's political structure seems to be experiencing a decisive change towards effective democracy. Mexicans have recognized for a long time that they live in a world where there has been an explosion of the economic national potentials of many countries, and that the integration forces are extraordinarily powerful. We have no doubt that the strengthening of conventional mechanisms and processes will keep playing an essential role in this integration process. We must create new competitive international markets, strengthen our financial systems, seek increasingly more effective and less polluting means of transport and communication, and extend the electronic networks to reach all the homes in the country, and so on. We should also preserve the impulse achieved by the search for efficiency, which is only a technical name for sound judgement and prudence applied to choosing methods of institutional design. Adequately transformed, the economy and management must carry on their significant roles in the regulation of integration. However, the recent democratic advances are an implicit recognition that we cannot go on considering neither the design of the integration processes nor the practice of maximizing efficiency as neutral or detachable from individual and collective historical and cultural traditions. We must face these traditions in order to understand them and design institutions suitable to their effective development. In order to have a productive and efficient integration of different cultural and social units as small as the workers and employers of an agricultural enterprise or an indigenous community, or medium-sized as the Mexican rural economy and the country, or as large as the nations of Europe and North America, there must be a definition and construction of projects for common existence that go beyond the establishment of economic individual or social contracts which seemingly reconcile the material incentives of the parties involved.

Notes

1. These were areas of high productivity in agriculture, subsidized by the government in several ways (Robles and Garcia-Barrios, 1994).
2. 'Reorganizing-restricted' indicates an institutional context that is unstable and developing, but under serious restrictions.

References

Bhaduri, A. (1983) *The Economic Structure of Backward Agriculture* (London: Academic Press).

Bonfil, G. (1989) *Mexico Profundo* (Mexico: Grijalbo).

De Janvry, A., Gordillo, G. and Sadoulet, E. (1997) *Mexico's Second Agrarian Reform* (San Diego: Ejido Reform Project, Center for US–Mexican Studies, UC).

Robles, G. and Garcia-Barrios, R. (1994) 'Fallas estructurales del mercado de maiz y la logica de la produccion campesina', *Economia Mexicana, Nueva Epoca*, vol. III(2), pp. 225–85.

4 NAFTA, the EU and Deficient Global Institutionality

Morten Ougaard

INTRODUCTION

The differences between NAFTA and the EU are clear, as stressed in some of the previous chapters of this book. Yet these differences should not obscure how much the two projects actually have in common. Fundamentally, they are both examples of regional market integration and political institutionalization. Although of very different vintage and shaped by different historical circumstances, there exists an historical link between the two, while their future trajectories are bound to be interconnected because both are building blocks in a wider process of international institutionalization.

Consequently, the inevitable interaction between NAFTA and the EU is likely to be among the decisive forces that will shape the evolution of the global polity. Deficient institutionality is not only a regional phenomenon: the two regional projects bring different patterns of deficiency to a larger and even more deficient arena of global institution-building. In this chapter, I will firstly present some theoretical arguments and evidence in relation to the emerging 'global polity', with the focus on why continued international institutionalization should be expected and how this process is shaped by inter-state politics. Secondly, I will describe the larger international institutional framework in which the two regional projects are located, including global and quasi-global institutions such as the World Trade Organization (WTO) and the Organization for Economic Co-operation and Development (OECD); broader regional arrangements such as the EU's agreements with neighbouring countries and the prospective Free Trade Area of the Americas (FTAA); and inter-regional arrangements such as APEC (Asia Pacific Economic Co-operation), ASEM (Asia Europe Meetings), the EU–Mercosur negotiations, and the Transatlantic relationship. Finally, I will

51

discuss the question of institutional deficiency in this global context, arguing that NAFTA and the EU are major building blocks in the global polity, that current political dynamics mean that they tend to strengthen rather than weaken global institutionalization, and that a likely effect of NAFTA – and the FTAA, if established – will be to serve as a lock-in of the American approach to international institutionalization.

THE GLOBAL POLITY

A central tenet of Marx's historical materialism was that when the economic basis of society changes, the political, cultural and ideological superstructures will also change. Applied to today's international realm, this proposition implies that an increasingly internationalized economy will bring about, in one way or another, an internationalized political superstructure. Marxists are far from alone in thinking along these lines. Much of the literature on the formation of international regimes shares the underlying assumption that increased interdependence, particularly economic interdependence, as a general rule of thumb leads to increased international institutionalization, regime formation and so on.[1] What regime literature emphasizes much more than Marxist literature, however, is that the actual shape of the resulting international political superstructure is not determined automatically, but is a result of complex national, international and transnational political processes.

Much writing on internationalization and globalization has focused on the liberalization of trade as a central feature of contemporary international political economy – and with good reason, since economic internationalization has taken a qualitative step forward in the period since the politics of neo-liberalism became dominant in most Western countries. But the history of modern economies has shown that even free markets require strong institutions, and it is no surprise that this also holds true for the international economy. In addition, all the other concerns that are addressed by states in developed capitalist economies – infrastructure, education, health, welfare, the environment and so on – increasingly acquire an international dimension, not least because of the reduction of states' capacities to solve problems at the national level. Therefore, it is reasonable to expect that in the process of internationalization, the breaking down of political barriers to trade will be accompanied by the building up of new *international* political structures as well as the expansion, strengthening and modification of existing ones.

Many contemporary international relations scholars share this line of reasoning. Moreover, it has become part of official American foreign policy thinking. In the words of National Security Advisor Samuel R. Berger:

> If we could look down on the earth from a distant planet, one of the most powerful phenomena we would observe are the effects of economic integration ... These forces of integration – economic... technological ... political – find practical if imperfect expression in international rules of the road ... These norms – alliances of like-minded countries ... adherence to the rule of law ... open and competitive trade rules ... major regimes to control dangerous weapons – are important in and of themselves. But they're also important because, brick by brick, they form a structure for security and prosperity. (Berger, 1997)

An even more significant pointer lies in the preface to the President's 1997 National Security Report to Congress, in which the notion of American leadership in a period of international institution-building is elevated to official foreign policy doctrine:

> We can – and we must – use America's leadership to harness global forces of integration, reshape existing security, economic and political structures, and build new ones that help create the conditions necessary for our interests and values to thrive ... Our responsibility is to build the world of tomorrow by embarking on a period of construction ... constructing international frameworks, institutions and understandings to guide America and the world far into the next century. (US President, 1997)

It would be wrong to interpret this as merely a rhetorical device, in response to the need for convincing new strategic concepts to help sustain the foreign policy consensus following the end of the cold war and the Bush administration's overselling of 'the new world order'.[2] The key phrase 'embarking on a period of construction' reflects the fact that intensified internationalization is already a reality and that international institutionalization has progressed in recent years. (Luard, 1990; McGrew, 1992). The establishment of the WTO, the broadening of the OECD's agenda, the progress made, in spite of delays and setbacks, in international environmental diplomacy, in arms control and in other areas, the proliferation and strengthening of regional and inter-regional co-operation schemes around the world, all testify to this.

Several writers have dubbed the phenomenon the evolution of a *global polity* (Luard, 1990; Brown, 1996), and although still a somewhat elusive entity, it can no longer be doubted that it is a real phenomenon. In the words of Robert Cox:

> There is, in effect, no explicit political or authority structure for the global economy. There is nevertheless something that remains to be deciphered, something that could be described by the French word nébuleuse, or by the notion of 'governance without government'.
>
> (Cox, 1994, p. 49)

'Nébuleuse' of course means nebulous, vague or woolly. But it is also a noun used in astronomy, where English speakers use the Latin word 'nebula'. In this context the term denotes, according to a French dictionary, 'tout corps céleste dont les contours ne sont pas nets', or is, according to the Encyclopedia Britannica 'formerly applied to any object outside the solar system that had a diffuse appearance and could not be resolved telescopically into a pointlike image'. In other words, Cox's remarks indicate that in the political realm a new combined national/international pattern is emerging, something that is real and visible, but whose precise contours and properties cannot be mapped by conventional methods of inquiry. American foreign policy strategy is based upon the expectation that this *nebula* will continue to grow, and current developments as well as a very large part of modern International Relations (IR) theory indicate that this is much more plausible that any alternative scenario.

In this growing forest of organizations, agreements, mutual understandings and regularized patterns of co-operation, more is known about individual trees than about the forest as a whole (for overviews and critical discussions see Hasenclever, Mayer and Rittberger, 1996; Levy, Young and Zürn, 1995). One reason is the sheer magnitude of the task of mapping the phenomenon itself and the political processes going on within it; another is the fact that it has no single centre of authority and is shaped by a multitude of actors and circumstances, without a commonly accepted blueprint. To add yet another metaphor, the *brick by brick* image used by Samuel Berger is very apt. The global polity is evolving through a process of adapting, expanding and strengthening existing international institutions as well as the creation of new ones; some regional, some inter-regional, some global, and some quasi-global; sometimes competing, sometimes complementary, sometimes clearly distinct from each other and sometimes overlapping geographically and/or functionally. New bricks are continuously added to the construction, but by masons that represent different artisan traditions, adhere to diverging architectural principles, and frequently disagree on the specific purposes the building is going to serve. They combine in different permutations to co-operate on one brick or the other, but the basic organizing principle is still the anarchy of the inter-state system, and to the extent that a measure of cohesion is imposed on the process, it is often the result of hegemonic leadership or coercion.

Returning to NAFTA and the EU, the point is that on the one hand their position in the global political framework will be one important factor in their own future development, while on the other hand they themselves are major building blocks in the global polity. The interesting question, then, is what will happen when two markedly different regionalist projects are brought closer together in a broader process of international institutionalization. To illuminate this question, I will first describe some main features of the patchwork of institutions in which NAFTA and the EU are set. A comprehensive account of all the international organizations and agreements in which the European and North American nations participate would be impossible to make and inappropriate here. I therefore focus on the most salient regimes and organizations of an economic nature.

NAFTA AND THE EU IN THE GLOBAL POLITY

All members of NAFTA and the EU are parties to the General Agreement on Tariffs and Trade (GATT) agreements and members of the WTO (as well as the World Bank group and the entire UN system, on which I will not comment further). Thus, they are firmly integrated in the global multilateral trading system and have accepted an array of obligations to liberalize trade, to facilitate foreign direct investment, to comply with the WTO dispute settlement procedures, and in general to work for greater economic openness in a growing number of areas. A major difference, of course, is that the EU participates jointly, whereas the NAFTA countries are individual members and negotiate their WTO obligations separately, resulting in differences in the pace and modalities of liberalization. Still, the NAFTA agreement explicitly stipulates that the free trade area is to operate within the GATT framework. Consequently, both regional projects are firmly situated within the context of multilateral liberalization and institutionalization.

All members of the two regional blocs also belong to the OECD (Mexico joined in 1994). Perhaps this organization is best known for its statistical and analytical output, but it is also a forum for consultation and political discussions on a large number of issues, covering 'practically the whole range of economic and social issues that are dealt with by its member governments' (Henderson, 1996, p. 13). It has no formal decision-making powers akin to the GATT agreements and WTO dispute settlement system, but it is an important arena for consensus-building among the industrialized countries, and it does issue substantial policy recommendations to its members. In other words, most of the issues that are dealt with by NAFTA and the EU respectively are also discussed in the OECD forum.

Furthermore, the OECD is not a closed club. Korea, Poland, The Czech Republic and Hungary have all joined recently. In addition, the organization has begun regularized discussions with several countries in the Third World. The East Asian NICs participate in this dialogue, of course, as did Mexico until it became a full member, but also India, Argentina, Brazil, Chile, Columbia, Peru, Uruguay and Venezuela participate with varying intensity. The system, which I propose to call *OECD+*, has two components officially known as 'The OECD/Dynamic Non-Member Economies Policy Dialogue' and 'The Emerging Market Economy Forum' (OECD website, July 1997). Both are still rather informal, but they seem to provide convenient mechanisms for integrating the 'emerging economies' further into the international economic order led by the industrialized nations. The range of issues being discussed is indicated by the titles of recent workshops and symposia: 'Trade, Employment and Labour Standards', 'Tax on Multinational Corporations', 'Competition Policy', 'Maritime Transport', 'Steel Trade', and 'Foreign Direct Investment' (OECD website July 1997).

Especially in the negotiations for a Multilateral Agreement on Investment (MAI) where the OECD has taken a leading role, it appears that the OECD+ can serve as a convenient and flexible mechanism for co-opting the dynamic and emerging capitalist economies of the Third World into the political structures of the developed world. Several Latin American nations participate in the OECD+

while at the same time they are partners in talks about a Free Trade Area embracing all of the Americas. At The Summit of the Americas in Miami, December 1994, it was decided to initiate negotiations for an FTAA. The deadline for the conclusion of an agreement was set in the year 2005. Preparations soon began and after two and a half years of preliminary talks the Third Ministerial Trade Meeting in May 1997 decided to enter the next and more serious stage. Reiterating the commitment to the 2005 deadline, they decided to recommend to their governments that formal negotiations for the FTAA be launched at the summit in April 1998 (Davidow 1997). Basic principles were also set out, including firm adherence to GATT principles and WTO obligations and the principle of open regionalism (Summit of the Americas, 1997). (The principle of open regionalism basically means that a free trade area, while liberalizing trade internally among the participants, should not enhance or create new barriers to outsiders). It is important to stress here that the FTAA talks also provide a wider framework for the NAFTA countries, in which goals are sought akin to those pursued in NAFTA, in the WTO and in the OECD+ – all working towards an open and rule-based international economy and creating the international or intergovernmental institutions necessary to maintain it.

Moreover, it must be noted in passing that other regional integration initiatives are being pursued in Latin America. Thus, the declaration from the 1995 'Ministerial on Trade' mentioned seven recent market integration agreements between countries south of the US (Summit of the Americas, 1995). Clearly then, NAFTA must be seen in the context of global institutions, the FTAA talks, and the recent surge in sub-continental integration efforts. In addition, the NAFTA countries, as well as Chile that is a prospective member, are partners in the Asia Pacific Economic Cooperation that has also decided to work towards the formation of a free trade area.

APEC was established with strong US backing in the early 1990s, and the effort reached a high point when it was decided at the Bogor summit in 1994 to create an Asia-Pacific free trade area by the year 2020 (Crone, 1993; Acharya, 1993; Saxonhouse, 1993). As indicated by the target date, this is a long-term endeavour, but preparations have begun. At the Osaka Ministerial meeting in November 1995 an action agenda was formally adopted, which identified 13 areas for economic and technical co-operation (Strange, 1996; Vernon, 1996). A secretariat has thereby been established in Singapore to co-ordinate a number of working groups involving the members in these different areas

(APEC website, July 1997). Not surprisingly, given the prominence of the US and other major trading nations, great care is taken to make this project fully compatible with the GATT/WTO system as shown by the adoption of open regionalism as a guiding principle. Although the realities of implementing this principle are much more complex and prone to conflict than signalled by the simplicity of the term (Oxley, 1996; Strange, 1996), the consensual commitment to the principle does show that APEC is meant to be a stepping stone, rather than a stumbling block on the road to global liberalization.

The European Union, too, is located in a wider network of partially overlapping co-operation and integration ventures. Over the years the EU has built a system of economic and trade co-operation consisting of three levels (WTO, 1995). At the core is the Union itself and those countries with which it has free trade agreements (The Baltic states, Norway, Iceland, Israel, Liechtenstein and Switzerland). At the next level are those countries in Central and Eastern Europe and the Mediterranean (Cyprus, Malta, Turkey) with whom the EU has reciprocal trade agreements as well as a host of other co-operative ventures, and all of whom are possible future members of the Union. The reciprocal trade agreements, however, fall short of the principle of free trade; so far they are frameworks for managed trade and negotiations about trade restrictions. Finally, the Union has a set of co-operation agreements with countries around the Mediterranean, as well as African, Caribbean and Pacific LDCs. In the technical language of the GATT they are classified as 'non-reciprocal contractual agreements', that is agreements that do not provide for trade concessions on a reciprocal basis.

A brief comparison with the North American pattern is pertinent at this point. The 1988 Canada–US free trade agreement also combined two developed countries in a liberalization project, which through the NAFTA agreement has been expanded to Mexico, and via the proposed FTAA is to be expanded to other less developed regions. Similarly, the EU and the inner circle of states referred to above are a free trade arrangement between industrialized nations. However, the agreements with the North African and Mediterranean countries (aside from Turkey where membership prospects are uncertain), although broad in scope, do not yet contain the perspective or ambition of a free trade area. Thus, the two regional patterns are similar in a broad geo-political sense, but the economic content is markedly different, the EU apparently set to maintain a higher degree of protectionism in its relations with its less-developed neighbours.

Following the decision at Maastricht to turn the EU into a genuine international actor with a common foreign and security policy, albeit on an intergovernmental basis, the EU has become more active globally. The Union has set out to establish inter-regional co-operative arrangements, both emulating and in competition with the American led APEC project. Engagement with East and South East Asia is being pursued along two paths, following the European Council's adoption of the document *Towards a new Strategy for Asia* in December 1994 (European Commission 1996b). One path is the system of regularized meetings between the Association of South-East Asian Nations (ASEAN) and the EU; the other is the more encompassing Asian-European Meetings, ASEM, involving political leaders from ASEAN, China, South Korea, Japan and the EU member nations as well as the European Commission.

Regular meetings between ASEAN and the EU began in 1978 and a Joint Co-operation Committee was established in 1980. At the 11th Ministerial Meeting in 1994, signalling a push to upgrade relations, it was decided to create an 'informal and ad-hoc eminent persons group from both regions to further enhance relations', clearly modelled on the Asia-Pacific eminent persons group that played a role in APEC's development (Strategy for a New Partnership, 1996). The 12th Ministerial meeting in Singapore, February 1997, reiterated 'the commitment to reinvigorate and to intensify our long-standing dialogue and co-operation' and noted that there is 'a strong network of mechanisms to drive ASEAN–EU co-operation. These mechanisms include the ASEAN–EU Ministerial Meetings, the Post-Ministerial Conference, the ASEAN Regional Forum, the ASEAN–EU Senior Officials Meeting and the Joint Co-operation Committee (Joint Declaration, 1997). In terms of concrete initiatives in economic matters, however, the picture is less impressive. There is a decision to 'initiate ASEAN–EU co-operation in customs matters'; and initiatives to increase consultation in several areas, but otherwise the main thrust of the Joint Declaration is to stress the importance of the WTO and note the potential for increased trade and investment between the two regions.

Turning to ASEM, at the first meeting in Bangkok, March 1996, it was unanimously decided *not* to institutionalize the forum (*The Economist*, 2 March 1996; ASEM website). Plans were nonetheless made for the next two summits (in 1998 and 2000) as well as an array of meetings between ministers and officials in order to 'enhance dialogue' in several areas. Among these are the control of illicit trade and the harmonization of customs procedures. A private/public working group is to consider measures to facilitate trade and investment, while in July 1996 a Senior Officials Meeting on Trade and Investment decided that a 'Trade Facilitation Action Plan' should be considered with a view to reducing non-tariff-barriers' (European Commission, 1997b). However, a genuine free trade area, or even reciprocal trade agreements, is not on the agenda. ASEM remains a rather weak effort to promote market integration, and although the examples show that some efforts are being made to create stronger and more durable structures of co-operation, ASEM is to remain non-institutionalized, and is far less ambitious than the FTAA and APEC.

In the opposite direction, geographically, the Union has also embarked on new co-operative efforts. A comprehensive strategy for relations with Latin America has been formulated, and relations between Europe and the US have entered a new phase with the establishment of 'The Transatlantic Dialogue'. In relation to Latin America, the dialogue with the Rio Group, which includes most of the Subcontinent, was launched in 1990 and is a forum for regular high level talks on a range of issues, including trade promotion, development assistance, human rights and democracy (European Commission DG1b, 1995). A similar arrangement with Central America, the San José Dialogue, has been in place since 1984. An agreement was signed with the Andean Pact nations in 1992, and in relation to Mercosur the Commission has been authorized to 'negotiate an interregional framework agreement on trade and economic co-operation'.

In 1995 the EU and Mexico agreed to 'conclude a political, commercial and economic agreement in order to develop their relations', which was still being negotiated in early 1997 (European Commission, 1997a). A framework agreement with Chile was signed in June 1996 with the 'ultimate aim to establish a political and economic association between the European Communities and its member states and Chile which will conform to WTO rules' and which will 'pave the way for progressive and reciprocal liberalization' (European Commission, 1996a). The results of these initiatives are yet to be seen, but it seems that on the one hand institutional ties are being genuinely upgraded and beginning to cover some of the hard economic and trade issues, at least in relation to Mercosur and Mexico. On the other hand, even in these two cases the European connection is of secondary importance compared to NAFTA and the FTAA process.

The last instance of international institutionalization to be mentioned here is the 'Transatlantic Dialogue' between the EU and the

US. There seems to be a little uncertainty about the name, since there is also talk about the New Transatlantic Agenda, the Transatlantic Partnership, the Transatlantic Marketplace, as well as the Transatlantic Dialogue. In terms of formally adopted documents, the 'New Transatlantic Agenda' of 1995 and the 'Joint EU–US Action Plan' of 1996 are the main instruments. To some extent this dialogue merely represents an initial shift to the Community level of the large number of existing bilateral co-operative arrangements between the US and individual EU countries, in keeping with the implementation of the Single European Market and the development of a common European foreign policy. However, it also reflects the fact that some institutions that for years were largely dominated by the US and Western Europe – the GATT, the BIS and the OECD – now have a much wider membership creating a need for new fora in which the two sides can discuss a multitude of issues.

Finally, it is yet another instance of increased international institutionalization in response to growing interdependence. It covers foreign policy issues, where it is probably merely an addition of little significance to existing co-ordinating mechanisms – NATO, the OSCE, the UN, bilateral consultations, and *ad hoc* groupings. It also contains negotiations on policy harmonization to facilitate market integration, going beyond what is possible in the wider global or quasi-global institutions. For example, concerning mutual recognition of standards and attempts to reach some convergence in the area of competition law (New Transatlantic Agenda, 1997). These cases illustrate that in spite of occasional trade friction, the EU and the US are already deeply integrated economically and have reached a very high level of mutual openness. The broadness of the relationship is furthermore illustrated by the other initiatives in the New Agenda, among them a Transatlantic Business Dialogue, a decision to strengthen 'people to people links', and the establishment of a Transatlantic Labour Dialogue.

The point that becomes clear, then, is that NAFTA and the EU are parts of a dense and growing network of regional, inter-regional, quasi-global and global institutions and co-operative arrangements, and that they are linked to each other in several ways through this network. Indeed, on the surface it seems that the international political economy suffers from excessive rather than deficient institutionality. The question is what these interrelations mean, what the specific nature of the interactions between the two regional arrangements is, and what this implies for the evolution of the global polity. These questions are to be discussed in the final section.

NAFTA, THE EU AND DEFICIENT INTERNATIONAL INSTITUTIONALITY

One important link between the two regional integration projects consists of the dynamic of neo-mercantilist competition and rivalry. The formative years of NAFTA coincided with the protracted Uruguay Round negotiations, and part of the reason for its creation was clearly the American need for an effective counter to the prospect of a Fortress Europe and European recalcitrance in global negotiations. NAFTA and the EU have, with some justification, frequently been seen as competing trading blocs. Indeed there are mercantilist elements in both of them. In NAFTA this applies especially to the fairly restrictive rules of origin which favour production within the North American region to the disadvantage of production elsewhere; and in the EU to remaining protective trade and industrial policies. But due to the firm commitment to the multilateral trading system and the whole panoply of global and quasi-global institutions and rules on both sides of the Atlantic, as well as the already achieved high degree of market integration between the two, the prospect of competing trading blocs engaged in a spiral of increasing protectionism seems very remote indeed.

Nevertheless, the perspective of competing trade blocs is not irrelevant. On the contrary, it is quite important, but it operates in a different way, and in present circumstances *in favour* of further global liberalization. The regional blocs are thus stepping-stones on the road towards global multilateral free trade, as argued by for instance Raymond Vernon (Vernon, 1996). The political logic behind this is that each bloc counterbalances the other, acting as a mutual disincentive to revert to protectionist policies. Both sides know that the other has regional alternatives to global co-operation, making it less tempting for either of them to engage in free riding. Each of them will also take care to ensure that the other maintains the principle of open regionalism, out of fear of being excluded from or restricted in access to the other most important market in the world. Since the respective regional groupings also strengthen the bargaining position of the leading powers in the two groups, NAFTA and the EU will consequently serve as powerful checks on each other in the evolution of the global polity.

These 'mechanisms of mutual deterrence' mean that the most likely effect of the two projects on the global regime structure is to press for greater international integration, rather than the opposite. Indeed much of the institutionalization described in the preceding section –

the FTAA, the Transatlantic Dialogue, the EU–Latin America initiatives, the OECD+ and so on – can be seen as evidence of this. The risk of being left out of major markets is a strong inducement to join the bandwagon, thus actually accelerating the process towards global integration. It might well be that the consolidation of this dynamic turns out to be the most important *long-term international political effect* of the establishment of NAFTA, reaching far beyond the short-term goal of concluding the Uruguay Round. NAFTA not only represents a 'lock-in' as it were of liberal economic policies in Mexico, but also a 'lock-in' of global liberalism, and even, perhaps, a 'lock-in' of the American approach to international integration and the evolution of the global polity.

It is in this context, then, that the question of deficient institutionality must be addressed. As discussed at length elsewhere in this book, the core of this notion is that economic institutions are created that fulfil some purposes effectively, but do not address problems created in other areas, especially societal side effects. This characterization is very appropriate as far as NAFTA is concerned, and in a more circumscribed way also the EU. The notion of deficient institutionality, however, also corresponds very well to the picture of the global polity presented by many observes. Susan Strange, for instance, writes:

> Now that the world market economy has outgrown the authority of the state, national governments evidently lack both the power and the will to make good the deficiencies of inequality and instability that have always gone with growth and change in market economies. No political authority has appeared that is both able and willing to prime the pump of a world economy that slips into recession ... What is lacking in the system of global governance ... is an opposition.
>
> (Strange, 1996, pp. 190, 198)

International regimes are strong in areas related to the liberalization of trade and capital mobility, but as regards equity and welfare issues they are far less developed (although in some policy areas regimes have been gaining considerably in strength; for instance human rights, arms control, and environmental protection). As indicated by Strange in the above quotation it is not only rules which are lacking, but also appropriate institutions where decisions can be made and where a wider set of opinions and interests can be represented – that is, arenas where broader political forces can be brought into the process of international and transnational policy-making.

The present proliferation of regional, inter-regional, quasi-global and global institutions described above should be seen in this light. The multitude of fora provide a degree of flexibility so that different permutations of 'like-minded nations' can pursue further steps towards greater openness – and avoid fora where undesired issues can be forced upon them. Issues are defined narrowly and treated separately in different fora with varying memberships. This process of defining issues, setting agendas and choosing institutions still takes place according to the anarchical rules of the inter-state system, giving the major powers, and especially the US, a dominant influence.

The point, then, is that the dynamics of EU–NAFTA relations described above support this pattern. First because it serves to consolidate the present approach to global institutionality. Secondly, because one of the crucial building blocs in the global polity, NAFTA (and most likely an FTAA in due time), is well-suited to further development in that direction, but ill-suited for remedying the deficiencies. In other words, NAFTA and the FTAA could serve as a *lock-in* of the American approach where multilateralism and a strong separation of issues are prevalent features. To the extent that the EU suffers from the same deficiencies, European integration will push global institutionality in the same direction. There are, however, some differences, and in the present context they are not insignificant.

The stronger element of supra-nationality in the EU, the role of the European Parliament, and the inclusion of a social dimension, mean that Europe represents a different approach to international institutionality. To some extent, perhaps, the European approach is already reflected in the broader contents of the Transatlantic Dialogue where macro-economic questions and labour issues are at least on the agenda. It is also significant that the NAFTA pattern continues to generate controversy and debate in the member countries, possibly leading to changes at some point. If Mexico and Canada were brought into the Transatlantic Dialogue, as suggested by the British Government (Foreign and Commonwealth Office, 1996, chapter 5), this could stimulate those debates further and give them a stronger international quality.

What all of this suggests is the possibility of an alternative scenario to that of a lock-in of the current American approach. In other words, if the social and environmental aspects of NAFTA continue to be a focus of political debate and the subject of pressures for change in the US, Canada and Mexico; if the EU continues to apply pressure for a broader agenda in multilateral and transatlantic discussions; and if the Transatlantic Dialogue is expanded to include the other NAFTA members, then a new pattern of truly transnational politics could emerge, involving the entire NAFTA–EU area. In this pattern domestic politics, transnational coalition-building and inter-state politics would interact in new and at present unforeseeable ways, with inevitable consequences for the emerging global polity. The number of 'ifs' in the preceding paragraph, however, clearly indicate that the 'lock-in' scenario is the most plausible of the two.

Notes

1. But in International Relations (IR) theory this basic idea has not got the attention it deserves. See however Kahles (1995).
2. Critics have frequently pointed to the Clinton Administration's lack of a convincing overarching 'foreign policy concept'.

References

Acharya, S. (1993) 'A New Regional Order in South-East Asia: ASEAN in the Post-Cold War Era' *Adelphi Papers*, No. 279 (London: International Institute for Strategic Studies).

APEC Website, July 1997.

Berger, S.R. (1997) Assistant to the President for National Security Affairs, 'A Foreign Policy Agenda for the Second Term', speech at the Center for Strategic and International Studies, Washington, DC, 27 March.

Brown, S. (1996) *International Relations in a Changing Global System. Toward a Theory of the World Polity*, 2nd edn (Boulder: Westview Press).

Cox, R.W. (1994) 'Global Restructuring: Making Sense of the Changing International Political Economy' in Stubbs, R. and Underhill, G. (eds), *Political Economy and the Changing Global Order* (Basingstoke: Macmillan).

Crone, D. (1993) 'Does Hegemony Matter? The Reorganization of the Pacific Political Economy', *World Politics*, vol. 45, no. 4, pp. 501–25.

Davidow, J. (1997) Assistant Secretary for Inter-American Affairs, 'Free Trade Area of the Americas', testimony before the Trade Subcommittee of the House Ways and Means Committee, 22 July.

The Economist, 2 March 1996.

European Commission (1996a) *Bulletin of the European Union*, no. 6.

European Commission (1996b) *Europe. Partner of Asia* (Brussels: European Community Instruments for Economic Co-operation).

European Commission (1997a) *Bulletin of the European Union*, no. 4.

European Commission (1997b) *Follow-up of the Asia-Europe Meeting (ASEM)*, homepage July 1997.

European Commission, DG1b (1995) *The European Union and Latin America. The Present Situation and Prospects for Closer Partnership 1996–2000*, Communication to the Council and the European Parliament.

Foreign and Commonwealth Office (1996) *Free Trade and Foreign Policy: A Global Vision* (London: Department of Trade and Industry).

Hasenclever, A., Mayer, P. and Rittberger, K. (1996) 'Interests, Power, Knowledge: The Study of International Regimes', *Mershon International Studies Review*, vol. 40(2), pp. 177–228.

Henderson, D. (1996) 'The Role of the OECD in Liberalising International Trade and Capital Flows', in *The World Economy. Global Trade Policy 1996*.

Joint Declaration 1997. Joint Declaration of the 12th ASEAN–EU Ministerial Meeting in Singapore, obtained from EU DGI homepage.

Joint EU–US Action Plan 1996.

Kahler, M. (1995) *International Institutions and the Political Economy of Integration* (Washington, DC: The Brookings Institution).

Levy, M.A. Young, O.R. and Zürn, M. (1995) 'The Study of International Regimes', *European Journal of International Relations*, vol. 1 (3), pp. 267–330.

Luard, E. (1990) *The Globalization of Politics. The Changed Focus of Political Action in the Modern World* (Basingstoke: Macmillan).

McGrew, A.G. (1992) 'Conceptualizing Global Politics', in A. G. McGrew, and P. G. A. Lewis (eds), *Global Politics: Globalization and the Nation State* (Cambridge: Polity Press), pp. 1–28.

New Transatlantic Agenda 1995. Adopted at the US–EU Summit in Madrid on 3 December 1995.

New Transatlantic Agenda 1997. New Transatlantic Agenda Senior Level Group Report to the US–EU Summit, The Hague, 28 May.

OECD website

Oxley, A. (1996) 'Achieving Effective Trade Liberalisation in APEC: The Limitations of "Open Regionalism"', issues paper no. 6, Australian APEC Study Centre, November.

Saxonhouse, G.R. (1993) 'Trading Blocs and East Asia' in J. De Melo and A. Panagariya (eds), *New Dimensions in Regional Integration* (Cambridge: Cambridge University Press).

Strange, R. (1996) 'Conference Report: Asia Consensus or Pragmatic Realism: APEC at Osaka', *Asia Pacific Business Review*, vol. 2(3), Spring, pp. 152–62.

Strange, S. (1996) *The Retreat of the State* (Cambridge: Cambridge University Press).

Strategy for a New Partnership 1996. Report of the Eminent Persons Group ASEAN–European Union, June.

Summit of the Americas 1995. *Trade Ministerial Final Joint Declaration*, Denver, Colorado, 30 June.

Summit of the Americas 1997. *Third Ministerial Trade Meeting Joint Declaration*, Belo Horizonte, Minas Gerais, Brazil 16 May.

US President (1997) *A National Security Strategy for a New Century* (Washington, DC: The White House), May.

Vernon, R. (1996) 'Passing Through Regionalism: The Transition to Global Markets', *The World Economy*, vol. 19(2), pp. 621–33.

WTO (1995) *Regionalism and the World Trading System* (Geneva: WTO).

Part II
Economic Integration and Societal Institutions

5 Economic Integration and the Construction of the Efficient Peasant

Hans Krause Hansen and Kirsten Appendini

INTRODUCTION

The Mexican constitution of 1917 established that rights of ownership of land belong to the nation, and that the nation has the right to impose restrictions on private property in cases assessed to be in the interest of the public. The state emerging from the Revolution (1910–21) was established constitutionally in the form of a presidential regime. Accordingly, the executive power became responsible for distributing and redistributing land (Gordillo, De Janvry and Sadoulet, 1997).

The principle of subordination of private property to public interest was a key component in the quest for social justice that resulted from the armed struggle. It evolved into a mixed land-tenure arrangement with three forms of property: private, public and social. The private form of property refers to land held by private individuals with limits to the extent of land allowed, whereas the public form refers to land held by the government. Such lands are used, sold, leased or transferred for any public purpose. The third form – social property – means lands used for communal or corporate purposes by designated local groups who use it in a productive manner. The institutionalization and transformations of social property became closely related to the different agrarian reform projects carried out by shifting revolutionary regimes (Siembieda, 1996).

This chapter analyses the situation of social property and the people who live on and with it in the Mexican countryside during the 1990s. Developing and applying an approach whose pivot is an analysis of state discourse in an economic and socio-political reality under change, we focus particular attention on the part of the Mexican peasantry who live in communities with reform-distributed land organized as social property: the *ejido* sector. Our aim is to explore how state discourse concerning the *ejido* peasantry was constructed and reconstructed as modifications of the state's relationship with society took place while processes of liberalization, regionalization and globalization of economic markets simultaneously crystallized into the hemispherical arrangement called the NAFTA. Originally proposed by the Salinas administration, NAFTA became effective on 1 January 1994. But it was immediately contested by the Zapatista National Liberation Army (EZNL) in Chiapas. Representing indigenous peasants and communities in Chiapas, the EZNL effectively articulated, among other things, its opposition to the strategy of economic liberalization of Mexican agriculture.

THE STATE, SOCIAL PROPERTY AND THE *EJIDO*

From the beginning of the formation of the new revolutionary state, social property was given a high priority. Being an important social force in the revolutionary process, the landless peasant population and its allies claimed use-rights over lands. Because the presidential regime had the power to expropriate lands from the haciendas or large landowners in the name of the nation and of social justice, these lands could be turned into corporate social property to the benefit of the peasants.

However, it was not the first time in Mexican history that corporate arrangements in terms of social property had been established between a central public authority and the population in the countryside. In fact, social property has had a tumultuous history in Mexico. During the Spanish colonization, special lands to corporate groups were allocated through royal decrees, including the Indians. The Indians were bestowed with a corporate identity, sanctioned by a specific body of laws pertaining only to them. After independence from Spain, liberal constitutional and anti-corporate reforms abolished the colonial system of state allocation of special lands to particular groups. Private property became dominant. The result was foreign investments and concentration of lands in large landholdings, the so-called *latifundio* system. This system marginalized the vast majority of the rural population and paved the way for the Mexican revolution. Article 27 of the 1917 Constitution laid the ground for a reconceptualization of social property, which was to crystallize into the corporate socio-cultural and economic organization of the *ejido*. Being a local unit of organization of peasants with land distributed as a response to the their petitions for land, Mexico's *ejidos* emerged from the rural communities which historically formed the basis for the petition of land. The nuclear population of an *ejido* community are the *ejidatarios*, heads of the households, and their families.

From the revolution through the early 1980s, a comprehensive redistribution of lands, known as the *reparto*, took place, culminating in 1936–39 under president Lázaro Cárdenas. By the 1990s as much as 54 per cent of the country's cultivatable land was controlled by approximately 28 000 *ejidos*. These contributed to the livelihood of 3.1 million *ejidatarios* and between 10 and 12 million dependants (Harvey, 1996; Stanford, 1994). Over time, the communities have grown and include people not attached to the *ejido*, and many *ejidos* have also been absorbed by expanding urban areas (Siembieda, 1996). Though the size of landholdings, access to resources, quality of land, crop patterns and local organization of members have varied greatly from one region to the other, *ejido* farming has typically been associated with small plots, basic crops and small livestock production. Most of the crop land is held individually and cultivated in small plots, while pasture, forest and uncultivatable land are held collectively by peasants belonging to the *ejido*. Food production for subsistence has been essential, and off-farm income has been an important complement to household income. In addition to the vast redistribution of lands which laid the ground for the *ejido* sector, a comprehensive institutional framework to service the *ejidos* was established from the late 1930s: public credit institutions, production of inputs for agriculture in parastatal enterprises, price subsidies, import permits to protect national production, and public marketing of basic crops. This protective institutional framework was established in the context of the economic strategy of industrialization through import substitution.

As a result of the constitutional conceptualization of social property, of the redistribution of lands through agrarian reform policies, and, not least, of the institutional framework established to support the *ejido* and protect it from foreign competition, the *ejido* developed as a unique corporate form of social and economic organization, becoming a symbol of economic nationalism. In this land-tenure regime, *ejidatarios* obtained use-rights to land which could not be legally sold, mortgaged or rented. Instead, it had to be cultivated by the possessor, and the rights were inherited by the family. The land could not be used as credit collateral, and the establishment of joint ventures with private capital was not allowed. These restrictions were aimed at protecting the *ejidatarios* from the loss of land and at preventing renewed concentration of land in a few hands.

The *ejido* sector also developed as a form of corporate political organization that connected rural Mexico to the national political system. On the one hand, the sector became strongly tied to the shifting revolutionary regimes and their administrative structures. The process of establishing *ejidos* has always been complex and highly centralized, not only due to land conflicts internally in the communities, and between the communities and other forms of property, but also due to administrative problems in the agrarian state institutions. As a result, thousands of *ejidatarios* have had to engage with the agrarian administration for many years to receive their titles and certificates that would accredit them their right in *ejido* land. Without the certificate, the peasant has had no security of tenure (Stavenhagen, 1986, p. 263). In the 1990s the authorities have still not settled the issue with thousands of peasants, and a huge backlog of unresolved land petitions exists. On the other hand, the *ejido* sector also became closely tied to the peasant sector of the government party, the PRI. Until the mid-1980s access to public goods and services required that *ejidatarios* belong to the National Peasant Confederation (CNC)[1], one of the PRI's key sectors (Gordillo *et al.*, 1997, p. 20). In summary, the *ejidos* have had a certain similarity with the forms of corporate community existing before the liberal reforms of the nineteenth century. They have been sanctioned by a specific and complex body of laws pertaining only to them, establishing a corporate and direct relationship with the state.

However, as structural adjustment policies of the 1980s led to a redefinition of the relationship between the state and the economy, the terms for economic, social and political integration of particular sectors changed drastically. By the mid-1980s the state withdrew much of its protection of agriculture, and on the threshold of the 1990s the way was paved for radical reforms. The reforms were aimed at reinforcing the shift of the 1980s to export-oriented agricultural production as global markets expanded, at the cost of the subsistence and domestic-oriented production in the *ejido* sector. In practical terms, the reforms officially put an end to the *reparto*, opened up for the privatization of *ejido* lands and for setting the conditions to integrate Mexican agriculture into the free-market arrangement of NAFTA.

It is against the backdrop of the *ejido* sector's symbolic relation to Mexico's past, in particular to the processes of formation and legitimization of the revolutionary state and its presidential regime, that we raise the question as to how the state conceived of the peasantry in the institutional discourse surrounding the reform of Article 27, as well as in subsequent government programmes related to the implementation of the reform.[2]

Given our focus on the period from 1989 to 1994, one key issue here is how the state constructed an identity for the peasantry that could comply with the new economic project of integration into NAFTA without breaking entirely the historical and symbolic links between the state and the peasantry. It is worth noting that unlike the attempts within the institutional framework of the EU to construct a social dimension (Bislev and Salskov-Iversen, this volume), NAFTA has from its very conception avoided developing co-operation on social issues. Social matters remained issues belonging to the national agendas, or as in the case of the expected increase in labour migration – including farmers pushed out of production by competition – from Mexico to the United States following the NAFTA agreement, issues to be dealt with in separate and bilateral negotiations between the three countries involved in the free-market arrangement.

With regard to the approach applied in this chapter, it should be emphasized that institutional discourses are neither neutral nor objective, though the discourse itself may claim or appear to be so. More generally, institutional discourses objectify cultural knowledge and forms of social consciousness. They are constitutive of social actors and social relations, making up techniques of government that may ultimately constrain and enable people to undertake or change everyday practices, though this constraint and empowerment may take place in ways that are different from those spelled out or anticipated in the discourse. Such techniques of government create a space of and for subject peoples, that is, state subjects, and they contribute to the construction of social groups, and particularly of client groups linked to the state. Being discursively constituted through the classificatory work in the registers, documents and programmes of the state apparatus(es), such groups become the target of the state's policies of distribution and redistribution of symbolic and economic resources within the national space.[3]

The institutional classification of client groups may be accepted or contested by the groups themselves or others, opening up for spaces of negotiation and bargaining. It is not our aim here to analyse this theme in depth, and we do not engage in a detailed study of the particularly complex situation in Chiapas, which led to the Zapatista uprising in

1994. But we do tentatively discuss how the *ejido* peasantry as a whole, inscribed in institutional discourse as a key societal actor and client of the state since the revolution, may have adopted and rejected the changes of its role in the national space, which are inherent in the institutional discourse of the late 1980s and the 1990s.

THE DISCOURSE OF EFFICIENCY, RATIONAL PEASANTS AND SOLIDARITY

As indicated above, the structural adjustment policies of the 1980s implied a major reduction of public investments in agricultural production, leading to a decline of agricultural productivity and continuing, if not increasing, rural poverty. Mexico's entrance into the GATT in 1986 and trade liberalization in the form of reduction and elimination of import tariffs also marked the gradual change from the subsidization of the *ejido* sector, to market-oriented policies. In political terms, organizations not adhered to the official peasant organization CNC had since the beginning of the 1980s tried to establish a space of independence from corporate state control, proposing that the administration of President de la Madrid (1982–88) should open up for more autonomy, decentralization and economic support for agricultural production in the ejido sector. In short, by critiquing the government's performance in the agricultural sector, these organizations focused on a democratic and participatory relationship with the state, and on access to and control over productive resources such as credit and support prices. However, the reduction of financial resources to agricultural production not only heavily undermined the economic capacities of the *ejidatarios*, but also the negotiating power of the peasant organizations, including the chief independent organization, UNORCA, and the official CNC (Appendini, 1996; Carton de Grammont, 1995). Thus, by the end of the 1980s the peasantry was not in a position to articulate a movement at the national level to oppose policy initiatives from a new administration.

It was in this context that the Salinas administration's National Development Plan of 1989–94 made privatization the key of continuing structural reforms. With regard to the national level, the aim was to create a modern, efficient and competitive national economy capable of acting in the global arena. With regard to the productive sectors of the national economy, these would have to be subject to processes of modernization.[4]

Drawing on a vocabulary rooted in neo-classical economic thinking, and by inserting this vocabulary in a reinterpretation of the Mexican revolution and its principal scripture, the Constitution of 1917, a major reform of the relationship between state and society was suggested (Salinas, 1990). From this perspective, a harsh rhetorical attack on the role of the state in the economy was launched. The Mexican society was to be freed from its scourges, such as government subsidies, protectionism and parastatal enterprises – all phenomena that the government condensed in the notion of state paternalism. State paternalism had to be abandoned, and a situation of shared responsibility, transparency, popular participation, democracy, social justice, solidarity and autonomy, as opposed to subordination, was to be established. Assessing the present capabilities of the Mexican population as opposed to the past, the government observed that Mexicans no longer seemed to be the passive subjects of the past, waiting for the government to resolve their problems, but were demanding, active, efficient and rational social agents.

In institutional terms, the government argued for a reform of the state that would mean a return to the original spirit of the Constitution of 1917 (Salinas, 1990, pp. 28,29). The state formation process that had led to a not very social but rather to a corrupt state who regarded civil society as its own property, would conclude as major sectors were privatized. In turn, the privatization would provide a revenue to finance solidarity programmes targeted at the poorest Mexicans living in the cities and in the countryside. In contrast to previous programmes which had been embedded in traditional state paternalism and populism, solidarity programmes would be democratically structured and transparent, involving popular participation, co-responsibility and respect for local traditions and autonomy (Salinas, 1990; Rojas Gutiérrez, 1992).

This strategy of redefining the state, and changing the relationship between the state and society by withdrawing the state in some areas while defining client groups subject for special treatment within the frame of solidarity, was incorporated into the programmes and plans for the different sectors of the economy, including agriculture. In the 1990 modernization programme for the agricultural sector (PROMO-CAM), the point of departure was a diagnosis of the economic situation of agriculture. The economic strategies of industrialization through import substitution prevailing before the structural adjustment policies had been based on an institutional structure that had limited the producers' freedom to make rational decisions, resulting in inefficiency, decapitalization, poverty and migration (PROMOCAM, 1990, p. 2). Though the macro-economic context of agriculture had turned more favourable during the late 1980s due to the implementation of structural adjustment policies, the situation was still, in spite of the government's effort, one of low productivity and decapitalization, hindering what was seen in the programme as a necessary development of economies of scale in Mexican agriculture, particularly in the *ejido* sector (PROMOCAM, 1990, pp. 4–5). *Ejido* peasants had made an important contribution to food and basic crop production, contributing in this way to their own subsistence and to the general food supply. Nevertheless, they had done so in the context of a protected economy and with state support, and this situation had led to low productivity.

Since the overall aim of the modernization programme was the improvement of welfare and justice in the countryside according to the original spirit of the Constitution of 1917, this could only be done by increasing the production and productivity of the peasants. To do this, policies would have to facilitate investments and enhance the mobility of production factors, avoiding at the same time the anachronistic state tutelage by promoting administrative simplification and decentralization. It was stressed that one of the main implications of the modernization policies was the enhancement of the producers' own decision-making capabilities. Clear policy definitions with regard to prices, inputs and foreign trade should enable the peasant to do this.

In the *ejido* sector, there were serious problems with declining yields and default on credits resulting in poverty. Together with its dependence on and subordination to the state, this situation put serious constraints on the *ejidatarios'* capacity to increase investments in agriculture and improve productivity. The *ejido* would have to become flexible by transforming it into an economic apparatus with integrated units of production (PROMOCAM, 1990, p. 21). This would increase the supply of rural jobs and enhance the autonomy, as opposed to the subordination to state, of the *ejidatarios*.

Two fundamental elements were incorporated into this strategy of converting the *ejido* into an efficient economic apparatus populated with rational and productive *ejidatarios*: the assessment of property rights in order to assure investment and efficiency in agricultural activities, and economic reforms in order to reducing state intervention in subsidizing the *ejido* sector. Both elements implied that the former identity of the state-controlled inefficient peasant-client was destroyed. The Mexican peasant would have to prepare for global competition and assume this new discourse as his own. On the other hand, if the Mexican peasant could not compete, he would be excluded by the market. In fact, a differentiation of farmers and of the implementation of policies was set up, classifying the peasantry in groups: economically viable, potential and non-viable (PROMOCAM, 1990, p. 24). Implicit in the classification of the peasants was a recognition of the hetero-geneity of the peasantry, of the need for differential policies and of a delimitation of a client group supposed to be the target of a new form of state intervention based on the notion of solidarity: the non-viable and poor peasant. Thus the differential discourse enabled the state, who was to dismantle its many agricultural institutions, to continue a certain engagement in the countryside.

With regard to the fundamental elements of property rights and dismantling of the inefficient institutional structure, the government mixed a critical assessment of daily reality with a privatization pro-posal. It argued that in spite of the constitutional security of tenure through social property, the reality in the *ejido* sector was already one of illegal renting of land and downright sale to outsiders. By incorpor-ating some of the demands for autonomy from corporate state control that had been present in the discourse of some of the independent peasant organizations of the early 1980s, the government classified the situation as a result of the malfunctions of the state institutions. These malfunctions had made peasants dependants on age-long state inter-ventions in terms of recognition of social property (certificates and titles), financing, prices, marketing, distribution and allocation of subsidies. In short, the state had established the general conditions for the development of the *ejido* sector on the basis of the principle of social property and institutional support. But it had failed, contributing instead to a situation in which peasants lacked security of tenure while being wrapped up in an institutional structure which made autonomy an illusion. Opening up for the privatization of the *ejido* would mean the legalization of hitherto illegal practices and provide the condition for security of property and for true autonomy.

In general, peasant organizations supported the idea of securing property rights in the *ejido* sector. But they feared the unrestricted freeing of land for privatization, arguing that it could lead to new manifestations of *latifundismo*. They also feared that since the institu-tional structure that had provided them with credits was to be dis-mantled, *ejidatarios* would engage in risky arrangements with private investors, leading to farm foreclosures and loss of land rights. How-ever, the government's project was not seriously contested by peasant organizations, but some of their demands were incorporated into the reform project (CAP, 1992; SRA, 1992)

In February 1992, the final legislation to reform Article 27 was approved in the Chamber of Deputies. The reforms proposed changes in matters of land distribution and tenure, economic relations between the *ejido* sector and the private sector, and economic and political relations between the *ejido* sector and the state. The reforms went to the core of a peasant identity which had historically been bound up in a corporate system and tied to the state with regard to access to land and institutional support.

First, the new reforms officially put an end to the *reparto*. This policy was based on the argument that there was no more land to distribute, and it provoked opposition among several peasant organizations, in particular in Chiapas. There, almost one-third of the backlog of un-resolved land petitions was concentrated. Some organizations wanted investigations into private possessions believed to exceed the legal limits. Second, the reforms established the legal procedures whereby *ejidatarios* may purchase, sell, rent or use as collateral the communal lands and individual plots that make up the *ejido*. Third, *ejidatarios* were given legal rights to enter directly into contracts with private national and foreign investors. The second and the third point opened up for a variety of possibilities for the *ejido* sector *vis-à-vis* private capital: coexistence, integration, subordination or exclusion. As in the former law, the new law recognized three kinds of rural property: private, public and social. Incorporating some of the demands presented by peasant organizations, the phenomenon of *latifundismo* was explicitly forbidden, and it was pointed out that to be made available for private ownership, the assembly of *ejidatarios* would have to approve the measure by a two-thirds majority.

At first sight, these changes meant a radical break with the original Article 27. By bestowing the *ejidatarios* with a legal independence of social property and economic independence through the recognition of private property in the *ejido* sector, the state sought to construct an identity of the *ejido* peasantry that could comply with its visions of modernization and globalization. By lacking private ownership of their *ejido* lands, the *ejido* peasants had also lacked incentives to invest in their own parcels. If *ejidatarios* were granted private ownership titles to their own land, they would increase agricultural investment and raise productivity. This would also lead to improved rural living standards. Thus the reform aimed at freeing the initiative of the producers, opening up for new forms of organization that could be instruments of social change, putting the final responsibility of change in the hands of the *ejidatarios*, who could now freely engage in private business as efficient, responsible and rational producers.

   In addition to the reforms to Article 27, the government privatized a major part of the institutional framework involved in the production and distribution of agricultural inputs and outputs. But, as we shall see, by opening up for privatization and reducing large state institutional presence in the *ejido* sector, the government was confronted with intricate political problems. To avoid unrest in the countryside, programmes aimed at providing support for those affected negatively by the swift reform process were elaborated. The implementation of these programmes contradicted the government's overall policies, involving not a deregulation in the neo-classical sense embedded in the modernization project, but a re-regulation to suit pragmatic political purposes. The programmes aimed at providing some basic conditions for the mere survival of large client groups who, against the backdrop of the dismantling of state institutions and opening for markets, would be excluded from the agricultural sector and not easily included in others if transitional arrangements were not invented.

BUILDING BRIDGES AND STRETCHING FLEXIBLE BLANKETS

The differential discourse towards the peasantry, initially set up in the PROMOCAM, broke with previous policies in which the peasantry to a large extent had been treated as a homogeneous group. But together with its downplay of a homogenous stance towards the peasants, the new discourse had also set up an agenda for how to deal with the different groups institutionally, and, hence, also how to keep the *ejidatarios* as a client group, though in a highly modified way. The programmes were tied to the regime's overall search for legitimacy, providing yet another discursive arena in which it could promote its re-invention of the past and tie it to the present conditions of regionalized and globalized economic processes.

   By the years 1992 and 1993, an institutional format with the modifications made to Article 27 of the Constitution at its core and a network of supporting programmes at its periphery had been constructed. The format crystallized into several programmes, of which three deserve special attention in this context: the certification and land titling programme PROCEDE, the subsidy programme

PROCAMPO, and the poverty alleviation programme PRONASOL. While the first two programmes were elaborated in the wake of the reform, the latter had already been constructed as an umbrella programme in the first months of the Salinas administration back in 1989. In the agricultural sector, this umbrella programme had been translated into different subprogrammes whose targets were different poor client groups of peasants (Rojas Gutiérrez, 1992).

Each of these three state-initiated programmes were aimed at offering different client groups within the overall concept of peasantry financial or symbolic resources in the context of the privatization and dismantling of state institutions, and each of the programmes were appropriated and responded to in different ways by different groups of peasants. Quite in contrast to the official policy of reducing the state's presence in the countryside, these programmes contributed to the appearance of new levels of bureaucracy which, in addition to the channelling of financial resources to the countryside, were empowered with the tasks of registering and demographically identifying target groups, and with geographically delineating boundaries in terms of property. The programmes also contributed to the creation of a space of bargain in which peasants could deal individually or locally with the state, as opposed to the former types of corporative arrangements which had run through the PRI and its peasant sector.

As already indicated, the programmes concerned the questions of security of tenure and property, subsidies, and poverty. First, to officially promote security in land tenure within the *ejido* sector, settling in this way the many conflicts over boundaries that had prevented the distribution of legal title to *ejidos* throughout Mexico (see the first section of this chapter), the government established the Programme for the Certification of Ejido Land Rights (PROCEDE) in 1993. To process individual certificates for the *ejidatarios*, the programme established a documentary practice according to which property rights could be regularized and secured. At the level of the *ejido* community, this regularization concerned the community as a whole by establishing limits between *ejidos*. At the level of the *ejidatarios*, the regulation was aimed at delimiting plots, prompting to solve individual conflicts on tenure rights, and giving certificates to individual holders.

The government justified the programme with reference to the need for settling conflicts over land and securing property rights (PROCAMPO, 1994, p. 14). As already indicated, there was a wide consensus as to bringing to an end the insecurity of property in the countryside. However, in terms of the practical implementation of the programme, two features stand out. First, as it was the specific purpose of the PROCEDE to document, resolve and certify a vast number of individual land titles and cases – some of which touched upon century old conflicts on land titles and territorial ownership and use, while others were to confound the regulation process since illegal sales of *ejido* lands had already taken place before the reforms – the programme involved the creation of an extensive agrarian bureaucracy with resources and extraordinary powers granted to oversee its implementation (Stephen, 1994). Preliminary investigations of the practical implementation of the PROCEDE suggest that officials have presented the titling process as highly positive for peasants themselves and the larger community, in this way putting pressure on the peasants to seek private title. Even though the programme eventually seeks to regulate peasants' tenancy rights, giving certificates to individual holders, many peasants have hesitated to enter into this relationship with the state. In general, they have shown little support for the titling process and regarded it with suspicion (Pisa, 1994; Stephen, 1994). Some peasants express the view that they see the regulation and its inherent registration process as a first step towards providing the state with tax liabilities, while others view the regulation as a vehicle for privatizations which in the end will lead to the dissolution of the *ejido* community as such, converting the peasants into contract farmers, day labourers on their leased land, or leading to a situation in which peasants lose their land outright. In urban areas, many *ejidos* prefer to get access to services such as water and electricity before securing legal title.

Second, the PROCEDE was closely connected to yet another agricultural programme, PROCAMPO, announced in October 1993 to offer producers of corn, beans, wheat, rice, soybeans, sorghum and cotton an income-directed subsidy. The subsidy was based on the size of landholdings instead of the level of agricultural output. The latter had been the case with the subsidy that PROCAMPO implicitly replaced: price supports. The programme was framed as part of the overall strategy of modernization, which aimed at more justice, equality and liberty among the peasantry through the withdrawal of the state and the capitalization and privatization of the countryside (PROCAMPO, 1993). PROCAMPO was attainable by all producers regardless of whether they marketed their products or not. The programme stressed as one of its fundamental aspects to provide support for the more than two million subsistence producers who had been excluded from the former price subsidy programme.

For producers who had benefited from price supports, PRO-CAMPO in fact constituted a means of compensation for income losses due to trade liberalization and decreasing prices. It thus contradicted the government's general modernization policies by not rewarding increases in productivity, basing instead its provision of subsidies on acreage (Appendini, 1996). Furthermore, in contrast to PROMO-CAM, the PROCAMPO was not designed as a differential programme. Rather, by treating the peasantry as a homogeneous mass, it opened up for a differential appropriation of resources. On the one hand large landholders ended up with the bulk of the PROCAMPO budget, on the other hand the peasants classified as non-viable by PROMOCAM in 1990 could claim a resource that was not aimed at them originally in that programme. Finally, but not stated as a legal condition in the programme, to qualify for this new subsidy, *ejidatarios* were required to provide legal documentation of their landholding and size. The PROCAMPO's connection to the PROCEDE was thus clear, providing the agrarian bureaucracy with a means to condition the provision of subsidies through the PROCAMPO with registration and titling through the PROCEDE.

PROCAMPO was launched as a subsidy that was not linked to production but to income in the new spirit of not distorting agricultural markets. However, as public resources and credit became scarcer in the aftermath of the 1994/95 financial crisis and grain farmers lacked working capital and were increasingly unable to compete with the imports being liberalized under NAFTA, PROCAMPO was directed towards uses far from its original purpose. In 1997 under a government programme for technical assistance (PEAT-97, 1997) peasants could cede rights to the PROCAMPO payment and accrue it to firms selling agricultural inputs and extension services. The subsidy again became linked to the supply of inputs – as had public credit before the reforms.[5]

Essentially framed as a poverty alleviation programme directed at the poor and the marginal (Gutiérrez Rojas, 1992), PRONASOL was presented within the project of a redefined role of the Mexican state: the programme both appealed to the idea of a new role of the state, and to the idea of democracy, participation and social justice. The state would be present among the peasantry as a reduced, modernized de-bureaucratized and transparent partner that supports but no longer replaces the responsible ejido peasant. PRONASOL defined that the support was directed to help subsistence activity. It emphasized the concept of solidarity also among its recipients, handing out credits that community groups as a whole was responsible for.

Structured as an umbrella organization whose task was to develop and improve the employment, infrastructure, nutrition, education, health and housing of the poor living in the cities and in the countryside, PRONASOL resembled programmes implemented by previous federal administrations in that it incorporated welfare and employment elements and strongly advocated popular involvement and participation. It also addressed the needs among poor, indigenous groups. However, it differed from previous programmes in one important aspect. Along with its messages of social improvement and the participation of the population, it explicity linked its policies to the administration's federal adjustment programmes aimed at economic liberalization, privatization and a reduced role for the state.

Dismantling the state and attacking bureaucratization would create a revenue that could be redistributed among the most needy (Rojas Gutiérrez, 1992, pp. 440–8; Salinas de Gortari, 1990, pp. 27–32). PRONASOL was thus an important element in the administration's restructuring programme in the sense that it provided a formula for linking democracy with social justice. This discursively articulated and economically manifested linkage was crucial at a time where the NAFTA was approaching and free-market economic strategies were dominant. PRONASOL made it possible for the administration to declare that the privatization strategy and the reduced role of the state were governed by social considerations.

Within the rural sector, the role of PRONASOL gradually changed from being targeted at the poor to stretching out to other client groups. PRONASOL offered a productive programme for the poor, which clearly defined that financial resources were aimed at supporting subsistence activity, and not to enhance productivity or market surplus. But the programme also provided support to thousands of peasants who had fallen in default with or could no longer gain resources from the former institutional structure, including the rural bank, which had been reduced. The programme thus appealed to a larger constituency, stretching further than for the poor and the marginal. Funds were also used to confront emergencies such as that of the coffee producers who faced declining world prices in the early 1990s at the same time as the withdrawal of the parastatal enterprise that had bought and processed much of the coffee grown by small producers. PRONASOL became a pool for bargained resources for organized groups. Peasant response to the changing rules of the game was pragmatic: while the discourse of peasant organizations still very much focused on the former demands for credit and support prices, bargaining around PRONASOL funds to support production and marketing on an organizational basis became more and more common. But the political ends of the programme became more and more evident as revelations of the selective and clientelistic distribution of resources according to the Salinas administration's political preferences became common.

CONCLUSIONS

In this chapter we have raised the question as to how the state conceived of the peasantry and tried to construct an identity that complied with its modernization project, whose pivot was a reform of social property and the project of establishing the NAFTA free-trade arrangement. It seems that the state did so by discursively changing the former picture of a state-protected and inefficient peasant to a rational autonomous producer, with options to develop flexible relationships with private capital and hence to the survival and improvement of the peasant and his family under conditions of rapid economic internationalization. For the peasants who could not comply, compensatory mechanisms such as transitional subsidy and poverty alleviation programmes were created and implemented. The non-viable were the poor, and, as such, they became the poor clients of the state in contrast to the autonomous, responsible, peasant producers that official discourse had classified as viable.

These changes did not imply the withdrawal or dismantling of the state. In fact, the state defined a new space for its presence in the countryside. It did so through a number of programmes of which three have been discussed above: PROCEDE entailed a registration and land-titling process which increased the state's visibility in the *ejido* sector, providing a symbolic link to the revolutionary promise of security of land tenure; PROCAMPO meant a return to the subsidiary principle incorporated in the former state conception of peasants as a client group with a corporate relationship to the state; and PRONASOL introduced the poverty concept through the conceptualization of the solidaristic state. PRONASOL, and in particular PROCAMPO, were directly linked to the government's overall strategy of economic liberalization, and in particular PROCAMPO was framed to alleviate the impact of the NAFTA free-trade arrangement on the economic situation of the peasants. Both programmes sought to build bridges to the revolutionary past by incorporating the issue of social justice. How did the *ejido* peasants respond to this contradictory state discourse?

Though a thorough assessment of this question has not been the intention in this chapter, a number of considerations can be developed for further inquiry.

The peasant organizations' discourse largely represented the peasants that benefited from the former subsidizing state, whether within the corporate system such as the official peasant organization, CNC, as well as the autonomous organizations such as UNORCA that emerged in the 1980s. These organizations by and large took a pragmatic stance, having little room for manoeuvring in a context of economic constraint and changes of institutional state discourse. They put a certain pressure on the reform process of Article 27; they pressed for a solution to the withdrawal of price subsidies (and trade liberalization) that resulted in PROCAMPO; and they managed to engage actively in appropriating some of the PRONASOL resources for their constituencies. But they were not able to identify with the discourse of efficiency nor to articulate an alternative discourse. They found themselves in a vacuum, giving rise to a hybrid organizational strategy in which they appropriated some of the elements from official discourse while presenting fragmented responses to state discourse.

Focusing exclusively on peasant organizational discourse, however, does not provide a sufficient perspective to peasant appropriation and resistance to institutional state discourse in present-day Mexico. In addition to the highly complex peasant and indigenous reactions in Chiapas to the policies of the Salinas administration and its impact on the Mexican peasantry in general, one would have to further investigate local and individual peasant practices. So far these seem to show a variety of reactions to the reform of Article 27, PROCEDE, PRO-CAMPO and PRONASOL, going from rejection and suspicion to pragmatic acceptance of the state's, not erased, but modified face in the countryside (Pisa, 1994; Stanford, 1994; Stephen, 1994). Research would also have to take into account regional differences, as well as socio-economic ones; generation, ethnic and gender aspects may also mould differences in the response of the peasants (Stephens, 1994). As a final reflection, more in the hypothetical spirit for future thought, it seems that both the state as well as the peasantry were relating to a discourse that underlined the identity of the peasant as an agricultural producer. The state sought to 'modernize' this producer and the peasant sought to retain and negotiate access to public resources that had supported him as such. Both discourses remained within what Kearney (1996) would call a concept of the peasantry constructed within a modernist and dualist perspective with distinctive notions of space and time. The complex and changing identity of the so-called 'peasant' – part-time farmer, wage-worker, artisan, merchant, informal urban self-employed and transnational migrant – are constructing new identities within the trends of globalization. What matters here is that these diversities may open up for new types of social and political associations at the local level, and to the construction of hybrid (peasant) identities that incorporate a variety of the changes that mould people in an agricultural sector under rapid transformation, not least due to the impact of the NAFTA free-trade arrangement.

Notes

1.   For full names in Spanish, see the list of acronyms at the front of the book and the References on pp. 87–8.
2.   In departing from the observation that much of what goes on between states and citizens takes the form of discursively mediated communication open for analysis, our approach is inspired by institutional ethnography and discourse analysis (Escobar, 1995; Cambell and Manicom, 1995; Burchell *et al.*, 1991; Hansen, 1998). We focus on documents and documentary practices of institutions, in this case of state institutions. Documentary practices are not only seen as anchored in a socio-political reality, but also as contributing to the construction and changes of this reality. Our principal data are a series of government programmes, development plans, presidential declarations and laws. These data all deal with aspects of the reform of the Article 27, as well as with subsequent programmes aimed at facilitating the implementation of the reforms.
3.   If we see the state as a set of institutions and personnel who administer a territorially demarcated area over which they attempt to monopolize the use of physical and symbolic violence (Bourdieu and Waquant, 1992), the population living in this space becomes subject to a constitution in institutional discourse along demographic, geographic, occupational, political and socio-ethnic-economic lines. When people are constructed as members of a particular community (such as the nation, region, locality) and as members of distinctive social groups (such as the peasantry), they are transformed into client categories subject to the potential intervention of the state.
4.   See also Garcia Barrios (Chapter 3) in this volume.
5.   'For the purpose of increasing productivity, that will result in a higher agricultural output and a better income for rural families, the federal government, through SAGAR-ASERCA, has launched this program for farmers that [are eligible] for the PROCAMPO program in order to give them a better access to the use of fertilizers, improved seeds and agrochemical inputs' (PEAT, 1997, p. 5).

References

Appendini, K. (1996) 'Changing Agrarian Institutions: Interpreting the Contradictions'. *Cerlac Working Paper Series no. 4*, York University.

Bourdieu, P. and Waquant, L.J.D. (1992) *An Invitation to Reflexive Sociology* (Cambridge: Polity Press).

Burchell, G., Gordon, C. and Miller, P. (eds) (1991) *The Foucault Effect. Studies in Governmentality* (London: Harvester Wheatsheaf).

Cambell, M. and Manicom, A. (eds) (1995) *Knowledge, Experience and Ruling Relations: Studies in the Social Organization of Knowledge* (Toronto: University of Toronto Press).

Carton de Grammont, H. (1995) 'Nuevos actores y formas de representación social en el campo', in Jean-François Prud'homme (ed.), *El impacto social de las políticas de ajuste en el campo mexicano* (Mexico, DF: Py V Editores).

CAP (Congreso Agrario Permanente), document, 32 pp. (1992).

Escobar, A. (1995) *Encountering Development. The Making and Unmaking of the Third World* (New Jersey: Princeton University Press).

Gordillo, G., De Janvry, A. and Sadoulet, E. (1997) 'Between Political Control and Efficiency Gains: The Evolution of Agrarian Property Rights in Mexico'. Paper for presentation at the *23rd International Conference of Agricultural Economists*, Sacramento, California, August 1997.

Hansen, H.K. (1998), 'Governmental Mismanagement and Symbolic Violence: Discourses on Corruption in the Yucatàn of the 1990s' *Bulletin of Latin American Research*, vol. 17, no. 3.

Harvey, N. (1996) 'The Reshaping of Agrarian Policy in Mexico', in L. Randall (ed.), *Changing Structure of Mexico. Political, Social and Economic Prospects* (New York: M.E. Sharpe).

Kearney, M. (1996) *Reconceptualizing the Peasantry: Anthropology in Global Perspective* (Boulder: Westview Press).

PEAT-97 (Programa Elemental de Asistencia Tecnica) (1997), 'Cesion de Derechos al Cobro del Apoyo de PROCAMPO. Adquisicion de Fertilizantes, Semillas, Agroquimicos y/o Servicios' (Mexico: Alianca para el Campo, SAGAR, ASERCA, INCA, Rural).

Pisa, R.A. (1994) 'Popular Response to the Reform of Article 27: State Intervention and Community of Resistance in Oaxaca', *Urban Anthropology*, vol. 23 no. 2–3.

PROCAMPO (Vamos al grano para progresar): Secretaría de Agricultura y Recursos Hidráulicos (SAHR), 1993.

PROCEDE (Programa de Certificación de Derechos Ejidales y Titulación de Solares Urbanos): Procuraduría Agraria, 1993.

PROMOCAM (Programa de Modernización del Campo 1990–1994): Secretaría de Agricultura y Recursos Hidráulicos (SAHR), March 1990.

Rojas Gutiérrez, C. (1992) 'El programa Nacional de Solidaridad: hechos e ideas en torno a un esfuerzo', *Comercio Exterior*, vol. 42 (5).

Salinas de Gortari, C. (1990) 'Reformando al Estado', *Nexos*, no. 148.

Siembieda, W. (1996) 'Looking for a Place to Live: Transforming the Urban Ejido', *Bulletin of Latin American Research*, vol. 15, no. 3.

SRA (Secretaría de la Reforma Agraria) (1992) 'Ley Agraria', *Diario Oficial*, 26 February.

Stanford, L. (1994) 'The Privatization of Mexico's Ejidal Sector: Examining Local Impacts, Strategies, and Ideologies', *Urban Anthropology*, vol. 23, no. 2–3.

Stavenhagen, R. (1986) 'Collective Agriculture and Capitalism in Mexico: A Way Out or a Dead End?', in N. Hamilton and T.F. Harding (eds) *Modern Mexico. State, Economy and Social Conflict* (Beverly Hills: Sage).

Stephen, L. (1994) 'Accommodation and Resistance: Ejidatario, Ejidataria, and Official Views of Ejido Reform', *Urban Anthropology*, vol. 23, no. 2–3.

6 Labour and Economic Integration: The Case of the Electronics Sector in Mexico[1]

Bodil Damgaard

INTRODUCTION

The North American Free Trade Agreement (NAFTA) represents a very different response to the globalization process than the European Union (EU), and the contrast between the two regions is exemplified by the approach to labour issues. Both regions have had to face global demands for increased competitiveness, but while the EU has adopted a series of institutional measures which seek to prevent the downward harmonization of wages and labour standards, for example in the form of regional and structural funds, the Social Charter, and the Social Dialogue, such initiatives are practically absent in NAFTA. Besides the weak 'parallel agreements' on labour and the environment which were attached at the very last minute to an otherwise purely commercial and financial treaty, there is no institutional framework in NAFTA designed to discourage downward competition on wages and labour standards (as opposed to competing in product design, quality, production capacity and so on), nor to alleviate the consequences for workers as they experience the adverse pressures of the free market.

Without the support of an institutional framework at the 'new' supranational level created by the NAFTA agreement, North American[2] workers are left to themselves and to traditional nationally-based institutions to defend their interests and to close the wide gap in labour conditions among the workers in the region. For Canadian and US workers, this means that they are to some degree dependent on their Mexican counterparts and the Mexican unions to avoid a downward harmonization of standards.

This chapter analyzes the interests and capacity of organized labour in Mexico to respond to the challenges presented by the globalization process, herein regional economic integration, and the prospects for

89

transnational labour cooperation in North America. The study focuses on the electronics industry which has been particularly affected by internationalization. While many studies have drawn attention to the harmful effects of globalization for high-wage countries, the first part of this chapter deals with the experience of Mexico, since in the 1980s the country abandoned four decades of protectionism in favour of a rather brutal,[3] neoliberal-inspired opening up of the economy combined with austerity measures. The second part examines how the power of the unions in the electronics industry has diminished due to the economic and political changes experienced over the past 15 years in Mexico; the means by which the unions have attempted to regain the lost terrain; and to what extent this has been advantageous to the workers in the electronics sector. The chapter closes by looking at the potential for and obstacles to advancing cross-border labour cooperation.

SOUR GRAPES: THE TRANSFORMATION OF THE ELECTRONICS INDUSTRY IN MEXICO

The electronics industry in Mexico can be divided into two scarcely comparable parts: the part located within manufacturing industry, and the *maquiladoras* (also known as assembly or in-bond industries). While both are concerned with the production of electronic devices and components, their histories are very different and direct links limited, although developments in one part have certainly had repercussions in the other.

Manufactured Electronics

The manufacturing part of the Mexican electronics industry was established in the 1930s and 1940s as a dual industry heavily influenced by the standard economic policies in Latin America of the time: the nationalization of industries and protectionism. The first and larger part grew in a monopsony relationship as provider of accessories to the national supplier of electricity (La Comisión Federal de Electricidad, CFE), and the demand from this company assured a stable production of electrical and electronic devices sheltered from foreign competition for four decades. The second part concentrated on the manufacture of electrical domestic appliances, enjoying protection from foreign competition as trade barriers pervasively excluded foreign products from the domestic market (Díaz Gonzáles, 1995).

This picture changed drastically when the Mexican debt crisis unfolded in the early 1980s. Part of the World Bank's conditions for granting debt relief to Mexico was that the CFE submitted its purchases to international tender. Faced with foreign competition, national suppliers came out as losers and consequently have had to close down a large part of their production capacity (*ibid.*). The situation for manufactured electronics went from bad to worse as the production of home appliances and other electronic devices was also stripped of protection from foreign competition as the economy was opened up. Consumers largely preferred relatively cheap imported goods (as the Mexican peso was overpriced in the same period) to low quality Mexican products, resulting in the closure of many local companies and the downsizing of others.

Figures from the Mexican Statistical Institute (INEGI) show that employment in the manufacturing part of the electronics industry fell by 21 per cent (from 91 268 to 71 756) between 1987 and 1995 – three and a half times the rate in manufacturing industry as a whole. In this same period, the value produced in manufactured electronics (calculated in real terms) declined by 9.4 per cent to 1.5 billion pesos per year (1994 prices).

These aggregate figures hide some enormous differences between the branches into which manufactured electronics can be further subdivided.[4] At one extreme there is a small, but very efficient computer branch dominated by a few large foreign-owned companies such as IBM and Hewlett-Packard, whose large capital investments and the implementation of efficient production methods caused the value produced per employee to rise by nearly 300 per cent between 1987 and 1995, reaching almost 500 000 1994-pesos per employee.(INEGI, 1996)[5] No other branch in electronics manufacturing has been able to invest on such a scale, and the markets they produce for are not nearly as attractive as that for computers. As such, the remaining branches have achieved barely increasing, and in some cases diminishing, values produced per employee, and are rather unattractive business prospects: The largest branch, measured by the number of workers, generated a mere 41.460 1994-pesos per employee annually (*ibid*).[6] Capital in search of favourable investments has every reason to look elsewhere.

Maquiladora Electronics

While most of the manufacturing part of the electronics industry has been severely hit by the change from protectionism and state intervention to free-market policies, employment in maquiladora electronics has soared at an average growth rate of 9.6 per cent annually between 1980 and 1997 (INEGI, 1998); a figure only other maquiladora industries have been able to match, and way in excess of other manufacturing or service industries in Mexico.[7]

There are some 600 maquiladora electronics plants in Mexico (up from 223 in 1980), currently operating with an average of slightly more than 550 employees each (335.000 in total), and generating more than 40 per cent of the entire gross production of maquiladora industries (INEGI, 1998).[8] In export figures this amounted to some $17 billion of electronics in 1997, or approximately 15 per cent of the total value of Mexico's exports; more than any other individual sector, oil included.

In spite of the fact that the maquiladora part is the *avant-garde* of the Mexican electronics industry, workers have seen their real wages decline over the past 15 years. The latest data available at INEGI does not specify trends in wages by occupational group, but the drop in the average wage level for all employees (including technicians and administrative personnel) following the 1994–95 crisis suggests that production line workers are presently receiving a real salary worth around 60 per cent of what they received in 1980. The average monthly basic salary for a blue-collar worker in maquiladora electronics (not including bonuses of various kinds) is currently around US $200 monthly (twice the minimum salary of 26.45 Mexican pesos per day). However, while wages have stalled, productivity has grown explosively. Calculated using 1985 as base year (= 100), by 1994 (latest available data specified by sector) the index had increased to 230.2.[9]

Then who has benefited from the tremendous productivity gains if wages have not risen commensurate with workers improved performance? According to a study released by the Institute for Policy Studies in 1995, 78 top executives from 26 US companies working in Mexico earned an average of $2.6 million in 1994 (Lobe, 1995). In the case of Allied Signal, the American CEO allegedly took home more in 1994 than the combined wage bill of the company's 3800 workers at its plant in Monterrey, Nuevo León. Furthermore, the study claims that if the American CEOs would make do with the US $411 200 a year that is the average pay of their Japanese counterparts, and the freed wage sum were redistributed among the corresponding Mexican workers, the latter would get a raise of more than US $1000 a year.

To sum up, the Mexican electronics industry has experienced an extremely uneven development over the past 15 years in various respects. The industry is divided between a stagnant and inefficient manufacturing part, unable to compete in an open-market economy (apart from a small but efficient computer branch) and a flourishing maquiladora part which is growing at a tremendous speed, achieving enormous productivity gains, and providing 15 per cent of Mexico's total exports. All of this rests upon the shoulders of approximately 300 000 employees, 80 per cent of whom are blue collar workers taking home 6–7 US dollars a day as their basic salary. While a case can be made that liberalization and formalized economic integration have greatly improved the productivity and competitiveness of the Mexican electronics industry as a whole – precisely as neoliberal theories advocating such political initiatives predict – these gains have been very unevenly distributed. The vast majority of workers in the manufacturing part face the threat of unemployment, and while employment in the maquiladoras is booming, there is no link between productivity increases and the wages workers receive.

ORGANIZED LABOUR IN MAQUILADORA ELECTRONICS

In the absence of supranational structures built into the economic integration framework of NAFTA, upward harmonization of labour conditions in North America depends primarily on the efforts of organized labour at the national level. The downward pressure on US and Canadian wages, particularly due to competition from the maquiladoras, makes the analysis of the performance of the unions in this industry particularly interesting.

Looking merely at the percentage of companies that have signed a collective contract with a labour union, one gets the impression that workers in maquiladora electronics are rather well represented, although the figures vary in the principal maquiladora locations: from an impressive 100 per cent in Matamoros (in the state of Tamaulipas, bordering Brownsville, Texas), over 70–90 per cent in Tijuana (Baja California, south of San Diego, California), to only 6 per cent in Ciudad Juárez (Chihuahua, south of El Paso, Texas) (Damgaard, 1997a, b; Quintero, 1992).[10] However, in reality the figures reflect three different ways of depriving workers of their right to organize, and the capacity of capital to dictate unilaterally the terms of industrial relations. This requires some explanation:

For both political and economic reasons, the Mexican government cannot afford to lose the maquiladoras. During periods when the rest of the economy is stagnating and struggling to survive, maquiladora industry is a virtual job-machine and, although low-paid, workers are more content with a job than without one. This means that social stability has come to depend on the expansion of the maquiladoras, not only with regard to the border regions, but also in many other areas of the country where unemployment is 'solved' by migration to the border regions and in many cases eventually to the United States. But this situation also implies a dependence on foreign capital, which demands favourable (that is union-free) labour relations in order to settle in Mexico; if this is not obtained, investments will go elsewhere.

Politically, however, it is a delicate task assuring foreign capital a union-free environment while at the same time sustaining a governmental system that rests upon the (1910–17) Revolution's demands for social justice and a corporative state-party, the Partido Revolucionario Institucional (PRI), which has organized labour as one of its three pillars.[11] While it is politically impossible to ban unions, the solution has been to control them, which is what the regime has practiced hitherto for more than half a century.[12]

Hence, the complete union coverage in Matamoros does not reflect a 100 per cent backing by the workers, but the fact that official unions are in a position to require (using exclusion clauses) all workers to be union members if they want a job. As any maquiladora that settles in Matamoros must sign a collective contract in order to be able to operate, the control over the workers by official unions is complete.[13] As for the 70–90 per cent union coverage in Tijuana, most, if not all, collective agreements signed in the maquiladoras are known to be 'protection contracts' (Quintero, 1992; Carrillo, 1994). Such contracts are signed between 'phantom unions' and the companies in order to shield the latter from genuine unions; a 'solution' that is possible because legally a firm may only sign one collective contract with one labour union per work site (as in the US, but contrary to, for instance, Denmark).

In Cuidad Juárez, the lack of labour organization stems not only from the authorities' illegal denial of registration to independent unions, without which the latter cannot operate. More important is the fact that the official unions are said to have agreed to abstain from organizing in the maquiladoras in order not to scare capital away, and some companies have allegedly insisted in a 'no-union guarantee' as a precondition to locating in Cuidad Juárez.[14] Furthermore, previous conflicts involving official unions have severely discredited any form of trade unionism, and workers quite rationally calculate that it is better to accept the various bonuses offered by the companies – transportation, two daily meals, heath and child care and so on – than to join a union and risk being fired and blacklisted.

Whatever the formal relationship between the unions and the maquiladora workers – forced, hidden or non-existent – it is evident that the situation is a categorical break with the traditions of Mexican trade unions, and that the formerly omnipresent official labour movement is losing power. The loss of political influence is especially debilitating as this has hitherto been the cornerstone of Mexican union strength. Traditionally, in exchange for supporting the government, the unions and the working class have been assured special favours ranging from political offices (mayors, governors, congressmen and so on), to access to a variety of organs in the state apparatus,[15] to an increase in the wage level above the level of productivity growth. This state of affairs existed in the 1950s and 1960s, but since the mid-1970s the practice of determining wages centrally via political negotiations between the government, the unions and employers' associations has resulted in wage settlements that fall far below increases in productivity.

One result of the democratization process taking place in Mexico is that the official unions are no longer 'automatically' assured a certain share of political offices. Although there are undoubtedly other reasons behind the PRI losing the elections in the northern states of Mexico and the main municipalities along the border, the detachment between the unions and the maquiladora workers must be considered a contributory factor.[16] For the unions it is a double loss: not only is local government no longer in the hands of the PRI, but still fewer of the political positions the PRI does hold are controlled by the labour sector within the party.[17] To regain influence both within the party as well as externally among the electorate (the workers), the unions need to reform their policies and the ways in which they operate. However, there are few indications that this is about to happen, especially at the local level.

The Official Unions' Capacity to Motivate Members and Supporters

Labour unions attract support either by offering financial or motivational incentives. The latter concerns the prospect of an alternative to the existing economic order which workers and supporters find attractive as well as conceivable (Robinson, 1994).

Empirically, workers have had little financial incentive to join unions in the maquiladoras because union leaders, acting upon the federal government's request to provide the best possible conditions for capital, have accepted conditions in collective contracts that in some cases even fail to meet the standards required by law (de la O and Quintero, 1995). On a rhetorical level union leaders pledge that productivity increases must be tied to improvements in wages and labour conditions and, furthermore, that 'showing workers the economic advantages of being a union member' is one of the key means of increasing union density.[18] However, in practice, even without the constraints placed on them by the government, the official unions lack the capacity to ensure that either of these two things happen.

A major obstacle is the incapacity of the local unions to negotiate effectively. Their understanding of the factors which determine the economic situation at the micro-level is poor, the sectoral level is not incorporated by the local unions into any analysis whatsoever, and the comprehension of how a union might capitalize on certain conditions[19] is alarmingly scarce. Furthermore, the whole approach of the local unions to negotiations with employers seems inadequate:

> Generally, when we negotiate with the company, we try to appeal to the conscience of the employer by showing him the conditions the workers live in. [Therefore we] gather newspaper clippings with information from those people who are on top of such things as inflation and the increase [in price] of the basket of basic products. That way we can show the employer that if the salary we receive is not increased, then after a while our purchasing power will decrease, and he becomes conscious of the needs we have for a rise in wages.[20]

Besides revealing the immense inequality between a multinational company that employs hundreds, if not thousands, of workers, and a local union using newspaper clippings as its main source of information, the quote illustrates that the productivity gains are never a basis for negotiating higher wages and improved conditions. As the company's market position is held to be irrelevant to levels of worker compensation, there is nothing that hinders a growing polarization of resources, and the famous neoliberal 'trickle-down' effect is instead a 'trickle-up' effect. Moreover, as the products manufactured in the maquiladoras are intended for export, the companies have no interest in developing the local market, in spite of the fact that no other area in Mexico has a demographic development as rapid as the border region.[21] Though the financial incentives are weak, the maquiladora unions could turn to motivational incentives to gain the support of workers and the public. At the national level certain sectors of the labour movement have begun the work of modernizing the official Mexican trade unions in these terms,[22] but locally in the maquiladoras the *status quo* prevails.

Local cadres formed under the traditional corporative system continue to see their task as being political, and give their unconditional support to the PRI-government. Although they accept that the only benefit of recent economic policies has been the quantity and not the quality of the jobs created, no one argues in favour of a dissociation between the unions and the PRI. The official line is that if the unions exercise discipline and support the traditional political system, then one day 'the bad times will be over' and the PRI will again name a president favourable to labour. However, in reality the problem is of a structural nature, and the globalization process severely obstructs – if not completely impedes – the possibility of reconstructing a populistic government founded on nationalism. For that reason no serious alternative to traditional unionism has been elaborated, and the official unions have nothing new to offer the workers and the public in general.

Along the same lines local union leaders reject the idea that official trade unionism needs new alliances beyond those established with the government, which is why independent unions are actively resisted, while local NGOs and foreign (US) unions are at best ignored.

THE POTENTIAL FOR CROSS-BORDER LABOUR COOPERATION

Although NAFTA as such provides no institutional support to promote improved labour conditions in the member countries, it has impelled an increase in transnational labour cooperation in two ways: by attaching the North American Agreement on Labour Cooperation (NAALC) to the core agreement, and by motivating contact between unions and pro-labour NGOs as a response partly to the treaty itself and partly to the possibilities created by the NAALC.

The Impact of the NAALC

The NAALC does not provide a new set of common labour standards for the three signatories to the NAFTA agreement, nor is it a new institution designed to ensure the implementation of domestic labour laws. It is merely a statement of good intent on the part of the three governments to improve national working conditions, and permits any party or individual to present a 'public submission' when a domestic labour law allegedly has been violated and the government in question has not brought the infraction to a halt. A violation may be denounced before a National Administration Office (NAO)[23] in one of the other two countries, upon which it will be decided whether or not to accept a submission for review. Having admitted a case for review, the NAO may recommend certain steps, the first and least compelling being ministerial consultations, which in specific cases may lead to trade sanctions.[24]

During the first three and a half years of operation only seven cases have been presented before NAOs; six regarding Mexico and one concerning conditions in the United States. As regards the issues concerned, six have dealt with the right to organize while the most recent case, which is still pending, has challenged the illegal practice found in the maquiladoras of requiring women to undergo pregnancy tests and on these grounds denying them work.

From the point of view of the workers involved, the results of the submissions have been rather futile. In two cases (General Electric and Honeywell), the submissions were granted the least attention possible: a review and a report issued by the US NAO, but no further action was taken. Thus, the dismissed workers were not rehired nor was the union involved in the dispute granted the right to affiliate the workers. On three occasions (Sony, Sprint and Pesca) ministerial consultations were recommended. Nevertheless the workers fired by Sony have not been reinstated and the company has allegedly not stopped intervening in union elections. Ministerial talks, seminars, public hearings, and in-depth studies on the issue of sudden plant closures have done little to speed up the Sprint case which after two and a half years is still pending before US national courts, although it is doubtful that any of the 177 dismissed workers will wait around long enough to see whether or not the company is ordered to rehear them. The ministerial consultations regarding Pesca have yet to be held and the union in dispute is still not recognised by the Mexican authorities.

In only one case (concerning Maxi-Switch in Cananea, Sonora) has a submission resulted in the union achieving its goal of recognition. The success of this case is also reflected in the fact that the situation was solved before the US NAO had finished its review: the complaint was withdrawn two days before a scheduled public hearing, which indicates that notwithstanding the weakness of the NAALC, the fear of negative public attention may compel companies and the authorities to put a stop to illegal practices. However, it is still too soon to assess whether this one case will become the turning point in the use of the NAALC.

The main achievement of the NAALC (and NAFTA itself) as regards labour issues appears to be that of having created a forum and a reason for union activists on both sides of the border to come together. However, neither of the main labour organizations have participated with enthusiasm; therefore initiatives at this level have been left to smaller participants.

It is not that the AFL-CIO has not wanted the contact: as the NAFTA debate unfolded; the US unions were in need of their Mexican counterparts to oppose the treaty (so as to avoid claims that their position was merely disguised protectionism), but the official Mexican labour movement, which hailed the agreement and increasingly stood out as authoritarian and oppressive, was not an option. Furthermore, the official Mexican unions found (and still find) that they have little in common with US unions and maintain that the latter are mainly interested in links with Mexican unions in order to return jobs to the United States.

This state of affairs has opened the door for the Frente Auténtico del Trabajo (FAT), the only Mexican labour federation that opposed NAFTA. Prior to the agreement, the FAT was a rather insignificant independent labour federation barely managing to survive, whereas now, still representing only some 35 000 workers but fortified by alliances with two US unions, it is about as well known in the US as the CTM which has several million workers affiliated. Utilizing its foreign ties (and donations), the FAT has consolidated its position at the national level as the leading independent federation of unions in Mexico. Nevertheless its inconsequential size and leftist positions make it more a partner by way of circumstances than by choice to the mainstream US labour movement, and close contacts have not been developed.

The closest alliance developed by the FAT is instead with the equally small United Electrical Workers' union (UE), which is among the most left-wing US unions and, significantly, not affiliated to the AFL-CIO. While it is obvious from UE rhetoric that the relationship with the FAT is to help strengthen independent unionism in Mexico, in terms of increased membership the co-operation so far has benefited the UE more than the FAT. For instance, support by the FAT has proven substantial in the UE's efforts to unionize predominantly Spanish-speaking low-wage workers in the United States.[25]

Surprisingly little cooperation among workers takes place where seemingly it would be easiest: in the border region. Besides the few cases where the FAT has been involved (GE and Honeywell), transnational labour cooperation is left to the NGOs, which participate with a greater or lesser degree of continuity and financial backing. One of the most important organizations is the San Antonio based Coalition for Justice in the Maquiladoras (CJM), where more than 100 organizations have joined forces, among them and as a principal contributor is the AFL-CIO.

As with the unions, US-based NGOs have been looking for Mexican contacts, but in the words of a labour lawyer from Ciudad Juárez:

> there are an enormous number of groups [in the US] that are trying to find a way to get into Mexico to help Mexican organizations. But they [find] that there are really no pro-labour organizations here. And those that exist have earned themselves a bad name in the US and in Canada because they have received economic help but...the money was not used for the purpose for which it was designated.[26]

As for the official unions in the border region, transnational labour cooperation tends to be regarded as close to treason and seen as putting the economic development of the country at risk. Consequently, local leaders do not dedicate any time to this issue and most have not taken the trouble to make themselves the least bit acquainted with the NAALC; some do not even seem to know of its existence.

CONCLUSIONS

Forty years of protectionism came to an abrupt end with the brusque opening of the Mexican economy, followed by the signing of a neoliberal inspired free trade agreement with the world's largest economy and Canada. Harsh consequences were bound to ensue – and did so. The Mexican electronics sector is a prime example of how the indiscriminate and rapid opening of an economy may radically convert a manufacturing sector in a developing country into a maquiladora industry.

Supporters of free trade point to the fact that the opening of the Mexican economy has greatly improved productivity rates, but regardless of the free market rhetoric which presupposes a link between productivity and real wages, workers have not seen any of the gains come their way. This is partly due to government policies that artificially keep wages down, guaranteed by a co-opted labour movement that controls workers and resists the emergence of independent unions. In this respect deficient institutionality in the case of Mexico applies not to the absence of institutions, but rather to the need to democratize and transform existing institutions.

The situation in the maquiladoras indicates that these same institutions are in fact changing, but not for the better, as previously it would have been unthinkable that Mexican workers in large companies and/or strategically important sectors were not unionized. Certainly maquiladora industries fit the bill in both respects, and the fact that labour organization is deliberately obstructed in this the most important economic sector suggests not only the abuse of existing labour institutions, but their complete decomposition.

The North American Free Trade Agreement failed to institutionalize solid measures that would ensure some redistribution of the benefits of regionalization either directly, as some kind of parallel to the structural and regional funds in the European Union, or indirectly by strengthening workers' capacity to assert their own interests. In this respect, the North American Agreement on Labour Cooperation has proven inefficient as a tool to improve labour standards in the maquiladoras but has, nevertheless, promoted contact among certain smaller unions in Canada, the United States and Mexico. The understanding and awareness of the common problems each labour movement faces has thereby been improved and the first joint organizing campaigns have taken place. Whilst it still remains a question to which degree the process of North American economic integration has resulted in a downward harmonizing of Canadian and US labour standards, the opening of the Mexican economy has surely not resulted in an upward harmonization of Mexican wages and working conditions.

Notes

1. This study forms part of the project 'Union Strategies After NAFTA: Mexico, the US and Canada' financed by the CONACYT and the Colegio de Mexico.
2. North America is referred to here as the United States, Canada and Mexico.
3. For example, very short phasing-out periods leaving little time for national industry to adjust to external competition, and not even permitting strategically important sectors to keep operating under some kind of protectionism. Furthermore, no government programmes were initiated to lessen the consequences of restructuring for the workers.

4.   For details on the development in the various segments see Damgaard (1997a).
5.   This segment produced in 1995 35.2 per cent of the total value generated in manufacturing electronics but employed only 1.5 per cent of the workforce.
6.   This is 'Fabrication of Parts, Spare parts, and Accessories for Electronic Equipment and Devices'. In spite of employing 41.5 per cent of the total workforce, this segment generates only 8.1 per cent of the value produced.
7.   The maquiladora industry exists due to a series of tax incentives. Since 1963 the US tariff code has included a stipulation that exempts US-made parts or components which are assembled abroad and which re-enter the country from being charged customs duties, except on the value added in the foreign country. In Mexico, both federal and local government provide tax breaks; most importantly in-bond industry is excepted from the value added tax and are generally not required to contribute to the development of local infrastructure.
8.   The latest figures from INEGI show that by May 1997 there were 3610 plants in the entire maquiladora industry employing 890 500 workers, and estimates from the industry's association predict that by the year 2000 there will be 5000 plants making use of 1.5 million workers (*Reforma* 30 July 1997). In terms of employment, the maquiladora industry has grown roughly 10 per cent annually since the beginning of the 1980s while exports since 1992 have grown by about 18 per cent per year. Banco de Mexico has released figures that indicate that the total value of maquiladora exports in 1996 amounted to 36 838.8 million dollars, or 38.4 per cent of Mexico's total exports.
9.   There are no official productivity measures calculated for the maquiladora industry; the index calculated is merely a rough estimate dividing the value of the production of maquiladora electronics by the number of employees it took to produce it. It should be noted that this measure is biased towards the market value of the products involved.
10. The more common measure of union density (share of the workforce affiliated with a union) is not available in Mexico, but must be constructed. For the present purpose, the difference is of less importance.
11. The 'official' unions – the name commonly used about the vast majority of labour organizations which support and in turn are supported by the PRI – have since 1938 been one of three basic pillars of this party. The other two are farmers and the 'popular movement' (neighbourhood organizations, small businesses, taxi drivers, street vendors, and so on). The PRI has ruled Mexico continuously since 1929.
12. On the role of organized labour in the Mexican political system and government control over unions, see Aziz (1989), Bizberg (1990), Middlebrook (1995).
13. Mexican labour law obliges employers to negotiate a collective contract when requested by two or more workers affiliated to a union. The law is not different in Matamoros than elsewhere, but it is the authorities' implementation of it is which explains the difference to other cities.

14. Solid proof of the existence of such an agreement is lacking, but union leaders have in essence accepted that this is the understanding (Schmidt, 1997).
15. For instance the Labour Conciliation and Arbitration Boards (LCAB), the National Commission for the Minimum Wage, the National Workers Housing Institute, the Mexican Institute for Social Security, and a long list of other organs and institutions that determine industrial relations and workers' conditions in many other respects.
16. The right wing party Partido Acción Nacional, PAN, won the election for governor in Baja California for the first time in 1988 and stayed in office after the 1994 elections. In the state of Chihuahua, PAN won the position for governor in 1992; the next elections are due in 1998. At the municipality level, both Tijuana, Ciudad Juárez, and Matamoros are presently governed by PAN
17. By 1991 none of the PRI representatives in the state congress in Baja, California, came from the labour sector (Quintero, 1992, p. 201).
18. This and the following is based on interviews with local union leaders in Ciudad Juárez and Tijuana, July and August 1996.
19. For instance the use of just-in-time principals (which make the company vulnerable to strikes), or whether the company's ownership or market relations are favourable for certain kinds of union activities and campaigns.
20. Interview with Jesús Díaz Monárrez, general secretary of the CTM in Juárez, 23 July 1996.
21. Legally, the provision that prohibited the sale of maquila products in Mexico is being phased out over the next couple of years as part of NAFTA, which should give capital a larger incentive to build up the domestic market. However, unless the US market plunges, the Mexican market is not overly interesting at least in the short run.
22. Most likely a new labour confederation will be created during 1997 that will unite both 'official' (that is PRI-supporting) and independent unions. The forces behind this initiative – notably the telephone workers' union and the teachers' union – intend to distance themselves from the old guard, the so-called 'dinosaurs', which dominate the largest Mexican confederation, the Confederación Mexicana de Trabajadores, CTM.
23. The NAALC obliges each country to create a National Administration Office under its labour ministry which (among other duties) receives the public submissions and conducts investigations into the cases.
24. These cases are violations of occupational safety and health, use of child labour, or infringements of the minimum wage standards – in other words, not infractions of the basic labour rights. For a critique of the NAALC see Cowie and French (1994) while Compa (1996, 1997) presents a more optimistic view.
25. Interview with FAT official, 4 July 1996.
26. Interview, Cd. Juárez, 25 July 1996.

104   *The Electronics Sector in Mexico*

References

Aziz Nassif, A. (1989) *El Estado mexicano y la CTM* (Mexico: CIESAS).
Bizberg, I. (1990) *Estado y sindicalismo en México* (México: Colegio de México).
Carrillo, J. and Ramírez, M.A. (1990) 'Maquiladoras en la frontera norte: Opinión sobre los sindicatos', *Frontera Norte*, no. 4, pp. 121–52.
Carrillo, J. (1994) *Dos Décadas de Sindicalismo en la Industria Maquiladora de Exportación. Examen en las ciudades de Tijuana, Juárez y Matamoros*, (Mexico: UAM-I/Miguel Angel Porrúa).
Compa, L. (1996) 'Another Look at the NAFTA Labour Accord', paper presented at *International Labour Rights and Standards After NAFTA*, Rutgers University Labour Education Center, New Brunswick, New Jersey, 2–3 May.
Compa, L. (1997) 'NAFTA's Labour Side Accord: A 3-Year Accounting', unpublished memo.
Cowie, J.R. and French, J.D. (1994) *NAFTA's Labour Side Accord: A Textual Analysis*, Duke, University of North Carolina, Program in Latin American Studies.
Damgaard, B. (1997a) 'Union Response to Economic Integration in North America: A Case Study of the Electronics Sector in Mexico', paper presented at the research workshop *Economic Integration and Inequality – Europe and America*, 20–22 March 1997, Copenhagen Business School, Department of Intercultural Communication and Management, *Occasional Paper # 31*.
Damgaard, B. (1997b) 'Sindicalismo y Globalización. El Caso del Sector Electrónico en México y Estados Unidos: Un Estudie Comparativo', Ph.D. dissertation, Facultad Latinoamericana de Ciencias Sociales, FLACSO-México.
de la O, M.E. and Ramírez, C.O. (1995) 'Trayectorias laborales y estabilidad en las maquiladoras de Matamoros', *Frontera Norte*, no. 13, pp. 67–92.
Díaz González, E. (1995) 'Estudio sectorial de las manufacturas eléctricas', *Seminario de Política Industrial*; División de Estudios de Posgrado; Facultad de Economía, UNAM, memo.
INEGI (Instituto Nacional de Estadística, Geografía e Informática) (1992) *Anuario Estadística de los Estados Unidos Mexicanos 1992*.
INEGI (1996) *Encuesta Industrial Mensual*, Electronic data base
INEGI (1998) *Industria Maquiladora de Exportación*.
Kenney, M. and Lowe, N. (1996) 'To Create an Industry – The Growth of Consumer Electronics Manufacturing in Mexico and Taiwan', memo.
Lobe, J. (1995) 'CEOs' Salaries/Mexican Workers Salaries', Inter Press Service 29 April.
Middlebrook, K.J. (1995) *The Paradox of Revolution. Labour, the State and Authoritanism in Mexico* (Baltimore: Johns Hopkins University Press).
Quintero, C. (1992) *Reestructuración sindical en las maquiladoras mexicanas 1970–1990*, tesis de doctorado en sociología, Mexico: El Colegio de México.
Quintero, C. (1993) 'Flexibilidad sindical en las maquiladoras: el caso de Agapito Gonzáles Cavazos', *El Cotidiano*, no. 52, pp. 92–6.

Robinson, I. (1994) 'NAFTA, Social Unionism, and Labour Movement Power in Canada and the United States', *Relations Industrielles*, vol. 49, no. 4, pp. 657–94.

Schmidt, S. (1997), *En busca de la decisión. La industria maquiladora de Ciudad Juárez* (Ciudad Juárez: Universidad Autonoma de Ciudad Juárez. Colección Sin Fronteras).

Zepeda Miramontes, E. (1993) 'El TLC y la industrialización en la frontera norte de México' in Covarrubias y Lara (ed.), *Relaciones Industriales y Productividad en el Norte de México: Tendencias y Problemas* (México: Friedrich Ebert Stiftung).

7 Environmental Cooperation before and after NAFTA

Blanca Torres

The North American Free Trade Agreement (NAFTA) expanded into issues which, until some years ago, were not normally part of formal trade negotiations. One of these was environmental protection. None of the three governments initially intended to include this issue in the negotiations. However, having been incorporated into the United States' political agenda, it was eventually accepted by the other two countries. This reluctant acceptance, in addition to US needs of reconciling opposing domestic interests, clearly anticipated the strong limits of the environmental agreements eventually reached by the parties.

Negotiations were far from straightforward given the sharp differences between the three countries concerning environmental priorities and laws. Canada regarded itself as having had an acceptable environmental record and was a well-known advocate for this kind of protection. However, its government did not seem interested in explicitly linking environment with trade. Mexico, as a developing country moving towards industrialization, had not considered environmental protection one of its top priorities, nor had it strictly adhered to its own environmental laws.

Environmental cooperation existed between the three long before NAFTA, though it has been much more extensive between the two developed countries (Abelson and Torres, 1995). In each case, cooperation had experienced several obstacles and delays and its scope had varied according to the type of problems involved. The polluter, regardless of the country's degree of economic development, usually postponed commitments or measures to solve or mitigate the specific transboundary problem to be dealt with. However, until the beginning of NAFTA negotiations, economic and political asymmetry proved to be the greatest obstacle to Mexico's cooperation with its two Northern developed neighbours. Mexico's level of economic development favoured different environmental priorities and methods to deal with problems and limited its ability to solve them.[1] Moreover, the broad power asymmetry *vis-à-vis* the United States also encouraged Mexico to prefer other options rather than bilateral cooperation.

NAFTA and The North American Agreement on Environmental Cooperation (NAAEC), reached by the three countries, will certainly modify the way this issue is dealt with between the three countries. However, analysts are not only divided regarding the possible impacts of the functioning of NAFTA on the environment in the North American region, but on the scope and eventual benefits or damages of changes in the management of transboundary problems provided for by the NAAEC.

In this chapter it will not be attempted to enter into the discussion about possible impacts of increasing trade on environment. Nor is it intended to deal with US–Canadian handling of the issue before and after NAFTA. Instead we will focus on explaining Mexico's unwillingness to include environmental provisions in NAFTA and to widen cooperation on the issue, which not only contributed to the shaping of the NAAEC but are still relevant to the performance of the newly created environmental institutions in North America in the short-run. Though it is too soon to evaluate the role of these institutions, their possible contribution to the opening of new avenues of cooperation between Mexico and its two developed partners, particularly the United States, is also discussed. This will be done on the basis of the agreement itself, of the environmental commitments in the NAAEC, and the initial performance of the institutions it provided for.

The strong shortcomings in the way environment is dealt with in the NAFTA's text and the parallel accord are admitted. However, here it is assumed that very few alternatives existed, given some structural factors and previous negative experiences which nurture Mexican fears of a too wide-ranging cooperation. It is proposed that economic asymmetry between Mexico and its two developed partners will continue to be one of the main obstacles to bilateral and trilateral cooperation. In keeping with its previous behaviour, Mexico will probably try, at least for some years, to limit the scope of a rather vaguely worded side-agreement. However, it is also proposed that the new institutions, in spite of their limitations, will gradually have an impact on the management of transboundary problems between Mexico and its two developed countries and on Mexico's environmental handling. Positive or negative impacts will depend on the way the NAAEC and other legal commitments are implemented. Attempts by its two partners, particularly the United States, to emphasize their contentious aspects or to interpret them as committing Mexico to a too wide cooperation, would only lead to continuous friction and litigation between the three countries. Conversely, if wisely used, the side-agreement could contribute to prevent the massive migration of polluting industries to Mexico and the new institutions could become mechanisms to encourage the gradual improvement of this country's environmental protection and to reduce transboundary problems. Experiences in other latitudes offer grounds for this proposition.

The managing of transboundary environmental problems has been made difficult by many factors, including scientific complexity and uncertainty about some environmental phenomena and different priorities mainly generated by differences in levels of economic development. On the very basis of the controversy, there is the existence of a system of states which still claim sovereign rights, in the sense of exclusive jurisdiction in their own territory. Certainly there are many voices asking for extensive supranationalism in environmental management. However, as some authors have noted, the prospects of the latter are remote and can be questioned. Therefore, this issue has been and probably would be dealt with in the near future taking into consideration political limits derived from state sovereignty (Hurrell and Kingsbury, 1992).

In spite of strong constraints to the development of international environmental norms, rules and regimes, some advances are noticeable. Although a 'soft law approach' still prevails, provisions of this type have frequently developed into more legally binding commitments. Moreover, outstanding authors propose, based on several experiences, that environmental institutions 'enhance the ability to make and keep agreements ... promote concern among governments, and ... build national political and administrative capacity' (Haas, Keohane and Levy, 1994). Encouraging revaluation of state interests has usually been a more important and successful activity of this type of international environmental institutions than that of direct enforcement.

MANAGING ENVIRONMENTAL TRANSBOUNDARY PROBLEMS BEFORE NAFTA

To explain Mexico's initial reluctance to incorporate environmental issues in NAFTA negotiations, and to evaluate the possibilities of changes in the management of Mexican environmental affairs and of transboundary problems in the region, a brief recount of Mexico's environmental conditions and US–Mexican handling of transboundary environmental problems before NAFTA follows.[2]

Mexico is faced with severe environmental problems, including most of those plaguing developing countries and many of those affecting industrialized states. Inadequate conservation measures threaten Mexico's extensive variety of plant and animal life, as well as migratory species from the north of the continent. Sewage and domestic waste disposal is inadequate in many cities as well as in the countryside. In the early 1990s, Mexico had the capacity to treat just 15 per cent of municipal and industrial waste, while 21 per cent of solid waste was not collected and half the waste collected was taken to open dumps. There were only three treatment plants and 10 confinement sites for the 13 000 tonnes of toxic wastes generated every day (Lujan, 1991). Mismanagement of industrial waste, including toxic materials, has contaminated rivers, damaging important water basins. Air pollution in Mexico's largest cities poses a serious threat to the health of millions of its inhabitants. Some of these problems have produced friction with their Northern neighbours because of the pollution's transboundary impact (Secretaria..., 1994).

Until the beginning of the 1980s, the Mexican government and large segments of the society shared with their counterparts in many other developing countries the belief that there was a clear-cut dilemma between rapid economic growth and environmental care. Pollution, and to some degree resources degradation, was seen as a price to pay in the short run for fast economic improvement. On the medium or long term, they thought, higher levels of economic development would provide the country with the technical and financial resources needed to improve environmental protection. Later on, domestic concern increased and stricter laws were adopted. However, this new trend coincided with the serious economic problems the country has faced during the last 15 years which diminished fiscal resources, encouraged other priorities and strengthened businessmen opposition to environmental requirements, seen as an 'additional burden'. Not surprisingly, enforcement of the new environmental laws was very lax.

Environmental issues were introduced into the US–Mexican bilateral agenda several decades ago. US concern for threatened migratory species of fauna and Mexican flora led to the negotiation of several bilateral treaties to improve their protection. By 1990, a handful of bilateral agreements providing for these types of protection were in force,[3] but most of these bilateral instruments were very limited.

The most controversial issues that emerged from the 1960s to the early 1980s were the US generation of excessive salinity in the

Colorado River waters and the pollution of the Texan coast by a pair of Mexican oil-rigs in the Gulf of Mexico. Worsening of environmental conditions along the 32000 km common border also came to light and began to be discussed regularly by the two governments, and these problems were increasing rapidly due to the acceleration of economic and population growth in the area, encouraged by the *maquiladora* (in-bond plants) programme (Rich, 1992).

The more institutionalized efforts of bilateral environmental cooperation before NAFTA were those intending to solve the problem of the poor quality of shared international waters and other sanitation problems in the border area. For many years, the two governments had relied on the International Boundary and Water Commission (IBWC) to deal with those problems. IBWC's responsibilities were first expanded to deal with water salinity, and subsequently to include problems of sewage and sanitation (Sánchez, 1991). Both countries have found the cooperative efforts of the institution to be adequate. This Commission has two national sections, each having jurisdiction over its own country. Although the IBWC can initiate the study of a problem, it can only make recommendations, and public participation, though gradually widening, is still very restricted. However, being perceived as a competent agency, the IBWC has wielded considerable influence in decision-making, encouraging or directly undertaking certain works (Mumme, 1993).

By the early 1980s, new mechanisms began to be discussed because IBWC's limited legal capacity to address the broad range of environmental border problems became clear. In 1983, as a delayed response to a US federal government proposal of a comprehensive bilateral environmental border cooperation agreement, the Mexican government submitted a draft which was signed during a visit of President Ronald Reagan to Mexico. The Agreement on Cooperation for the Protection and Improvement of the Environment in the Border Region (commonly called the La Paz Agreement) is a framework which provides for the negotiation of executive agreements to be incorporated as annexes. Over the following years, five appendices were concluded to address specific problems. It is noteworthy that research carried out related to the negotiation of some of the annexes eventually demonstrated that Mexico was not the only polluter in the area.[4] Data showed that US companies and individual citizens also contributed to the pollution on the Mexican side of the border.[5]

In the early 1980s the linkage between trade competition and environmental protection emerged for the first time in the bilateral environmental agenda. It was related to Mexican smelters' emissions in the Sonora-Arizona border.[6] A few years later a second case arose: the highly-publicized tuna/dolphin problem which eventually led to a US embargo on Mexican tuna imports (Torres, 1993). As in the first case, many Mexicans claimed that the true goal of this measure was to protect US economic interests. The Mexican authorities clearly showed its preference for multilateral organizations over bilateral cooperation when the government turned to the GATT. Both experiences nurtured the perception of Mexico's government and large segments of the society that environmental complaints and demands from developed countries were covering other kinds of interests and not expressing genuine concerns for the environment. They did little to encourage bilateral cooperation.

Here it is worth making a parenthesis to focus on the actors involved. Until the beginning of the 1980s, most border environmental issues were raised in the United States by local or the national governments – or sometimes by national media. In the few cases where Mexico was the complainant, as in water salinity for example, the issue was also raised by local or federal authorities.

US national NGOs were relatively active regarding protection of Mexican flora and fauna. In fact, they lobbied for most of the agreements signed by the two governments before the eighties. Large US environmental NGOs were also involved in the two contentious problems linking environment with trade mentioned above.[7] However, until the late 1980s, US border non-governmental organizations (NGOs) were not very active on the issue, while on the Mexican side they were almost non-existent. However, mounting environmental problems at the border stimulated the emergence of NGOs, particularly on the US side, which began demanding the strengthening of the La Paz agreement.[8] NAFTA negotiations provided them with an excellent opportunity to advance their petitions. National NGOs soon joined them perceiving the chance of introducing environment in a major trade agreement (Mumme, 1993).

NAFTA AND THE NORTH AMERICAN AGREEMENT ON ENVIRONMENTAL COOPERATION

It is a well-known fact that the environmental issue was included in the agenda of NAFTA negotiations largely as a result of environmental NGO (ENGO)s' activity. Their main concerns were further deterioration of the border zone, the possibility of massive migration of 'dirty industry' to Mexico, 'unfair competition' from products coming from a country with a low level of environmental protection and potential pressure by domestic businessmen to reduce US environmental standards in order to deal with competition.[9] Widespread opposition to NAFTA enhanced the ENGOs' appeal.

US ENGOs did not maintain a united strategy (Esty, 1994). Those favouring free trade tried to ensure that the proposed trilateral trade agreement included significant provisions to address environmental concerns, while opponents fought to defeat the proposal entirely. Two Canadian ENGOs were also active: the Canadian Environmental Law Association (CELA) opposing NAFTA, and Pollution Probe, which tried to impose conditions on it. Soon, some Mexican NGOs did the same. However, US NGOs took the lead, playing the key roles of agenda-setting, establishing the terms of the discussion and advancing the main proposals. Asymmetries between countries extended to their social organizations.

The concerns of environmental groups were not allayed by the hurriedly composed bilateral plan for environmental cooperation at the US–Mexico border, provisions incorporated into the foreword and text of the NAFTA, nor by President Bush's last minute offer of a trilateral commission to foster cooperation. Neither were most of them satisfied with the final parallel agreement negotiated by the Clinton administration. This administration faced difficult two-level negotiations: while dealing with their two partners-to-be, it had to reconcile US businessmen's concerns about the distortion and inhibition of trade and investment with ENGOs demands.

Although advances in environmental safeguards and shortcomings have been fully discussed by several authors, a brief summary of both is useful. The foreword to NAFTA explicitly recognizes the purpose of pursuing free trade in a way consistent with the protection and preservation of the environment. The three parties also recognize a handful of international agreements on environment ratified by them, as superseding NAFTA in case of inconsistency.[10] The parties also agreed to promote an upward harmonization of environmental standards in the three countries, although no incentives were provided for.

The NAFTA text also recognizes the right of each party to adopt the standards it considers most appropriate, according to the level of protection it desires, even if they are stricter than those established internationally. In this way it acknowledges the diversity between the countries involved. Some analysts consider that NAFTA gives member countries more freedom than the GATT to establish their own standards and enforce them on imports[11] (Spalding, 1997; Wilkinson, 1993).

Likewise, parties may also adopt, maintain or apply any sanitary or phytosanitary measure (SPS) or standard-related measure (SRM) necessary 'for the protection of human, animal or plant life or health in its territory', including a measure more stringent than an international standard. In this matter, NAFTA is also considered to be more flexible than the GATT as the latter requires that these measures be 'least trade restrictive'.[12] NAFTA provisions on SPSs and SRMs are also seen as having influenced the Uruguayan Round on the issue.

In an attempt to provide reassurance for ENGOs fearing migration of industry to Mexico, the NAFTA text considers it improper to attract investment by relaxing domestic health, safety or environmental standards. However, the relevant article has also been strongly criticized because it merely provides for consultations if a country fails to comply with this provision and there is no provision for the imposition of sanctions. However, the risk of public exposure could discourage foreign investors intending to move to Mexico to avoid environmental regulations.

As regards dispute settlement, the NAFTA text deals with controversies involving sanitary and phytosanitary measures and other standard related measures which may be considered trade-protectionism by one of the parties. Here it is worth noting that the party facing the charge has the right to choose the organization where the demand is to be filed (NAFTA or the WTO) This may be seen as an additional important concession to ENGOs. A significant difference between NAFTA and the WTO dispute settlement mechanism, for example, is that in NAFTA the complainant has the burden of proof (Johnson and Beaulieu, 1996).

Though strongly opposed up to the last minute by both Canada and Mexico, monetary and trade sanctions for ineffective enforcement of domestic laws were finally accepted by the latter (Winham, 1994). However, Mexico succeeded in introducing a long process for reaching such a decision.

Finding solutions to these controversies, enforcement of environmental laws and sanctions for non-compliance probably are, as it has been noted, the main focus of the NAAEC and the trilateral Commission for Environmental Cooperation (CEC). To promote environmental cooperation, including regulatory improvement in the three countries, is its second main task. The two bilateral institutions provided for the NAAEC, the Border Commission for Environmental Cooperation and the North American Development Bank will promote and support infrastructure projects along the US–Mexican border to help clean it up and provide support for community adjustment related to NAFTA.

Several ENGOs admit as gains the guarantees included in the NAFTA's text that the level of environmental protection would be maintained, as well as state and local power to determine the degree of environmental protection considered adequate and the establishment of the three institutions. Some ENGOs saw promise in the CEC's right to investigate complaints of non-compliance by governments submitted by groups and citizens throughout the NAFTA region; in provisions for majority voting in the Commissions on important procedural matters; in the introduction of sanctions; in new fora for lobbying and in the reinforcement of national and transnational networks (Munton and Kirton, 1996). Some US NGOs also found relief on the issue of a Statement of Administrative Action (SAA) committing the United States to withdraw from NAFTA with regard to either Canada or Mexico if any country denounced the environmental parallel agreement (Inside US Trade, 1993).

However, most ENGOs were certainly disappointed with the limited degree of autonomy of the Secretariat; with the mechanisms to finance investments for environmental infrastructure and clean-up; with the limits on citizen's petitions, participation in conflict resolution, access to information flows and right-to-know (Kelly, 1993).

US and Canadian studies of the side agreements have usually focused on the shortcomings mentioned by ENGOs of the two developed partners. It is therefore useful to recall some Mexican ENGOs' and researchers' concerns that have been largely ignored. This is particularly important because it shows that NAFTA instruments mainly address US ENGOs' concerns and priorities. The main criticism of Mexicans is the emphasis of equality of efforts, including financial disbursements. Given the wide gap between Mexico's laws and its actual capacity to enforce them in the short run, the lack of a schedule for stricter compliance is seen as opening the way for numerous complaints and disputes. Immediate stricter enforcement of the law is not only regarded as difficult to achieve because of that gap and because hundreds of norms are still lacking, but would also result in bankruptcy for many small and medium-sized industries. Industries battered by the recurrent economic crises affecting Mexico would need extensive financial support to meet environmental requests.

Strong US demands for high Mexican investment in environmental cleaning up along the border, where less than 4 per cent of the Mexican population live, is also perceived as having potentially negative effects of discrimination and lack of geographical fairness. Furthermore, investing an excessively large proportion of limited funds and technical resources in the border zone could also reproduce the same vicious circle as in Mexico City, where huge investments for many decades to appease a relatively more politicized society led to more population migrating to this city. The fact that the problem of acute water shortage in the border zone was not addressed, and in general the lack of importance given to the protection of natural resources, were additional shortcomings highlighted by some Mexican ENGOs and scholars (Sanchez, 1991).

Summarizing, environmental provisions in NAFTA and the NAAEC have had opposing interpretations: 'environmentally friendly' or 'opening the way for more degradation'. Indeed, they reveal the negotiators' efforts to reconcile the interests of both the developed and the developing parties, and the specific interests of domestic actors within each country. The same holds true of the absence, heavily criticized by ENGOs, of any consideration of the processes and production methods and a weak call for policy harmonization. As Esty has suggested, the incremental approach adopted

> allows differences in environmental priorities, natural endowments, and levels of development to shape the starting point for common environmental programs. It also permits parties to identify together the most promising areas for convergence as part of an ongoing process. (Esty, 1994)

Though critics of the three countries coincided on the accord's vagueness and loop-holes, a handful of ENGOs and researchers did recognize the opportunities that the interpretation of the vague provisions of the side deal might offer. They perceived an immediate opportunity to continue advancing: the agenda setting of the new institutions. However, their participation has been limited by recent developments in the United States and in Mexico. This country entered into an acute economic crisis in December 1994, just a few months after the new institutions were established. US ENGOs have largely withdrawn from Mexican issues, concentrating instead on domestic affairs, as they have perceived a trend toward less strict regulation, since the shift in Congress from Democratic to Republican control. Canadian ENGOs have also perceived a threat to environmental laws and programs, both as a result of budget cuts and the delegation of greater responsibility to provincial governments (NAMI, 1995).

THE NEW INSTITUTIONS' PERFORMANCE

The bilateral Border Commission and Nadbank have advanced very slowly. Priorities for the first phase were established (water, waste water and solid waste disposal projects). However, project certification and financing have proved difficult because both institutions are expected to reconcile the criteria of showing sensitivity to social considerations with the assurance of technical and financial feasibility.[13] Developing the general criteria with broad public participation, as stipulated, took several months and the criteria remain quite vague. Equity and sustainability are emphasized, although the definition of both concepts is still controversial.[14] Controversy surrounding priority criteria for funding has led to the postponement of the certification of several projects. Increasing participation of inhabitants of the two sides of the border is encouraging.

The trilateral Commission's work also began slowly. The CEC sees itself as an entity created to help the parties prevent negative impacts of trade and to generate development alternatives less damaging to the environment. To avoid becoming involved in continuous litigation, given NAAEC focus, the three parties have emphasized the 'collaborative agenda'. Information-gathering and capacity-building are the main goals of most of the programmes already approved. Ecomaps of the region, toxic release inventories, a common framework to limit pollutants in the region, beginning with the drawing up of trinational guidelines to deal with DDT, PCBs, chlordane and mercury are some of the programmes currently being implemented. Additional initiatives include a joint effort to identify important areas for North American migratory birds, the establishment of protected pilot areas and the improvement of legislation to protect them; the creation of a task force to encourage cooperation on climate change issues; a comparative analysis of environmental impact studies in the three countries; the creation of a North American Environmental Fund; greater information access to the public through the Commission's home-page; and a North American Center for Environmental Technology Information Service.

However, contentious issues have already arisen in the CEC. The first two were submitted against the US government. One was the complaint lodged by US and Mexican ENGOs against provisions attached to a new US law, which not only reduced the United States Fish and Wildlife Service budget for environmental enforcement, but forbade the agency from making any 'final determinations that species or critical habitat are endangered for the remainder of the fiscal year of 1995' (*Inside NAFTA*, 1995). The second complaint was filed by US Mexican and Canadians ENGOs charging the US government with violating the side agreement. The ENGOs' goal was to prevent Congress from suspending all laws forbidding tree felling in the Pacific Northwest for eighteen months. This measure was regarded as a threat to certain endangered species, particularly the Douglas fir owl in Oregon (*Inside US Trade*, 1995). Both complaints were dismissed by the Commission, on the grounds that they challenged the laws themselves rather than their enforcement.

A closer look at the complaints against Mexico sheds light on its government's strenuous efforts to limit the interpretation of the side-agreement and particularly to introduce restrictions concerning the Secretariat's autonomy. It is aware that the Commission's responses set precedents which will gradually eliminate the ambiguities and gaps in the accord. Clearly none of the three governments was willing to establish supranational institutions. However, during the negotiations, the US government did press for greater powers for the Secretariat including the authority to initiate reports and gather information. Only the joint opposition of Canada and Mexico prevented the inclusion of this proposal in the agreement.

Under the terms of articles 13 and 14, the CEC is authorized to investigate and issue reports on situations of non-compliance and non-enforcement of existing environmental laws. One complaint against Mexico concerned the pollution of a lake in central Mexico. The Commission appointed a nine-member panel charged with identifying the causes of the deaths of a number of migratory birds, making recommendations to prevent similar problems in the future, and suggesting areas of trilateral cooperation in this field.

Another complaint focused on the failure by the Mexican government to request the appropriate environmental impact assessment of a project to construct a pier which some Mexican and US ENGOs claim could endanger the world's second largest coral reef system, either directly or indirectly. This project had previously aroused the concern of the local governor, but was approved by the federal authorities. The

Mexican government reacted strongly against what it regarded as mishandling of the problem by the Secretariat. According to Mexican authorities, the claim should have been rejected by the Secretariat on several grounds of a procedural nature. They also claimed that the Secretariat showed an anti-Mexican bias.

However, to avoid a majority vote at the Council, the Mexican representative joined its partners in ordering the Secretariat to proceed with the preparation of a factual report. The Mexican government, however, stated that as a result of this experience, the three parties should be prepared to revise the specific mechanisms that would allow the elimination of any possible distortions in the interpretation of the side-agreement and ensure that the CEC's actions were kept on track in the spirit of cooperation that was the basis of its creation.

The strength of the Mexican government's initial reaction reveals its desire to prevent any further advance on the part of the Secretariat.[15] To a certain extent, it also shows the dilemma faced by developing countries between economic growth on the one hand and better environmental protection.

It must be said that restraint has been shown by US and Canadian ENGOs regarding claims against the Mexican government. In addition to their concentration in domestic affairs, as mentioned above, other factors may explain this restraint. Some ENGOs probably became aware of the negative effects that continuous litigation would have on environmental protection in Mexico, a country with few financial and human resources. Much of top Mexican environmental officials' efforts, for example, have been spent on the handling of the Cozumel (coral reef) case, not to mention considerable expenditures during NAFTA negotiations on efforts to solve specific environmental problems to please a handful of US ENGOs.[16] Some of these organizations have finally realized their requests were not always wise or necessary, and in some cases led to the abandonment or neglect of other better designed projects. However, a fresh onslaught of pressure cannot be ruled out.

These developments have certainly given Mexico breathing space. Environmental agencies are working hard on legislative changes. Some of them are intended to move away from command-and-control policies, trying to rely more on market mechanism to improve protection. It is also possible to perceive the beginning of a self-policing strategy currently being promoted by certain multinational and large domestic companies. They are encouraged by business' expectations of a stricter law enforcement. If this pattern becomes widespread, emissions and other pollutants would be reduced.

CONCLUSIONS

Reluctant acceptance of incorporating the environmental issue in NAFTA negotiations by Canada and Mexico, and the US government's need to reconcile different domestic interests had an impact on the scope of the commitments eventually reached by the three governments. However, in spite of their limits, those commitments went far beyond what Mexico had previously accepted.

The bilateral and trilateral environmental institutions established parallel to NAFTA had started, though slowly, to increase environmental cooperation between Mexico and its two developed partners, particularly the United States. Not surprisingly much of the work done by the Commissions has centered on encouraging research and improving Mexican capacities. More data about environmental problems at the US–Mexican border and, in general, in Mexico's whole territory are badly needed, and could lead to a better understanding of those problems and a more adequate establishment of priorities and courses of action. In this way, it could possibly influence a revaluation of national interests.

A good priority-setting by the Mexican government, favoured not only by better information and higher personnel capacity, is specially important to channel efforts and funds, including those coming from its developed partners, to deal with its most urgent environmental problems. This is particularly important given limited Mexican domestic resources and the low magnitude of the flows of financial and technological assistance from its Northern neighbours. A clear priority setting would also allow Mexican authorities to choose more adequately their responses to foreign demands.

It is not possible to deny that Mexico's margins, options and possibilities to advance its own environmental agenda have been reduced while accepting formal cooperation. However, they have not disappeared. Alliances with the Canadian government, although not always possible, could prove useful in dealing with intermittent US pressures which often respond to purely domestic political motives and purposes. Closer contact with some of Mexico's own ENGOs and those of the other two countries that have shown a sympathetic attitude, would enable the Mexican government to make them aware of its priorities, increasing its chances of advancing its positions. Better informed ENGOs, who certainly will continue to be important actors, could prove useful allies in the extremely difficult task of improving environmental protection not only in Mexico but in the region as a whole.

Though until now the three parties have shown their willingness to avoid as much as possible the NAAEC's wide contentious aspects, it is clear that cooperation could encounter severe obstacles and lead to frequent recriminations and litigation. Requests for cooperation that would entail substantial changes in the pattern of economic development pursued by Mexico, the economically weaker country, would strongly be resisted by the latter. However, the Commissions have provided fora for a continuous dialogue between officials of the three countries, and also to the interested public. This could help to improve mutual understanding and to gradually reduce Mexico's suspicions.

In sum, though many ENGOs do not agree with the incrementalist approach provided by the NAAEC, it could prove to be, if its more contentious aspects are put aside, the best way to advance toward the improvement of law enforcement in Mexico and eventually an upward harmonization of policies and legislation in North America.

Notes

1. Here it is convenient to remember that Mexico's GDP is 20 times smaller than that of the United States, whereas its population is a little less than a third and it is growing at a much faster rate.
2. Collaboration between Mexico and Canada has increased, including a flow of funds for $1 million in environmental assistance, agreed on 18 March 1992. However, for reasons of space, this chapter will focus on US–Mexican cooperation.
3. They were related to the protection of migratory birds, mammals, plants, wetlands and winter habitats. Alberto Szekely, 'Establishing a Region for Ecological Cooperation in North America', *Natural Resources Journal*, vol. 32, summer 1992.
4. They openly or implicitly admit San Diego's sewage contribution to the pollution of its own beaches, and the high US copper smelters' emissions in the Sonora-Arizona border area. Roberto Sánchez, 'La negociación de los conflictos ambientales entre México y Estados Unidos', in *Frontera Norte*, vol. 1, January – June 1989.
5. For example, appendix III deals with the maquiladoras' (in-bond plants) failure to comply with their commitments of sending back toxic wastes to US territory. It also tries to deal with the illegal sending of these type of wastes from the United States into Mexican territory. Sánchez, 'La negociación', *ibid.*, p. 28.

6. It seems that US copper smelters that raised the issue were less concerned for the environment than for the competition of an expanding facility in Mexico. This conflict is analyzed in: Steven P. Mumme, 'The Cananea Copper Controversy: Lessons for Environmental Diplomacy', *Inter-American Economic Affairs*, 1, 38, Summer 1984, pp. 3–22.

7. Greenpeace, the Arizona Clean Air Coalition, the Environmental Defense Fund, Sierra Club and Friends of the Earth, approached by US copper producers, joined the opposition. A California-based NGO submitted the complaint that eventually led to the embargo. Conversely, Greenpeace worked closely with the Inter-American Tropical Tuna Commission (IATTC) to find a multilateral solution to incidental dolphin killing and supported the lifting of the embargo.

8. Problems on the Mexican side increased while growing slum areas in the US side also experienced infrastructure deficits. 60 per cent of the 'colonias' in Texas have running water but just 1 per cent have sewers. The figures for New Mexico are 80 per cent and 7 per cent. SEDUE, *Plan Integral Ambiental Fronterizo, Primera Etapa 1992/1994*, SEDUE, México, 1991, pp. 26, 50–1. See also Ingram *et al.*, *op. cit.*, pp. 18–19.

9. Local NGOs provided them with data about the most urgent problems. Geoffrey Land, 'North American Free Trade and the Environment: Border Environmental Groups and the NAFTA', in *Frontera Norte*, vol. 5, July – December 1993, p. 102.

10. '[T]o the extent of the inconsistency, provided that where a party has a choice among equally effective and reasonably available means of complying with such obligations, the Party chooses the alternative that is least inconsistent with the other provisions.'

11. A country may refuse access to imports it considers dangerous to the environment, health or security on the basis of scientific principles, whereas GATT requires scientific proof.

12. According to NAFTA the application of the standard is considered 'only to the extent necessary to achieve its appropriate level of protection, taking into account technical and economic feasibility'.

13. For example, interests rates of the loans are expected to be just below commercial ones, discouraging poor communities.

14. Following Agenda 21 of the Rio Conference, some ENGOs advanced the need to include, among other elements, carrying capacity and commitment to future generations. However, to date the selection has emphasized the ability of the community to properly maintain the facilities for its life-cycle. These definitions are to be revised in 1997. *NAMI News*, issue 17, 1996, p. 9.

15. This does not disregard the Mexican government's assurances that there would not be any damage to the reef and that developers were complying with Mexican law.

16. For example, Carlos Salinas's administration hurriedly introduced several measures to protect turtles, which badly hurt poor fishermen who were not given job alternatives or any other help.

References

Abelson, P. and Torres, B. (1995) 'The Politics of Environmental Cooperation: A View from Ottawa and Mexico', mimeo, ITAM.

Esty, D.C. (1994) *Greening the GATT. Trade Environment and the Future* (Washington, DC: Institute for International Economics), pp. 29, 32, 185–92.

Haas, P.M., Keohane, R.O. and Levy, M.A. (1994) *Institutions for the Earth. Sources of Effective International Environmental Protection* (Cambridge, Mass.: The MIT Press).

Holsti, K.J. and Levy, T.A. (1976) 'Bilateral Institutions and Transgovernmental Relations between Canada and the United States', in Fox, A.B., Hero, A.O. Jr. and Nye, J.S. Jr. (eds), *Canada and the United States, Transnational and Transgovernmental Relations* (New York and London: Columbia University Press), pp. 282–309.

Hurrell, A. and Kingsbury, B. (1992) *The International Politics of the Environment* (Oxford: Clarendon Press).

Inside NAFTA, 9 August 1995, p. 4.

Inside US Trade, 1 September 1995.

Inside US Trade, (1993) 'Administration Pledges to Exit NAFTA if Side Pacts are Abandoned', 12 November.

Johnson, P.M. and Beaulieu, A. (1996) 'The Environment and NAFTA; Understanding and Implementing the New Continental Law' (Washington, DC, and California: Island Press).

Kelly, M.E. (1993) 'Review of the Environmental Side Agreement: Does it meet expectations?', *Frontera Norte*, vol. 10, July – December, pp. 133–47.

Lujan, S.R. (1991) 'Working within the Legal Framework for Environmental Protection in Mexico', paper presented at the conference *Exporting Environmental Know-how Workshop*, San Francisco.

Mumme, S. (1993) 'NAFTA and the Future of Mexico – US Border Environmental Management', *Frontera Norte*, vol. 5, July – December, p. 89.

Munton, D. and Kirton, J. (1996) 'Beyond and Beneath the Nation-State: Province–State Interactions and NAFTA', paper presented at the International Studies Association Annual Meeting, San Diego, California, April

North American Institute, *NAMI News*, issue 14, May 1995.

Rich, J.G. (1992) 'Planning the Border's Future: the Mexican – US Integrated Border Environmental Plan', the University of Texas at Austin, Lyndon B. Johnson School of Public Affairs, *US – Mexican Occasional Paper No. 1*, March.

Sánchez, R. (1991) 'El Tratado de Libre Comercio en América del Norte y el Medio Ambiente de la Frontera Norte', *Frontera Norte*, vol. 6, July–December, p. 14.

Secretaría de Desarrollo Social, Instituto Nacional de Ecología (1994) *Informe de la situación general en materia deequilibrio ecológico y protección del medio ambiente 1993–1994*, Mexico, SEDESOL, Institute for International Research, 26 June.

Spalding, M.J. (1997) 'Lessons of NAFTA for APEC', *Journal of Environment and Development*, vol. 6 (3), September, pp. 252–75.

Torres, B. (1993) 'La cuestión del medio ambiente en la agenda bilateral (1991–92)', in G. Vega (ed.), *México, Estados Unidos, Canadá, 1991–1992* (México, El Colegio de México), pp. 381–428.

Wilkinson, D.G. (1993) 'NAFTA and the Environment: Some Lessons for the Next Round of GATT Negotiations', *The World Economy*, vol. 17 (3), pp. 395–412.

Winham, G.R. (1994) 'Enforcement of Environmental Measures: Negotiating the NAFTA Environmental Side Agreement', *Journal of Environment and Development*, vol. 3 (1).

8 Constructing Europe: The Role of Social Solidarity

Sven Bislev and Dorte Salskov-Iversen

INTRODUCTION: ECONOMIC INTEGRATION AND SOCIETAL EFFECTS

Unlike other regional integration projects, the European Community/ Union[1] has a social dimension. From the outset, that dimension was part of the conception of the Communities – as a pre-condition for and corollary of market-building. However, much ambivalence has surrounded the social aspect of the communities – the 'European social model' is regarded by some as a protectionist, inflexible burden of the past; the liberal economic regimes of the EU are there to remedy such ills. For others, the very same model is the epitome of human achievement in the field of community and state-building.

This chapter looks at the political implications of the social dimension – notably its role in creating legitimacy and identity. The first section establishes the interconnection between social solidarity on the one hand and legitimacy and identity on the other hand – and points to the particular relevance of this correlation for an institution like the EU which, on some counts, is assuming state-like functions. The second section sets out briefly to trace the discursive constitution of the social dimension as a political field in the EC/EU. In the third section, we pursue this discussion in an analysis of two Commission documents prepared for the Intergovernmental Conference 1996. It is because the political function of social solidarity is ultimately concerned with the conceptualization of a framework for action capable of containing the inherent ambivalence of project Europe that we find the Commission's discourse a promising site for investigation.

Most other free trade areas are minimalistic in their approach to integration. As another exception, however, NAFTA is quite ambitious in the number of sectors included and the areas regulated. But NAFTA most emphatically avoids establishing cooperation on social

matters. In Europe, social matters have largely been left to the care
of those nation-states, for whom it is a traditional policy area. In
North American states, social policy as such is a strongly disputed
area. Mexico, the weaker member of NAFTA, has its own problems,
peculiar to a third world country – among them is the problem of
affording social programmes and organizing efficient representation
of interests.

European nations all have both social policy and European integration high on their political agendas – although with large variations,
according to social structure, culture and the ideologies of incumb-
ent governments. At present, however, these two goals seem to be in
conflict, and the political ambitions of the EU are challenged: the
integration agenda has been successful in the sense that a vast
number of areas are regulated through the Union – so many that the
need for political legitimacy is rising fast. But the most obvious
means for building legitimacy in modern democracies – redistribution
and social initiatives – are very hard to transfer to the supranational
level.

The problem we examine in the following is political by nature:
the community spawned by the postwar integrationist efforts has
become increasingly political, and the legitimacy dimension is being
addressed in the ongoing attempts at deepening and widening the
Union – but how effectively? There is already a quite considerable
literature (Caporaso, 1996; Münch, 1996; Schmitter, 1996; Weiler,
et al., 1994; Jachtenfuss *et al.*, 1997) discussing 'the nature of the
beast', that is, the sort of creature that is emerging out of project
Europe. Precisely because the EC/EU – according to these analyses –
approximates a state-like construction on several counts, the community-building process needs to institutionalize social solidarity as
a crucial legitimacy-building factor. The problem for European integration however is that social solidarity remains tightly attached to
the identities associated with the nation-state, and as such it is not
readily accessible for the supranational state in its legitimacy-building
efforts. In recent policy documents from the EU – white papers,
declarations, treaty amendments – a number of solidarity-semaphors
are being raised. Action, however, remains tardy and ambivalent. In
particular the Commission of the European Communities (CEC) has
been trying to advance the process by rearticulating the field, constructing a formula for social solidarity – and by implication a framework for figural action (see below) – acceptable to the member states'
governments.

AN INTERNATIONAL COMMUNITY ASSUMING STATE
FUNCTIONS: THE ROLE OF LEGITIMACY

> a single currency, as a major integrating factor for those operating in
> the economy at large and for individual citizens, calls for a strong
> political and social identity.
>
> (The European Commission, February 1996, p. 7)

The EU is probably not going to be a nation-state in the classical sense.
Even with a very 'activist' notion of state- and nation-building (Smith,
1986), and despite the growing confidence of Europeans towards each
other and the Union (Dogan, 1993), it is highly unlikely that the
fragmented and dispersed elements of European identities can be
assembled into anything resembling even a modest version of the
national identity necessary for a modern state (Schmitter, 1996; Obradovic, 1996).

But, in several aspects, the process of European integration is,
nonetheless, reminiscent of the classical historical process of state-
and nation-building as we know it from European history: a set of
regulations are being established for a territory (an expanding one, but
at each moment precisely defined). Those regulations are superior to
other types of regulation. Common regulations of external affairs are
being made, decision-making mechanisms are being established, and,
in the process, legitimacy is attempted.[2]

Building a state-like body implies a need of generating legitimacy:
both the mechanisms of power allocation and the distribution of
resources must be justified in terms of moral and political principles
acceptable to a sufficient number of citizens. Legitimacy may be
defined as including three aspects – a legal aspect, a value aspect,
and a will formation aspect (adapted from Beetham, 1991). The EU
has gone some way to integrate its legal systems through the accepted
supremacy of the European Court of Justice (Stone, 1996), but the two
other aspects are still gravely underdeveloped: a set of integrating
ideas is sometimes declared, but has not really taken root; and the
will formation process – the deliberative aspect of politics – in the
Union lacks the broad input from all walks of life that demonstrates
the existence of a mature democracy (Jacobsson, 1997).

Redressing EU's legitimacy deficit is sometimes held to be a question of diffusing more information. Technocrats and politicians think
that fears and suspicions, or 'pockets of resistance', stem largely from a
lack of information:

A lot more needs to be done to promote the Union. There is no substitute for politicians going out and explaining European policies and aims to voters as often as possible to get the message across.
(Abel Matutes, Spain's Foreign Affairs Minister, April 1997, p. 54)

But the problem obviously cannot be reduced to one of disseminating more information. It is a question of the conceptualization of project Europe, the discursive constitution of solidarity, identity and legitimacy. Denmark is a case in point: although according to Eurobarometer surveys the most knowledgeable and well-informed about European matters, the Danes are also just about the most negatively inclined towards integration; and the question most pertinent to Danes in relation to EU integration is the question of the welfare state, broadly defined.

The building of a European identity presupposes the formulation of Europeanness in a language that can express the values and qualities that supposedly make up Europeanness. That is, it needs a political discourse capable of expressing and, eventually, constituting identity. Presently, a number of discourses on European integration can be identified, each constructed around a specific set of images and oppositions: harmonization versus autonomy; integration versus sovereignty; regulation versus market; and so on. The formation of a European identity demands an ideological solution to those dualisms – the possibility of 'figural action' in Wuthnow's sense (1989, p. 14): a set of values, concepts and modes of behaviour that – at least in principle – can provide solutions to those contradictions and dilemmas.

Such a European political discourse has yet to be established (Schäffner *et al.* in Musolff *et al.*, 1996, p. 10). Europe hardly constitutes a political field (in Bourdieu's sense) in its own right. In particular, it is extremely difficult to point to a well-defined 'discourse practice' – that is, production, distribution and consumption of texts – which embraces and engages all the stakeholders in European integration. The official EU discourse is, to a large extent, an example of internal political discourse (politicians/bureaucrats talking to other politicians/bureaucrats, the production of texts that are instrumental in policy-making), while the external dimension to EU's discourse is only emerging (that is, politicians/bureaucrats talking to the wider public, still mainly argumentative and persuasive texts (*op. cit.*, p. 9)). Project Europe's discursive vacuum is arguably one of the hardest obstacles to further political integration.

Historically, since the late nineteenth century and especially after WWII, legitimating national discourses in Western Europe have revolved around a particular set of basic values and shared beliefs: those of nationhood, popular sovereignty and democracy, as embodied in liberal-democratic institutions.[3] The states are there to organize nations and they are governed by institutions that function in such a way as to organize the will of the people and to serve the general interest (Beetham, 1991, pp. 135 ff., 163 ff.). This sort of justification makes the social question particularly important: in this democratic setting citizens are politically equal, but how much equality should be implemented in practice among the democratically equal citizens, and what social rights should ensue from the status of being a citizen?

In the second half of the present century, Western Europe gradually developed a mechanism whereby the wealth of the nations could be redistributed on a scale satisfactory to the masses; known as 'the welfare state', it nonetheless assumed several forms. The degree of egalitarianism has varied widely: from Scandinavian universalism and redistribution, via continental welfare states which reproduce labour market inequality, to liberal Anglo-Saxon models which only provide a residual protection (Esping-Andersen, 1991). But in terms of state-building the emerging welfare state has played a major role every-where in the democratic consolidation of the nation-states (Dunn, 1995; Banting, 1995).

This, accidentally, provides a contrast to American discourse: in the US it is much more frequent to denounce outright the welfare state and argue for its dismantling. In neo-conservative discourse, 'welfare state' has a negative connotation, derived partly from its association with 'welfare', meaning social assistance (Hoover and Plant, 1989; Piven, 1995). Historically, the welfare state never gained a secure foothold in the US. The absence of a social dimension in NAFTA is in complete correspondence with this US tradition – and serves to demonstrate how much NAFTA is a US creation: neither Canadian nor Mexican political discourses, however different, are by tradition inimical to the concept of a welfare state.

The substance of politics is transformations of power – however defined. And the process of politics is about getting access to power in various ways. But politics are to a large extent constituted – that is, reproduced, challenged or changed – through discursive processes (Fairclough, 1995, p. 131). The case for scrutinizing the discursive dimension as part and parcel of an analysis of a particular social practice, in particular in the political sphere, is also stressed by Bourdieu (see for example Bourdieu 1991). The political arena provides a prime example of the workings of language and symbolic power, mobilizing and legitimizing forces in support of specific social projects. Symbolic power reflects the capacity of a social agent to establish the imperative of a project, to naturalize or normalize the ideological construction of a given field.

THE PROCESS OF A COMMUNITY-BUILDING INITIATIVE: POLITICAL AND DISCURSIVE ASPECTS

The European Community, like any community in the making, had to develop a common identity, mutual trust and a sense of solidarity demonstrating that the goals of the Community were to the benefit of all participants. But the constitution of an EC identity took place in an ambiguous space, where, firstly, the community's raison-d'être was initially based on grounds of peace/security, and economic gain. And secondly, the subjects/agents carrying or developing that identity were both states and citizens.

These ambiguities were politically conditioned: several ideologies were represented among the actors in the community-building process. To retain cohesion among all the interested parties, a discourse developed that was sufficiently oblique and fluid to contain the different perspectives – and correspondingly precise on matters where agreement could be reached. Thus, trade liberalization soon acquired truly common policy status, complete with legally-binding formulations. Social issues, on the other hand, were duly proclaimed but were never invested with the same degree of symbolic power as the liberalization issues and have never been acted upon in any systematic and collective fashion.

According to the Treaty of Rome, the 'essential objective' of the European Economic Communities was a very broad and social one: 'the constant improvement of the living and working conditions of their peoples' (Treaty of Rome 1957, preamble). And its tasks were to promote economic development – stability, harmony, expansion... plus: 'an accelerated raising of the standard of living and closer relations between the States belonging to [the Community]' (Article 2). To achieve these ends, a number of economic policy measures and economic regulations were introduced (Article 3). It seems, then, that the *economic* or 'welfare' goal was placed before the *security* one, although it was at the same time clearly presented also as a means to security – especially in other official communication from the EU.

The means adopted to implement these activities and to reach those goals was the establishment of a state-like structure, with political representation, administrative structures, and a legal system (Article 4). In this structure, *states* were the actors or participants. Over the years, the idea of a more direct relationship with *citizens* evolved – finally formulated in the declaration of a European citizenship in the Treaty of European Union.

The Treaties, and other important policy documents, interwove the themes of inter-state cooperation, of economic rationality and of community building. The social question was rarely discernible as a theme in its own right, and when it surfaced it was mostly as a sub-issue in connection with arguments about community-building. The general goal of welfare generation (Treaty of Rome, Article 2) does not specify any directions or principles as to the distribution of the welfare generated. Article 117 declares a goal of improving the lot of workers, and of geographical equalization. Article 118 demands wage equality between the sexes. Articles 123–128 institute the Social Fund, which aims to increase the possibilities of workers to adapt themselves to new and larger markets. These social articles contrast with the economic sections in their vagueness and in the absence of implementation mechanisms – except where they are very closely related to market-building processes (Hantrais, 1995).

As the 'regulation density' of the Community grew, the necessity of building identity and legitimacy at the level of citizens increased. With the launching of the single market initiative (1986), the Commission took upon itself the role of promotor of a social dimension, as a corollary of advancing commercial liberalization. The social dimension had two aspects – employment creation and social corporatism – neither of which, however, could pass the barrier of conflicting ideologies and national interests. Policies remained narrow or vague. Discursively, however, a certain territory was established: the subject of employment creation was put on the European agenda. And a dialogue between labour market organizations at the European level became part of the EC political structure.

Shortly after, in 1989, came the 'Social Charter' ('Community Charter of the Fundamental Social Rights of Workers'). Encoding the social question in a charter constituted an interesting shift of genre, which can be construed as the discursive facet of attempts at reconfigurating the existing social order. From this perspective, changes in social practice are both manifested at the level of language in changes in genres, and in part effected through such changes. A 'charter' is a solemn pledge containing important mutual commitments. In its present-day context, a charter forges a moral nexus, rather than a legal nexus, between the parties, and it invests the issuing authority with a human face (it becomes less of an abstraction) and with a certain amount of symbolic power.

The Social Charter declared the social aspects of integration to be as important as the economic and to be developed at the same pace. However, while the charter did mark a concerted effort on the part of the Commission to regain the political and moral high ground, its immediate effects were negligible. Besides being still limited to the labour market (thereby neglecting vast areas of social problems), it was signed without the UK, and thus constituted as much of a problem as a solution.

In the 1993 Treaty of European Union (TEU), the EU's goals both continued and expanded the formulations of the EC Treaty: while the primary goal was still economic and social progress ('mainly through...' and then Article B listed the components of the economic union), the Treaty elaborated it somewhat, making the political elements more explicit: international politics, Union citizenship, the strengthening of EU legal infrastructures.

On the question of identity, the TEU declared itself as constituting 'a new phase in the process towards an ever closer union between the European peoples' (Article A).[4] Europeanness and common European principles of democracy and social solidarity were presupposed, that is taken for given in the Treaty, as well as in a lot of documents emanating from the Council and the Commission. The notion of subsidiarity, on the other hand, was introduced as a new core element in European Union discourse: common Europeanness notwithstanding, as many affairs as possible would be handled at a sub-European, (sub)national level, 'close to the people' – especially in the case of social and labour market issues.

After Maastricht, the social initiative was continued in a Green – and later White – Paper on Social Policy (WPSP), and a White Paper on Growth, Competitiveness and Employment (GCE). The WPSP was an extension of the Charter – more ambitious, also in terms of broadening social policy beyond the labour market. In this document, the Commission escalated its discourse on the extension and importance of social policies – but it was constricted by political factors: Britain's opt-out, member states' unwillingness to harmonize social policies, and by the tendencies towards a 'post-industrial' social policy. The WPSP, following the political trend, argued for privatization and mini- malization of social security, and for initiatives that depoliticized the social policy area (Kuper, 1994) – arguments that extracted social policy from the identity and legitimacy context in which it potentially plays a crucial role. This development was sought reversed by the Commission before the 1996 IGC, with solidarity and social policy reembedded in the Commission's discussion of the broader political context (see below).

The emphasis of the GCE White Paper was on employment initiat- ives – a subject still dividing EU governments, with policies still largely unimplemented.[5] The controversy about the establishment of the Eur- opean Central Bank and the formulation of its goals, followed by the deflationary policies to meet the 'Maastricht criteria' of economic and monetary union, show how employment is still low on the EU's poli- tical agenda.

THE COMMISSION'S DISCURSIVE CONSTRUCTION OF SOLIDARITY

While the main thrust of EU policies clearly still reflects the conspic- uous absence of a binding commitment to social solidarity in the EU's founding documents, the discourse originating from the EU institu- tions, especially the Commission, is increasingly oriented towards social issues and the related themes of citizenship and democracy – themes that, as we will show below, seem less controversial in an EU context.

But why bother with the Commission in the first place? It can be argued that the Commission is still labouring under the legacy of Jacques Delors – the embodiment of the dominant Franco-German discourse in the 1980s – and that it may be increasingly out of tune with the political and economic interests currently at play, witness the ease with which the Commission's recommendations in the social sphere seem to be disregarded. The reason for focusing on the Commission nevertheless, and not on some of the EU institutions presently on the offensive in these matters, is, firstly, that it is mostly in (some of) the Commission's writings that we find examples of an EU discourse that allows for the notions of social solidarity, identity and legitimacy – and their imbrication. And secondly, the Commission's powers are uniquely reflexive and discursive: among the EU actors, it is primarily the Commission which – abiding its role in the constitution of the EU[6] – strives to conceptualize the integration process and eventually encode it into a language capable of containing rivalling projects, including its own.

In this section, we will look at two minor, but for our purpose central, policy documents from the Commission. We are not so much concerned with the question of the eventual realization of the utterances and visions in the texts (their truth value). Rather, if we accept that ideation is prior to action, they can be considered attempts to constitute reality in an ideational sense – as exercises in the realm of symbolic power. Material effects may or may not follow.

Both documents appeared before the 1996–97 Intergovernmental Conference (IGC). The *Commission Report for the Reflection Group* (European Commission, 1995) outlines the Commission's initial thoughts on the then forthcoming IGC, in response to the mandate of the Corfu European Council that the Community institutions each review the operation of the Treaty of European Union (TEU). Thus, in terms of ideas the 1995 report articulates the themes and foci to be addressed in the run-up to the IGC, and is the first stage in the deliberation process prior to the Commission's final report before the IGC, which is the second document under scrutiny here: *Commission Opinion. Reinforcing Political Union and Preparing for Enlargement* (European Commission, 1996). The latter document proposes appropriate policies, instruments and methods to ensure successful further integration.

Taken together, the documents are conspicuous in the way they construct a platform for *social solidarity*, latching it onto several other, dominant discourses. Without directly challenging it, the documents insist on problematizing the implicit premise in the TEU that there is such a thing as Europeanness, that legitimacy will develop further as a matter of course and that the social question will go away as Europe reaps the economic benefits of its integrationist efforts – and that such social problems as persist will somehow be solved at the national level. Given the function of the 1995 publication, mapping out the discursive terrain of the IGC, it is remarkable that the social question receives so scant attention. It is not entirely absent but is only mentioned briefly, and mostly as a subordinate or derivative issue. In the 1996 *Opinion*, it features more prominently, but still under the auspices of a dominant discourse about identity and legitimacy. The first document in a sense prepares the ideological ground for launching the social dimension in the second document, where its cautious inclusion suggests that the Commission is still struggling to mobilize support for its views.

In the preface to the 1995 publication (pp. 3–8) the Commission identifies two main concerns, the continued existence of 'a degree of scepticism about European integration'[7] and the accession of the new Eastern European democracies. Consequently, Europe must rise to the challenges of making 'Europe the business of every citizen' and making success of future enlargement (the latter will not be commented on here).

The organization of the remainder of the 1995 document bears out the emphasis on identity and legitimacy. Under the heading 'Heightening the sense of belonging to the union and enhancing its legitimacy', the first section in Part 1 (Democracy and Transparency in the Union, p. 19) reviews the concept of European citizenship since its introduction in the TEU and assesses the institutional response to the demand for legitimacy, new legislative and implementing procedures and the review function. However, as the analysis and arguments contained herein are hardly suitable for consumption by the wider public – that is, the very people who according to the preface need to be convinced of the Union's relevance for their lives – our investigation will focus mainly on the preface pp. 3–8, whose more life-world qualities (in a Habermas sense) anticipate its likely mediatization.

In the first section, headed Two Major Challenges for Europe (pp. 3–4), there is only one reference to *solidarity*, otherwise the text is on how to make Europe's citizens understand European integration and its relevance for their lives. The two perspectives are not unrelated, but a discourse on relevance carries less risk of connoting costly and controversial social and economic policies than a discussion revolving around the notion of solidarity:

> The Commission will be listening to the views of ordinary men and women, and focusing on ways in which Europe can combat unemployment, safeguard the environment and promote solidarity.

Still, the main concern in this first section is to address the Union's popular deficit. Alarmist interpretations of this observation are however defused by establishing an analogy between the alienation of many ordinary people from the EU and what is allegedly the accumulated experience in individual EU member states. The implication is that the EU is not necessarily more unwieldy, more inaccessible, less transparent, less democratic than these member states. By presupposing these similarities, the Commission posits interpreting subjects, that is readers and especially ordinary people, with particular prior (textual) experiences and thus contributes to the ideological constitution of these subjects (Fairclough, 1992, p. 121). It taps into ordinary people's presumed loyalty with their own country and possibly also their grudging acceptance of the shortcomings of domestic politics, the national version of the legitimacy crisis that pervades most western democracies.

It seems, therefore, that 'consolidating the ordinary citizen's sense of being a part of the process of building Europe' (European Commission, 1995, foreword to Chapter 1) does not involve reconstituting the social identities of 'ordinary men and women' and their relationship to the Union. Notions of élitism linger, and the citizens of Europe are not recast in a more participatory, active role capable of informing/influencing the integration process in a way more directly than at present

The next section, 'The achievements of four decades of European integration' (pp. 4–5), reminds the reader of how peace was the fundamental objective of European integration. However, Europe's success in this field is used as a vehicle for introducing the social question:

> Despite the tragedy of unemployment, and the social exclusion which tears at the fabric of our societies today, Europe has, since the 1950s been through a wholly unprecedented period of development: this should never be overlooked.

The Commission lists Europe's two most salient characteristics: firstly, that it is based on law – this feature is celebrated at some length – then, secondly and more succinctly:

> This Community is also based on solidarity: solidarity between member states, solidarity between regions, solidarity between different parts of society, and solidarity with future generations. The European model forges a fundamental link between the social dimension, human rights and civic rights.

Summing up its reflections, the Commission concludes that the main focus of the IGC will have to be improvement of decision-making mechanisms. This is related to the enlargement question, which is in turn connected to how to tackle different speeds of integration. It is at this point, just before closing the preface, that the Commission relaunches the social question, this time using the (technical and legal) enlargement prospects as a vehicle for its introduction:

> Permanent excemptions such as that now applying to social politics, which in the last analysis have had the regrettable effect of excluding the Social Charter from the Treaty, create a problem, as they raise the prospect of an 'à la carte' Europe, to which the Commission is utterly opposed. Allowing each country the freedom to pick and choose the policies it takes part in would inevitably lead to a negation of Europe.

The next document under scrutiny is the Commission's final opinion on the eve of the IGC 1996. In the following, we will unpick a few examples of language that offers insight into how also this text tries to resolve/fudge the contradictions contained in project Europe, even though 'Promoting the European Social Model' is in fact the first major policy area to be addressed in Chapter 1, A People's Europe – a heading which connotes the themes of legitimacy and identity rather than social policy. The main thrust of the report is 'how to give the Union a genuine political dimension' and to base future initiatives 'on a clear political project'. Thus, compared with the 1995 text, the case for a political and social dimension is made more explicit.

But, again, a number of discursive features detract from the efforts at addressing effectfully the EU's conflicting strands. An example can be found in the introduction: spelling out the broad twofold aspiration on which the TEU is arguably based, it backgrounds political integration, listing it as the second objective after economic integration. One concern could be to defuse potentially hostile reactions to seeing the political question on the agenda by first mentioning the relatively speaking less controversial objectives of European integration. The remainder of the comments to this publication will relate to Chapter 1, A People's Europe, pp. 9–10, in which efforts to further develop the concept of European citizenship are being inextricably linked to cementing and expanding the social dimension.

Importantly, the existence of a European social model is simply presupposed, for instance by using the definite article when talking about this model. Likewise, when the text states 'that Europe is built on a set of values shared by all its societies', it makes it difficult to refute the case for promoting it. When the Commission argues the case for strengthening the model and making it more explicit, it presumes that it is already in place. 'The social dialogue' is also cued by the definite article so as to suggest its existential meaning. And 'new forms of solidarity' invariably implies old forms!

Another discursive feature instrumental in constituting the assertion of the reality of a European social model is overwording, which occurs when there is dense wording of a particular domain, often by means of near synonyms. Citing Fowler, Fairclough explains it as 'a sign of "intense preoccupation" pointing to "peculiarities in the ideology" of the group responsible for it' (Fairclough, 1992, p. 193). In this text it is the lexicalization of the presumed characteristics of the European social model which shows signs of overwording. Significantly, the one term the texts omits is *the welfare state*. Examples include: a model 'whose members are committed to mutual support'; in the EU freedom of movement and establishment is 'to be enjoyed with a proper level of security'; the values on which Europe is built 'include the access for all members of society to universal services or to services of general benefit, thus contributing to solidarity and equal treatment; and (e)ach Member State strives to secure social goals for all its people'.

Again compared with the 1995 document, the political project that emerges from this report is marginally more participatory. In the text, this is reflected by the way citizens are invested with a capacity for action, though they are not necessarily represented as agents yet: the opening statement in Chapter 1 is particularly ambivalent when it stipulates that 'ordinary people must feel actively involved'. This is a very modest ambition indeed.

In sum, in this document we see a more outspoken, a less timid, a more openly political Commission, using its institutionalized role as policy initiator to the full. Its concern with identity and legitimacy makes it argue openly for a binding social dimension, and for more participatory structures to be implemented. The absence of a political field where a social dimension could be constituted reveals itself in the presuppositions of the text, and its overwording of the *social model* which attempts a semantic reconstruction of the term, ditching 'welfare state' associations. Likewise, the formulations in support of more participatory structures speak into an institutional vacuum and there-fore have to be rather vague: the sort of participatory democracy sketched in the Commission's opinion does not fit into the contemporary institutional configuration of the EU.

The Commission's dilemmas when advocating a somewhat different strategy leave important traces in its texts and are in part sought mediated by attempts at restructuring the issues discursively. The many contradictions and inconsistencies are evidence of an ambition to invest project Europe with a differently balanced ideology while observing the hegemonic relations at play.

CONCLUDING REMARKS

Becoming a union is no easy process. The transformation from a unique Community creature to the state-like species of a Union involves several difficult transformations: the powerful German and French member states want a common currency and a central bank, the European Parliament wants democratic institutions, and the European Commission wants that, plus identity and legitimacy. All these transformations encounter difficulties, but of a different nature. Monetary union can be seen as a logical next step in the economic integration process (Balassa, 1975; Robson, 1987), democratic institutions as a link in the very slow and gradual development of the role of the Assembly/ Parliament (Cot and Corbett, 1993). If they are not part of an evolutionary process, at least they can be constructed through the building of formal institutions – no small task, but feasible in the traditional way of negotiation, compromise, political decision and implementation.

Not so with identity and legitimacy, however. They belong to the state-building process, but they are feelings, states of mind, ideational constructs. They may result from institution-building efforts, but neither unequivocally nor immediately.

Our contention has been that to obtain identity and legitimacy one must, at least in the present era of welfare states, establish a notion of social solidarity. We have tried to show how the social dimension has been present in the community-building process, although in shifting disguises and with varying emphasis. The lack of emphasis on that dimension creates a problem growing in importance with each new phase of integration.

In this chapter, we have pointed to the absences and equivocations in the symbolic and material construction of European social solidarity. Identifying the Commission as the main discursive agent of the EU, and as the spokesperson for social matters, we have looked at important policy documents from the Commission to investigate its symbolic construction of social solidarity. What we found was that the social dimension, while obviously important to the political totality, remains inserted in more dominant discourses. Identity, legitimacy and democracy are still easier to stage as values for the Union than social solidarity.

Most analyses of the EU have stressed that it is a unique creature, neither an international organization nor a new nation-state. Its level of ambitions, however, leads it to assume state-like functions and features. In the process it has encountered its own inbuilt limitations of an absent social dimension, which have so far denied it the sort of legitimacy recquired for stateness. The Commission's discourse does – perhaps increasingly – address the central notions of social solidarity and citizens' rights, but its message remains sufficiently opaque to accomodate to a situation in which the social dimension is still contested and as yet unconstituted.

Returning briefly to the interregional comparison of the introduction, we maintain that the EU approach still has a lot going for it: addressing the societal effects of integration remains a more rational policy than neglecting them or maintaining an illusory distinction between economic and social questions. But perhaps the troubles of the EU social dimension point to inherent problems of creating a supranational state out of a patchwork of old nation-cum-welfare states: because of the sheer complexity of the forces and decision making layers involved, the formation of common identities and construction of legitimacy is more difficult at the supra-national level than at that nation-state level, to which identities have traditionally been tied and legitimatory processes directed. Furthermore, the welfare state at the national level is no institutional fixture: present developments suggest a possible need for major revisions of those welfare states as we know them.

Notes

1. The European Community, formed in 1956–57, still exists, and has been given a social dimension. Two new areas of cooperation among the member states were added with the Treaty of European Union, and conventional usage now is to refer to the whole arrangement as the 'EU' whenever the post-1972 period is implied.
2. In Rokkan's classical scheme (1975, pp. 570 ff.), the temporal phases of state-making are called '1-Penetration; 2-Standardization; 3-Participation; 4-Redistribution'. It is not hard to see the EU as being between phases 2 and 3, and the fourth step awaiting in the future. Neither is it difficult to realize the complexity which arises from the fact that the participants in EU state-making are fully-fledged states, where phase 4 is part and parcel of their political structure and discourse.
3. Some European states came to be liberal-democratic later than others; but European cooperation in the twentieth century has generally assumed liberal democracy to be the norm.

4.   '...in which decisions are made as close to citizens as possible'. The contradiction between a close union and decentralized decision-making is, like so many other incoherences in the very pluralistic TEU, simply ignored in the text.
5.   The issue was addressed as this book went to press, at the extraordinary European Council Meeting on employment in Luxembourg, 20–21 November 1997.
6.   The Commission holds the monopoly of initiative – according to the Treaty of Rome, Article 4, it is legally the privilege and duty of the Commission to put forward suggestions for legislation. The political reality is of course that new initiatives can emanate from all parts of the institutional structure.
7.   In the following, quotation marks denote verbatim quotes from the two Commission texts.

References

Balassa, B. (ed.) (1975) *European Economic Integration* (Amsterdam: North-Holland).
Banting, K.G. (1995) 'The Welfare State as Statecraft: Territorial Politics and Canadian Social Policy', in S. Leibfried and P. Pierson (eds), *European Social Policy. Between Fragmentation and Integration* (Washington: The Brookings Institution), pp. 269–300.
Beetham, D. (1991) *The Legitimation of Power* (London: Macmillan).
Bourdieu, P. (1991), *Language and Symbolic Power* (Cambridge: Polity Press)
Caporaso, J.A. (1996) 'The European Union and Forms of State: Westphalian, Regulatory or Post-Modern?', *Journal of Common Market Studies*, vol. 34, no. 1, March, pp. 29–51.
Cot, J.-P. and Corbett, R (1995) 'Democracy and the Construction of Europe', in and Rieu, A.M, Duprat, G. and Parker, N. (eds), *European Democratic Culture* (London: Routledge), pp. 235–55.
Dogan, M. (1993) 'Comparing the Decline of Nationalisms in Western Europe: The Generational Dynamic', *International Social Science Journal*, No. 136, pp. 177–98.
Dunn, J. (1995) 'Crisis of the Nation State?', in J. Dunn (ed.), *Contemporary Crisis of the Nation State* (Oxford: Blackwell).
Esping-Andersen, G. (1990), *The Three Worlds of Welfare Capitalism* (Cambridge: Polity Press)
European Commission (1995) *Commission Report for the Reflection Group* (Bruxelles: EC), May.
European Commission (1996) *Commission Opinion. Reinforcing Political Union and Preparing for Enlargement* (Bruxelles: EC), February.
Fairclough, N. (1992) *Discourse and Social Change* (Cambridge: Polity Press)
Fairclough, N. (1995), *Critical Discourse Analysis* (London: Longman)
Hantrais, L. (1995) *Social Policy in the European Union* (London: Macmillan).
Hoover, K. and Plant, R. (1989) *Conservative Capitalism* (London: Routledge).
Ifversen, J. (1996) 'Modernitet og Modernisering – Demokrati og Demokratisering', Århus: *GRUS*, no. 50, pp. 5–23.

Jacobsson, K. (1997) 'Discursive Will Formation and the Question of Legitimacy in European Politics', in *Scandinavian Political Studies*, vol. 20, no. 1 1997 pp. 69–90.

Kuper, B.-O. (1994) 'The Green and White Papers of the European Union: The Apparent Goal of Reduced Social Benefits', *Journal of European Social Policy*, vol. 4, no. 2, pp. 129–37.

Leibfried, S. and Pierson, P. (eds) (1995) *European Social Policy. Between Fragmentation and Integration* (Washington: The Brookings Institution).

Matutes, A. (1997) 'Europe Must Convince Public Opinion', in E. Bonino *et al., How Much Popular Support is There for the EU?* (Brussels: The Philip Morris Institute for Public Policy Research).

Musolff, A., Schäffner, C. and Townson M. (1996) *Conceiving of Europe: Diversity in Unity* (Aldershot: Dartmouth).

Münch, R. (1996) 'Between Nation-State, Regionalism and World Society: The European Integration Process', *Journal of Common Market Studies*, vol. 34, no. 3, September, pp. 379–401.

Obradovic, D. (1996) 'Political Legitimacy and the European Union', *Journal of Common Market Studies*, vol. 34, no. 2, June, pp. 191–221.

Piven, F.F. (1995) 'Foreword', in S.F. Schram (ed.), *Words of Welfare* (Minneapolis: University of Minnesota Press), pp. ix ff.

Robson, P. (1987) *The Economics of International Integration*, 3rd edn (London: Unwin Hyman).

Rokkan, S. (1975) 'Dimensions of State-Formation and Nation-Building: A Possible Paradigm for Research on Variations within Europe', in C. Tilly (ed.), *The Formation of National States in Western Europe* (Princeton: Princeton University Press).

Schmitter, P.C., (1996) 'Democratizing the European Union', unpublished manuscript, European University Institute, Firenze

Smith, A.D. (1986) 'State-Making and Nation-Building', in J. Hall (ed.), *States in History* (Oxford: Basil Blackwell), pp. 228–63.

Stone, A. (1996) 'Constructing a Supranational Constitution: Dispute Resolution in the European Community', unpublished paper, Robert Schuman Centre, European University Institute, Firenze.

Van Kersbergen, K. (1996) 'Double Allegiance in European Integration: Publics, Nation-States, and Social Policy', unpublished paper, Robert Schuman Centre, European University Institute, Firenze.

Weiler, J.H.H. Haltern, U.R. and Mayer, F.C. (1994) 'European Democracy and its Critique', *West European Politics*, vol. 18, no. 1, pp. 4–39.

Wuthnow, R. (1989) *Communities of Discourse* (Cambridge, Mass.: Harvard University Press).

9 The Europeanization of Politics in the Southern Members of the EU

Susana Borrás-Alomar

INTRODUCTION

The homogeneous level of socio-economic development within the EC changed dramatically in the 1980s with the membership of three new Mediterranean countries: Greece, Portugal and Spain. However, the enlargement to the south meant more than just greater disparities within the EC. These new members were in a process of accelerated transformation, and their economic dynamism and young democratic systems added a new dimension to the European Community. New issues came onto the European agenda, such as the cohesion or solidarity principle, and European citizenship; while old ones acquired renewed political direction, such as agriculture, fisheries and external relations. Conversely, the political and legal structures of the EC have had a profound effect upon the nature of Greek, Portuguese and Spanish domestic politics. The accession processes were based on the gradual but complete adoption of the principle of *acquis communautaire*, with important institutional and legislative implications at national level. On top of this, the special dynamics of the European integration process since the mid-1980s, with the SEA (Single European Act), the TEU (Treaty on European Union) and the recent Amsterdam Treaty have influenced decisively the autonomy of member states.

In the wake of recent academic discussions about the Europeanization of national politics and policy, this chapter will focus on the socio-political and institutional effects of EC membership on Greece, Portugal and Spain, with special emphasis on the latter. Europeanization is essentially a political process 'reorienting the direction and shape of politics to the degree that EC political and economic dynamics become part of the organisational logic of national politics and policy-making' (Ladrech, 1994, p. 69). In other words, a process by

which the EU is gradually becoming a powerful factor in shaping
domestic politics. The main questions in this chapter relate to the
role of EC membership in the institution-building process that has
been taking place in these countries over a longer period (since the
mid-1960s), and how national institutions have adapted to developments in European integration.

The purpose of this chapter is threefold. Firstly, to contribute to the
theoretical debate about Europeanization that is currently taking
place, and to introduce a southern European perspective by addressing
the question of modernization. For this purpose, the first part gives a
critical review of the literature and identifies the special characteristics
of this process in the three southern European member states. The aim
here is not to invalidate the theoretical framework of studies on the
Europeanization process, but rather to pinpoint some current analytical shortcomings. Secondly, the chapter summarizes the most salient
socio-political and economic changes in Greece, Portugal and Spain
since the mid-1960s, in an attempt to provide a synthetic approach to
internal dynamism prior to EC membership. In this sense, the second
part aims at addressing the question of why EC membership was
perceived by political élites in these countries as a means of reinforcing
the transformation, and why the modernization discourse included so
many references to Europe. Thirdly, a brief analysis will be made of
the Europeanization of Spanish policies and politics during the 10
years of its EC membership from an institutional perspective. The
transformation of three national policy areas will be used to explore
the different patterns through which the process of Europeanization
has been taking place in a national context of weak policy articulation
and deficient institutionalization.

THE EUROPEANIZATION OF NATIONAL POLICIES AND POLITICS

The Concept of Europeanization within EU Studies

It has become commonplace in European studies to refer to the
sui generis nature of the EU political system and of the process
of European integration. Academic interest in the overall picture of
European political change has been strongly renewed in the wake
of the Maastricht Treaty. This can in part be explained by the difficulties experienced in ratifying the treaty in individual member states,

which has served as a powerful reminder of the legitimacy problem underlying European integration and raised concern about national politicians 'losing touch' with their civil societies (Hayward, 1996).

The rapidly changing scenario in Europe, including the latest treaty reforms agreed in Amsterdam, has encouraged observers to view European integration as an unpredictable process. This perception coincides with an important shift in the theoretical framework of European studies. Whereas the 'classical schools' tried to identify the elements and dynamics of the integration process (O'Neill, 1996), current scholars are more interested in institutional changes and structures of governance (Risse-Kappen, 1996; Bulmer, 1994), that is, in the nature of the system itself. Today, it is generally accepted that the EU constitutes a unique form of political governance (Schmitter, 1996), characterized by a certain degree of discontinuity, uncertainty, and a multi-tier pattern of governance mechanisms (Wallace, 1996, pp 440–5). A core question in European studies since the inception of this political system is the relationship between nation-states and the EU, with the focus on issues such as the transfer of sovereignty (Christiansen, 1994) and challenges facing parliamentary democracy both at national and EU levels (Andersen and Burns, 1996). The relatively recent focus on the Europeanization of national policies and politics clearly stems from this line of research. The main starting point here is concrete but wide; namely, to what extent and how has the EC transformed the contents and structures of domestic policy-making and politics?

The process of European integration cannot simply be interpreted as the homogenization of national politics, economy, society or culture (Ladrech, 1994; Olsen, 1995), disregarding the importance and persistence of specifically national frameworks of organization. On the other hand, the alternative of analysing events at European and domestic levels separately seems equally artificial. It is thus no longer possible to view the socio-political and economic dynamics of EU member states as completely disentangled from the policy contents and political institutions of the European integration project. The 'Europeanization' approach constitutes a solution to this apparent dilemma, by taking into account the impact of the EU on the transformation of national politics and policies in recent decades. As Ladrech puts it, 'Europeanisation preserves the legitimacy and authority of national government, but suggests that it will become progressively permeated by environmental inputs which become, over time, internalised in politics and policy-making' (Ladrech, 1994, p. 70).[1]

Taking the changes at national level as the object of study, Europeanization is considered an 'exogenous factor' influencing the nature of organizational and institutional change. However, the notion needs further conceptualization. In this sense, I distinguish here between two complementary interpretations of the notion of Europeanization. The first of these is broad, and relates to the transformation of sociopolitical and economic institutions. In this sense, the teleological dimension of European integration and the way in which the European polity and its institutions are constructed have direct implications for *the future of the nation state*. 'The impact of Europeanisation on the nation-state, then, will depend on the...relative priority given to building a European polity, a market, a welfare society or a culture' (Olsen, 1995, p. 25). Alternatively, and in a more narrow sense, Europeanization can be interpreted as a crucial external factor in *the transformation of national policy-making and policy development*, by introducing new modes of understanding public policies and administrative management. These two understandings of Europeanization are interdependent; the difference between them relies on the scope and level of analysis rather than on a divergent account of the dynamics. It will be argued later in this chapter that the main impact in the case of Spain has derived from Europeanization in the narrow sense.

The Southern European Perspective

In the literature on Europeanization, a general pattern emerges. When accounting for the European elements in the transformation of national politics and policy-making in France (Ladrech, 1994; Lequesne, 1996), Germany (Goetz, 1996) and Denmark (Pedersen and Pedersen, 1995), an interesting common analogy can be identified in the form of a move from a neo-corporatist model towards a more pluralistic one, where networks of actors operate in a more atomised decision-making process. Europeanization has also meant some substantial changes of a constitutional nature, from the transformation of articles in accordance with the Maastricht Treaty, to the role of institutional and political actors in specific policy areas (for example EU regional policy is modifying the relationship and balance of power between national and sub-national governments in France).

However, these examples provide a perspective on the Europeanization process which is only of partial use in the analysis of Greece, Portugal and Spain. There are at least two crucial differences. First, these countries joined the EC at a relatively late stage, but since their accession there have been important changes in the EC polity. Thus, for the new southern European members the process of adopting the principle of *acquis communautaire* has taken place in a period when the European Community has been undergoing rapid transformation. The methodological implication of late membership is that it is impossible to separate out the impact of these rapid changes in the EC polity (given the need also to implement the previously existing body of EC laws), and, therefore, to explore how substantial changes in the 'external factor' affect internal developments.

A second difference relates to the assumption that internal variables are relatively static. These three countries have been in a process of unparalleled socio-political and economic changes since the 1960s, which were the basis for the political changes of the mid-1970s when authoritarian regimes were replaced by parliamentary democracies. The paramount significance of 'internal factors' in this transformation process invalidates the implicit 'static' assumptions of previous work on Europeanization. Moreover, Europeanization in these three countries has gone hand in hand with the process and discourse of modernization, an element not present in previous empirical analyses. Modernization is understood here as a social phenomenon, by which a society experiences rapid changes in societal values and patterns of behaviour in line with those prevailing in western, industrially-developed countries. It is interesting to see that modernization has been a continuous process since the early 1960s, but that the most significant impetus in institutional terms was directly related to EC membership.

TRANSFORMATIONS BEFORE EC MEMBERSHIP

The Three Dimensions of Change since the 1960s

The transformation of socio-economic and political structures in Greece, Spain and Portugal since the 1960s can be categorized into three: economic and industrial development; changes in terms of social values, patterns of behaviour and stratification; and, last but not least, the transition from dictatorship and authoritarian rule to democratic regimes. The similar nature of these changes and their almost simultaneous occurrence are powerful arguments for undertaking 'Southern Europe' as an analytical entity (Williams, 1984).

The autarkic *economic policies* of the two decades after the Second World War created a protectionist environment shielding weak national industry in Greece, Spain and Portugal. Facing serious structural economic deficiencies and imbalances due to these strategies, all three undertook important economic reforms during the early and the mid-1960s, leading to a partial liberalization of the economy. Related to this a certain degree of economic internationalization occurred, of which there were three main features: the expansion of foreign capital investment and an incipient process of technology transfer; the emigration of workers to Northern Europe; and the development of the service sector, where tourism had a prominent position.

Parallel to this economic transformation, a profound and rapid process of *social change* was experienced from the 1960s, shaped by the following key elements. The migration from rural areas into large cities produced not only unbalanced territorial development,[2] but also an 'urbanization' of social, working and consumption patterns. Of particular significance were the changes in family structure (from extended to nuclear family), variations in birth ratios (from the period of baby-boomers in the 1960s to an ageing population with the lowest birth rate in Europe in the 1990s), and the transformation of the role of women in the family, the labour market and education. The secularization of society has also had important political consequences, namely the weakening of the clericalism/anti-clericalism socio-political cleavage which was especially strong in Spain (Giner, 1984; Perez-Diaz, 1996). Last but not least, the expansion of the middle classes and the improvement of the education system were further key elements explaining the changes in the Greek, Portuguese and Spanish societies in this period.

The *transition to democratic regimes* occurred in the mid-1970s in these three countries. With the exception of Greece, which endured a comparatively short military regime between 1967 and 1974, these transformations took place after long-lasting dictatorships. Both Salazar in Portugal and Franco in Spain came to power before the Second World War and established repressive, isolated and in ideological terms poorly articulated political systems. Despite their almost simultaneous occurrence, the transitions to democratic regimes were country-specific developments deeply linked to the nature of their respective political contexts and forces.

In Portugal, the (progressive) military coup in April 1974 started a short transitional revolutionary period until 1975. Several provisional governments succeeded one other, but eventually free general elections were organized leading to the promulgation of the demo-cratic Constitution in 1976. The distinct feature of the Portuguese transition to democracy is not only its intrinsically revolutionary nat-ure, but also the role of a progressive group in the military. This was entirely different in the other two countries, where the military was an homogeneous and reactionary force. In Greece, the turbulent end of the junta-government of the colonels in 1974 gave way to a centre-right government headed by Karamalis, who undertook important initiat-ives, such as the legalization of the communist party, the organization of free general elections, and a referendum on a republican state (Kurth and Petras, 1993; Kohler, 1982). In Spain, a similar transforma-tion took place under the first government of Adolfo Suarez, with the legalization of trade unions and political parties, free general elections establishing the constitutional assembly, and a referendum on the newly written Constitution by the end of 1977. The Spanish transition had a distinctive feature, however, in that the transition occurred peacefully after the death of the dictator, rather than from political convulsions in the form of a revolution (Portugal) or a political col-lapse (Greece).[3]

In the wake of political transition, the three countries faced similar challenges, most notably the need to substantially transform economic institutions, to build up a modern welfare state based on principles of social justice and equality, and to emerge from decades of political isolation in the international system.

The Modernization Discourse and EC Membership in Southern Europe

In this renewed socio-political context one of the first concerns of political elites was to rethink security and foreign policy, and EC membership was seen as a central option. In Portugal and Spain the modernization discourse and EC membership went hand in hand. Left-wing parties accepted the idea that entry into the EC would imply a step forward in terms of social equality, worker protection and prosperity. Consensus was built upon a broad agreement that the EC would stimulate social and economic progress.[4] However, such a consensus did not exist in Greece, which had joined the EC earlier than Portugal and Spain (in 1981) under a different political scenario. The negotiations for entry were conducted by the centre-right govern-ment of Karamanlis, against the strong opposition of the PASOK socialist party, which did not share the vision of a socialist Greece entering the capitalistic and bourgeois structures of western Europe (Kolher, 1982, p. 152). However, despite these socialist principles, PASOK did not question Greek membership once in power, accepting it as a means of enhancing the modernization process.

But why did the political élites in these countries identify EC membership as important to the process of socio-economic transformation? Why did the modernization discourse include so many references to Europe as an abstract idea, meaning northern and central European modes of organizing society, the economy and political life? The modernization discourse reflected a collective spirit shared by most citizens in favour of change, which became especially strong in the mid-1970s in relation to political transition. Public debate at the time centred upon political visions of a desirable future for each of the three societies, and in this sense upon the meaning of modernization.

At the same time the transition to liberal democratic regimes implied the emergence of a new political culture (Perez-Diaz, 1993), which went hand in hand with the development of a discursive process by which society and political élites constructed *a new meaning for themselves*. In Spain, for example, such a discourse meant a renewed interpretation of the Civil War, and a projection of national identity into a European identity as a mechanism defining a desirable future. As Perez-Diaz put it:

> It was generally believed that Spain could arguably aspire to a type of society such as that embodied in present-day western Europe, and that Spain was in fact already becoming more and more like a western European country. In fact this European reference, and the construction of a European identity for Spain, has been one of the most crucial mechanisms at work throughout the entire process of transition to and consolidation of democracy.
>
> (*Ibid.*, p. 5)

The strategy towards EC membership agreed by political élites in Greece, Portugal and Spain was matched by a parallel perception among European élites. It was widely believed in diplomatic and academic circles throughout Europe that EC membership would reinforce the new democratic regimes and economic development of these three states. In other words, an enlargement of the EC would unequivocally contribute to the political stability of the Mediterranean region (Payno, 1982).

THE EUROPEANIZATION OF SPANISH POLITICS AND POLICIES

The Impact of the EC on Public Policies

It is not possible in this chapter to review 10 years of Spanish EC membership.[5] The aim is to pinpoint some of the effects of membership on national politics and policy areas.

At the time of accession to the EC, Spain had already adopted substantial political and economic reforms. Democratic institutions were well established 10 years after the new Constitution, which had introduced a new form of state (a parliamentary democracy with decentralized powers). The same can be said of important economic institutions, such as property rights, commercial regulations and independent trade unions. In spite of this, it is maintained here that Spain suffered from weak institutionalization in two senses. Firstly, many policy areas were underdeveloped or inadequately implemented. Examples include environmental regulations, regional policy, consumer protection and technology policy. The generalized weak articulation of public policies was in many cases due to the unclear distribution of powers between national and sub-national authorities. Secondly, weak institutionalization was reflected by the fact that the new organizational structures lacked institutional routines, 'rules of the game', and their own culture of regulation.

EC membership has partly solved the problems of weak institutionalization with the adoption of new legislative frameworks and organizational structures shaping previously non-existent or unarticulated policy strategies. However, the impact has only been indirect in regard to the establishment of routines and informal norms within administrative structures.

Environmental regulations in Spain, for example, were few and badly implemented in the early 1980s. EC environmental policy has *de facto* meant the establishment of a comprehensive regulatory framework in this domain, and the articulation of a public administration structure to fulfil the implementation tasks. Similarly, regional policy was non-existent as a set of articulated and economically significant measures directed towards the reduction of socio-economic disparities (Cuadrado-Roura and Suarez-Villa 1993). By means of co-authoring and co-financing nation-wide regional planning (the Community Support Framework), EC regional funds have established the major policy instrument for territorial redistribution in Spain.

A final and illustrative example of the 'Europeanization' of public policy is in the domain of scientific research. Government financial support for technological development in Spain was meagre and resources were poorly coordinated between the ministries concerned. The first national plan aimed at solving such important deficiencies, and followed the model elaborated a few years before by the EC Commission with the so-called Framework Programme (Sanz-Menendez *et al.*, 1993).

The Limits of Europeanization

However relevant this Europeanization of Spanish politics might have been in terms of policy and administrative impact, there is a wider understanding of how European integration has affected national politics. As stated in the first section of this chapter, the wider notion of Europeanization refers essentially to the idea that the EU has also affected key elements in the structures of member states' political systems. Manifestations of this include the constitutional reforms of some countries after the Maastricht Treaty, changes in the form of neo-corporatist models within states, and the changed nature of region–state relations resulting from the increased political role of sub-national levels in European politics and policy formulation. The balance between the role of 'internal' and 'external' (or European) factors in these transformations is, once again, crucial. This chapter contends that the 'external' European factor has played only a minor role in the deep transformation of the political system in Spain before and after EC membership, an argument supported by the three examples just mentioned.

Firstly, Spain did not need to change any of the articles in its Constitution after the ratification of the Maastricht Treaty. Written in the mid-1970s the text was already elaborated on the basis of a flexible understanding of national sovereignty in an increasingly integrated Europe. In other words, the text was prepared with the assumption of a wide transfer of competencies to a supranational political system.

Secondly, the evidence from other member states that the Europeanization of policy-making serves to weaken models of neo-corporatism finds no parallel in Spain (Streeck and Schmitter, 1991). The main reason is that such a model did not exist in the first place.[6] Despite the political importance of tripartite agreements during the transition period as well as the first two terms in office of the Socialist party, a neo-corporatism similar to the ones prevailing in the Scandinavian countries or Germany has never been established in Spain.[7] Today, more than ever, territorial interests (in the form of minority national government alliances with nationalist–regionalist political parties) seem to dominate the articulation of interests in the formulation of most policy strategies.

Thirdly, the crucial European element in recent changes in region–state relations, through which sub-national entities have gained (limited) participatory power, as in the French case (Lardrech, 1994; Balme and Jouve, 1996), only partially applies to Spain. The need to fulfil the political aspirations of diverse territorial identities in Spain resulted in the creation of the so-called 'State of Autonomies' in the Constitution. Of a semi-federal nature, the division of powers between regions (autonomous communities) and the national government is ambiguous and complex, and has given rise to constant political and judicial controversy, especially during the 1980s. The difficulties in establishing mechanisms through which the regions could bargain collectively with the central government has resulted in a bilateral pattern of negotiation, which means that the question of the distribution of powers is still not settled.

The European Union has only affected this scenario in a relatively indirect manner. Whereas regional participation in the decision-making process of the Spanish national position in EU negotiations is still insufficient and unarticulated (Morata, 1996), regions now seem to play a gradually increasing role in the implementation of EU laws and the administration of regional funds. The partnership principle, an EU provision whereby local and regional authorities participate in negotiations and in the implementation of regional policy, has been applied under quite restrictive terms (Morata and Muñoz, 1996). On the other hand, most of the Spanish regional governments have increased their presence on the European political scene, either by trying to influence Community decisions (informally through lobby activities, and formally through the Committee of the Regions), or by establishing cooperation agreements with other European regions (Borrás, 1995). However, the political results of such activism at the European level are unclear and rather insignificant as regards national politics. To sum up, the dynamics and nature of territorial politics in Spain depend more on the characteristics of the 'State of Autonomies' (an open model of power distribution) and on the controversial nature of territorial politics in this country, rather than on any sort of European imperative.

CONCLUSIONS

By the mid-1970s, Greece, Portugal and Spain were undergoing a political transition towards democracy. In the process they constructed a new socio-political discourse in which EC membership was a crucial element. Belonging to the EC was perceived as an important external stimulus to continue and consolidate social, political and economic transformation. Ten years on, it is quite evident that there has been a salient Europeanization of the politics and policies of these countries. However, this process has not been homogeneous, nor has the institutional impact of EC membership affected all spheres of the domestic polity equally.

As the analysis of Spain shows, the effects that EC membership has had on various policy areas and on the structures and dynamics of the political system have been uneven. These two distinct forms of understanding Europeanization have served here as complementary analytical tools to explore this process in Spain. Thus the 'external' European variable was found to be important in explaining the tremendous changes in the contents of public policies and in implementation procedures. The weak institutionalization of many of these policy areas prior to membership meant that the Spanish system was permeable to European regulations and strategies. Yet, paradoxically enough, the Europeanization process does not appear to have been so relevant seen in a broader perspective. As has been shown EC membership has not played a direct role in the nature and dynamics of Spanish territorial politics nor in the forms of interest representation. In determining the structures and characteristics of the Spanish political system, internal variables are still predominant.

These broad conclusions need further investigation, yet they are already of interest for the political problem they reveal. Structural political change during the transition of Spain, ending with the signing of the new Constitution, occurred with a high degree of social participation and mobilization. Similarly, territorial politics has been at the centre of political life in Spain. However, the degree of social participation in the changes within individual policy areas reveals a completely different picture. The Europeanization of public policies has in general terms been de-politicized. With the exception of fisheries and agriculture (where sectoral interests are very well organized), no open public debate appears to have taken place. The formal and informal mechanisms for the elaboration of the Spanish position in EU negotiations, concentrated in the national government and ministries

(Morata, 1996), have certainly not helped to solve this problem. A lack of democratic accountability, both in the formulation and implementation of EU decisions, and reflected in the lack of formalized access of social agents, might constitute one of the most salient future risks of Spanish EU membership, mainly in terms of social legitimization.

It is important to note here that the analysis of two distinct dimensions at the national level, namely the public policy dimension and the nature of the political system, is in fact artificial. There are still many unanswered questions that relate to both simultaneously. For example, how far has the transfer of competencies from the national level to the EU been one of the factors preventing political attempts to establish a neo-corporatist model of interest representation in Spain? What have been the changing political interpretations of the partnership principle in regional policy, relating to region–state negotiations in territorial politics, and what does this imply for the 'State of Autonomies'? This is the main reason why a future research agenda needs to focus on empirical analysis, providing a comprehensive approach to the institutional relevance of European integration to Spanish policies and politics during the last 10 years, and to pinpoint future bottlenecks and risks.

Notes

1. Goetz goes even further in this point, stating that the Europeanization of the German state not only has acquired the form of adapting public institutions to the imperatives of EC/EU membership, but that 'there is a growing evidence to suggest that over the last decades the country's key institutions have become progressively programmed for integration' (Goetz, 1996, p. 24). This, in turn, poses problems to distinguish between German national interest and a European interest, due to this 'in-built integrationist orientation' of the German state.
2. Tsaloniki and Athens in Greece, Lisbon and Porto in Portugal, and Madrid and Barcelona in Spain, have been the fastest growing areas in terms of population and economic development.
3. In other words, the Spanish transition to democracy was somehow negotiated before hand involving all the political forces, between the opposition groups (still illegal) and the moderated sector of the late Francoist regime, under the so-called 'ruptura pactada'. This is the reason why some authors refer to a 'reform within continuity' (Kohler, 1982, p. 5).
4. Despite important differences in the political visions about the nature and development of European integration, no serious opposition to joining the EC could be found in the Spanish political spectrum at the time. The same cannot be said about NATO membership, about membership of which most of the Spanish population was initially strongly reluctant

(Del Arenal, 1992). The Spanish socialist government successfully managed to present both memberships as being deeply interlinked, and by 1987 this country belonged to both international fora (Holman, 1996).

5. Spain submitted its official application for EC membership in July 1977, after the first democratic elections and the establishment of the constituent parliament (the parliament that should write the text of the Constitution). Negotiations started in 1979 and concluded some years later with the signature of the protocol on June 1985 and the effective membership from 1 January 1986.

6. It has been argued that the Francoist Spain included a peculiar and weakly articulated form of corporatism, characterized by 'exclusion rather than inclusion, subordination rather than mobilization' (Giner and Sevilla, p. 119) and that was never socially legitimized.

7. Some authors describe the transformation from state corporatism (during the dictatorship) to a societal corporatism as one of the main structural elements that help explaining the peaceful transition to democracy in Spain (Holman, 1996, pp. 55–61), or more normatively, the possible and desirable move towards a democratic model of neo-corporatism (Giner and Sevilla, 1984, pp. 130–6). In any case, whether it is societal corporatism or a movement towards a desirable one, the formal inclusion and articulation of non-party interest representation in the policy-making process in Spain is still quite weak.

References

Andersen, S.S. and Burns, T. (1996) 'The European Union and the Erosion of Parliamentary Democracy: A Study of Post-parliamentary Governance', in S.S. Andersen and K.A. Eliassen (eds) *The European Union: How Democratic Is It?* (London: Sage).

Balme, R. and Jouve, B. (1996) 'Building the Regional State: Europe and Territorial Organization in France', in L. Hooghe (ed.), *Cohesion Policy and European Integration: Building Multi-Level Governance* (Oxford: Oxford University Press).

Borrás, S. (1995) 'Interregional Cooperation in Europe during the Eighties and Early Nineties', in N.A. Sørensen (ed.), *European Identities. Cultural Diversity and Integration in Europe since 1700* (Odense: Odense University Press).

Bulmer, S. (1994) 'The Governance of the European Union: A New Institutionalist Approach', *Journal of Public Policy*, vol. 13, no. 4, pp. 351–80.

Christiansen, T. (1994) 'European Integration between Political Science and International Relations Theory: The End of Sovereignty', *EUI working paper* no. 94/4.

Cuadrado-Roura, J.R. and Suarez-Villa, L. (1993) 'Thirty Years of Spanish Regional Change: Interregional Dynamics and Sectoral Transformation', *International Regional Science Review*, vol. 15, no. 2, pp. 121–56.

Del Arenal, C. (1992) 'La posición exterior de Espana', in R. Cotarelo (ed.), *Transición política y consolidación democrática. Espana 1975–1986* (Madrid: CIS).

156   *The Europeanization of Politics in the Southern EU*

Giner, S. and Sevilla, E. (1984) 'Spain: From Corporatism to Corporatism', in A. Williams (ed.), *Southern Europe Transformed. Political and Economic Change in Greece, Italy, Portugal and Spain* (London: Harper & Row).
Goetz, K.H. (1996) 'Integration Policy in a Europeanized State: Germany and the Intergovernmental Conference', *Journal of European Public Policy*, vol. 3, no. 1, pp 23–44.
Hayward, J. (ed.) (1996) *Élitism, Populism, and European Politics* (Oxford: Clarendon Press).
Holman, O. (1996) *Integrating Southern Europe. EC Expansion and the Transnationalization of Spain* (London: Routledge).
Kohler, B. (1982) *Political Forces in Spain, Greece and Portugal* (London: Butterworth Scientific).
Kurth, J. and Petras, J. (eds) (1993) *Mediterranean Paradoxes. Politics and Social Structure in Southern Europe* (Oxford: Berg).
Ladrech, R. (1994) 'Europeanization of Domestic Politics and Institutions: The Case of France', *Journal of Common Market Studies*, vol. 32, no. 1, pp. 69–88.
Lequesne, C. (1996) 'The French EU Decision-making: Between Destabilisation and Adaptation', in S.S. Andersen and K.A. Eliassen (eds), *The European Union: How Democratic Is It?* (London: Sage).
Morata, F. (1996) 'Spain', in D. Rometsch and W. Wessels (eds), *The European Union and Member States: Towards Institutional Fusion?* (Manchester: Manchester University Press).
Morata, F. and Muñoz, X. (1996) 'Vying for European Funds: Territorial Restructuring in Spain', in L. Hooghe (ed.), *Cohesion Policy and European Integration: Building Multi-Level Governance* (Oxford: Oxford University Press).
O'Neill, M. (1996) *The Politics of European Integration. A Reader* (London: Routledge).
Olsen, J.P. (1995) 'Europeanization and Nation-State Dynamics', ARENA working paper no. 9/95.
Payno, J.A. (1982) 'La segunda ampliación desde la perspectiva de los nuevos miembros', in J.A. Payno and J.L. Sampedro (eds), *La segunda ampliación de la CEE: Grecia, Portugal y Espana* (Madrid: Servicio de Estudios Economicos. Banco exterior de España).
Pedersen, O.K. and Pedersen, D. (1995) 'The Europeanization of National Corporatism. When the State and Organizations in Denmark Went to Europe Together', *COS-rapport*, no. 4/1995.
Perez-Diaz, V.M. (1993) *The Return of Civil Society: The Emergence of Democratic Spain* (Cambridge, Mass.: Harvard University Press).
Pollack, M.A. (1994) 'Creeping Competence: The Expanding Agenda of the European Community', *Journal of Public Policy*, vol. 14, no. 2, pp. 95–145.
Risse-Kappen, T. (1996) 'Exploring the Nature of the Beast: International Relations Theory and Comparative Policy Analysis Meet the European Union', *Journal of Common Market Studies*, vol. 34, no. 1, pp. 53–80.
Sanz-Menendez, L. Muñoz, E. and Garcia, C.E. (1993) 'The Vicissitudes of Spanish Science and Technology Policy: Coordination and Leadership', *Science and Public Policy*, vol. 20, no. 6, pp. 370–80.

Schmitter, P.C. (1996) 'Examining the Present Euro-polity with the Help of Past Theories' in G. Marks *et al.* (eds), *Governance in the European Union* (London: Sage).

Streeck, W. and Schmitter, P.C. (1991) 'From National Corporatism to Transnational Pluralism: Organized Interests in the Single European Market', *Politics and Society*, vol. 19, no. 2, pp. 113–64.

Wallace, W. (1996) 'Government without Statehood: The Unstable Equilibrium', in H. Wallace and W. Wallace (eds), *Policy-Making in the European Union* (Oxford: Oxford University Press).

Williams, A. (ed.) (1984) *Southern Europe Transformed. Political and Economic Change in Greece, Italy, Portugal and Spain* (London: Harper & Row).

Part III
Unbalanced Integration in America

10 Regionalism: The Case of North America

Edmé Domínguez Reyes

INTRODUCTION

The North American region is only starting to undertake a process of integration that at present limits itself to certain economic aspects like trade and investment. Although the goal has never been to engage in such an accomplished integration as the European Union, certain non-economical aspects, like environmental and labour issues, are already taken into account. Can this sort of integration limit itself to the trade and investment level or can something deeper be achieved? And in the latter case, what role do certain structural factors like cultural differences, national identities, experiences of nation-building, internal conflicts, and the process of homogenization, and so on play in the process of integration or of regional institutionalization?

We propose to examine how the three members of NAFTA represent three different cultures, built through different historical trajectories, while the mode of institutionalization of economic cooperation in NAFTA represents only one of these three cultures – the American one, and its values, concepts and traditions. Hence, this one-sidedness of NAFTA's institutionalization as an integration project is heavily reflected in the type of economic regulation, a very neo-liberal one, and severely limits the possibility of a regional identity formation.

REGIONAL IDENTITY: SPANISH, FRENCH AND ANGLO-SAXON HERITAGE

Canadians, USA's citizens and Mexicans are separated not only by the language; their history, religion, race and philosophy are totally different. The United States and Canada are nations with only 500 years of history but they are well advanced into the twenty-first century while Mexico with a history of several thousand years is still attached to its past.

161

One of the fundamental contradictions opposing the North and the South, the Anglo-French and the Spanish heritages has been their difference in mentalities and traditions – regarding the role of the market, of the aristocracy and the bourgeoisie, of the state and the church – that has shaped the development of two radically different societies within the same geographical region. Moreover, the European paradigms of 'development', 'democracy', 'progress' and 'modernity' have not only been interpreted differently according to an Anglo, French or Spanish tradition, the original, so called 'Indian' cultures have made these differences even deeper.

However, the European – and specially the Anglo-Saxon – paradigm of modernity has had a very strong influence over Mexico's educated élites. This, together with the impact of the 'American way of life' in the Mexican middle and upper classes, concerning their projects of life has become one of the pillars on which the project of regionalization and institutionalization of this regionalization may be built.

NATION AND STATE BUILDING

Experiences of Nation-Building

The American nation-building experiences have been enormously different even if all these countries shared the experience of colonization, European immigration and independence from Europe.

North America had a certain ethnic identity before European colonization. However, while the North American populations were mostly nomads with no urban experience, the meso-American peoples had attained a high level of urbanization and cultural and scientific development. This diversity, the conflicts among them, together with the different cultures of the European colonizers made the way for two processes of conquest and colonization: one in the United States and Canada and another in Mexico.

In the United States and British Canada the English–Protestant tradition moulded a certain type of nation-state that denied any legitimacy to the native-Indian populations and traditions. These were rapidly conquered and physically eliminated in large numbers. The model of economic development was based on private initiative – first rural and commercial, then industrial. The European settlers themselves became the labour force in the case of the northern territories and Canada; whereas in the southern plantations of the United States this role was taken by slave labour.

In French Canada the settlements were mainly rural, under the strong influence of the Catholic Church, and very conservative. Also, because of their rupture with France in 1759, they were isolated from the Enlightenment period and all the liberal ideas that preceded the French revolution. French settlers refused to mix with the British or other immigrants. From Britain they obtained a certain autonomy after 1774. Moreover, Canada 'officially' became from the end of the eighteenth century, two nations: Upper and Lower Canada, where English and French Canadians respectively predominated; the first increasingly commercially and trade-oriented, the second overwhelmingly rural. Despite some liberal uprising – the French Canadian rebellion of 1837–38 – French Canada remained very traditional, rural-oriented and underdeveloped. Besides, because of British migration policies, the French became a minority by the middle of the nineteenth century.

In the case of the Spanish colonization the situation was very different. The European settlers recruited the Indian population as a working force and thus kept some of them alive in extremely rude conditions, physically and culturally. The model of development: state controlled, inefficient, aristocratic, nearly feudal and export oriented, sealed Latin America's underdevelopment.

Identity and 'national belonging' also differed within the region. In Canada and the United States, the European settlers became 'American, French or English-Canadian citizens' without losing their European cultural identity or religion (although this identity somehow got adapted to the new context – that is, Americanized). However, the black slaves and afterwards other non-European waves had problems finding their place in the new national entities.

In Mexico the mixture of cultures and races produced an identity confusion: most Mexicans are neither European nor Indians, they are 'mestizos'. The nation-building after independence was forged through a century of devastating civil wars and foreign invasions. The Indian groups that survived maintained their culture and language in a marginal way, and they have never felt themselves as part of the Mexican nation.

The Process of State-Building

The state-building process in the countries of the region has also been different. Canada and the United States followed the European patterns of democratic institutions (Canada – parliamentarian, the United States – presidential) inherited from the British parliamentarian tradition. Their state-building was influenced by regional interests (Canada – French-British, USA – South-North) which laid the ground for a strong federalism and full respect for the provinces/states autonomy.

Mexico inherited a very authoritarian tradition both from the pre-Hispanic world and from Spain. After independence and endless struggle between Liberals and Conservatives the Liberal victory shaped a presidential federal republic that nevertheless allowed for a powerful and centralized presidential power that left little power to the Congress or the provinces. Neither the Mexican Revolution nor the reforms brought by it changed a centralized, authoritarian state that also became corporative.

DOMESTIC CLEAVAGES

Canada

In Canada the main social cleavage is between the French and the Anglo-Saxon parts of the population. In the beginning of the 1990s the French-speaking Canadians comprised 25 per cent of the total population of Canada but 80 per cent in Quebec (World Directory of Minorities, 1990). In spite of the fact that the Constitution of 1867 guaranteed certain language rights to the Francophone minority French Canadians found themselves increasingly disadvantaged.[1] This resentment was directed not only towards English-speaking Canadians but at economic domination by Canadian and US firms.[2]

The political mobilization behind nationalistic aims started in the 1960s. Quebec accomplished a late transition from a rural society and isolationism to modernization. A search for identity through direct contacts with France and Francophone countries and increasing socio-economic difference with British Canada gave way to a strengthening of autonomy and independence goals which found their expression in the 1970, nationalistic terrorist groups' actions and the 1976 victory of the PQ under the leadership of René Levesque in Quebec.

By 1980 this nationalistic period had lost momentum.[3] However, Quebec has not yet found its place within the Canadian federation up to now. The failure of the different attempts to give Canada a constitution satisfying all regional and national interests reflects a crisis in the Canadian national formation.[4] The 1995 referendum concerning

Quebec's sovereignty again saw the defeat of the separatists.[5] But Quebec's French speakers (four-fifths of its electorate) voted 60–40 per cent for independence and it's doubtful they will be satisfied with only some changes to the Canadian constitution and a few more powers devolved to Quebec's provincial assembly (*The Economist*, 11 November 1995). The native people's (5 per cent of Canada's population) grievances are also part of the internal problems Canada faces, and this concerns mainly Quebec where there are still conflicts of interests between French-Canadians and Indians regarding territorial rights.

The USA

The USA's internal cleavages are also related to ethnic and socio-economical differences. All immigrants were supposed to have an equal opportunity to develop their abilities and fortunes, but American Indians, African slaves and many non-European groups of immigrants lacked such opportunities. American society became, in fact, a conglomerate of different social and national groups that didn't mix with each other: the opposite to the 'melting pot'.

Ethnic and socio-economic conflicts oppose native Americans,[6] African-Americans (the largest minority, 12 per cent of the USA's 255 million in 1990[7]) and Latinos on the one side, to Asian-Americans and Whites (or 'European-Americans') on the other. Several social movements have legally given minorities equal rights to those of the rest of the population,[8] but in spite of the fact that some of their members have attained middle-class status, racial and socio-economic marginalization has continued.[9]

On the other hand, Asian-Americans (2.7 per cent of the American population) in spite of their heterogeneity and of having come as manual labourers or extremely poor refugees seem to have far less socio-economic problems than the other minority groups.[10]

The 'Whites' or Europeans do not constitute a homogeneous group. Nevertheless, they statistically form the core of the 'average middle class' and they have been able to become integrated into American society without major conflicts.

Contradictions between these minorities and between them and the white European majority are one of the most destabilizing problems the United States faces today.[11] Poverty, segregation, unemployment, lack of education and lack of alternatives reflect deep ethnic, class and cultural contradictions.[12] Within politics, one can notice that the racial and social questions have penetrated and divided the ideology and programmes of both the Democratic and the Republican parties, and besides this the political system is going through a deep crisis of representation and alienation from politicians.[13]

Mexico

In Mexico, social and regional cleavages are even deeper, especially after the 1994 crisis.[14] Already during the Salinas period the average income of the wealthiest 10 per cent of the population was 36 times higher than that of the poorest 10 per cent. In Western Europe such a relation is usually around 10 (Pipitone, 1994, p. 22). By the beginning of 1996, according to some calculations, two-thirds of the Mexican population lived in poverty.[15]

The social contradictions reflect themselves at the internal regional level. The north of Mexico is rather industrialized, partly as a result of the *maquiladoras* scheme which has been in place since the 1960s, and partly because the internal industrialization efforts since the 1940s took place mostly in the north.[16] The north got more transport, urbanization and industrial infrastructure and became a place of reception for workers migrating from the southern states (for example from Oaxaca). Even politically, since the 1910 revolution the north has been better represented in central government.

The south, where most Indian groups still live (15 millions in the whole of Mexico), remained rather rural, with lower rates of employment, education and health. In 1993, seven of the southern states (65 per cent of the population) had incomes of less than two minimal salaries (1 minimal salary = US $3 per/day).[17]

Social unrest in these regions (but also everywhere else) had a violent outcome with the Zapatista movement in Chiapas in January 1994. In Chiapas social and ethnic contradictions are reflected at its utmost.[18] Chiapas was only the beginning of a deeply rooted social crisis that erupted in new guerrilla movements, in new social movements and even in a political crisis within the official party.

RECORD OF COOPERATION AND CONFLICT

Certain key conflicts have opposed mainly the USA and Mexico. The first one, the territorial conflict, although more than a century ago, has left definite traces since then that have marked the relationship between Mexico and the United States. Mexico's loss of half of the Mexican territory in 1848 marked the Mexicans with a profound distrust of American motives and contributed to Mexico's xenophobic tradition (further reinforced by the French intervention in the 1860s). Further on, Mexico's independent position in international affairs confronted the US both in the case of the Cuban revolution and in that of Nicaragua during the Sandinista period.

Mexico refused to back and comply with the US-inspired Organization of American States (OAS) resolution to exclude Cuba from the organization in the early 1960s, to break diplomatic relations with its government and to enforce an embargo against the island for its subversive activities.[19] The conflict remains unsolved and has even escalated with an increasing embargo (the Helms–Burton Law) to which both the European Union and Canada as well as Mexico and many other countries of Latin America have reacted.[20] This has gone as far as the creation of special laws both within Mexico and Canada that try to protect their national firms from the effect of the American law.[21] Moreover, this is creating a serious conflict to be solved within the conflict resolution mechanisms foreseen in NAFTA.

The Central American conflict during the 1970s also placed Mexico's position (together with other Latin American countries and even Canada sometimes) in opposition to that of the USA. Mexico and Venezuela tried to counteract the region's polarization and its transformation to a North–South conflict. The Contadora initiative was a response to this polarization; its failure demonstrated once more a typical American mistrust for all initiatives not taken by their unconditional allies. On the whole we can say that the record of cooperation and conflict has been determined to a high degree by US security, political and economic interests. Cooperation has only succeeded when these interests have permitted it to succeed and conflict has surged whenever these interests have been or seemed to be at stake. Once again cooperation has meant a sort of US institutionalization framework.

Apart from all three being members of the Organization of American States they have also collaborated in different sub-regional economic (since the Alliance for Progress) and even defence schemes (like the Pact of Rio) inspired by the USA's security and economic interests, what can be called hegemonic regionalism. Besides, Canada has had a long-standing cooperation with the USA regarding defence matters, as a member of NATO. However, more than an integrated pattern of cooperation – where partners are equal – we have different bilateral relations with the US at one end and Canada or Mexico at the other.

Although there have been several integration schemes within Latin America, since the 1960s none of them included the USA and Canada. NAFTA is the first to do so. Moreover, this has been interpreted as an effect of the global trends towards regionalization in other areas. But does NAFTA really place North America in a framework of regional integration? Only a few years ago the idea of a free trade agreement between Mexico and the United States would not have been accepted by Mexican political élites. The situation was different for Canada who signed a first free trade agreement or 'Reciprocity Act' with the United States in 1854. In 1989 – after several years of negotiations – the Free Trade Agreement (FTA) between the US and Canada started to be implemented. This confined itself to trade and investment issues and as such would be the model for NAFTA.[22]

NAFTA is not comparable with the EU integration scheme. Its aims can be compared in principle to those of EFTA (European Free Trade Association) in the sense of being a differential trade area that does not entail any elements of supranationality. But NAFTA is also an 'institutional framework', fostering and guaranteeing the continued pursuit of neoliberal policies at the domestic level in countries party to the agreement, within an asymmetric relation where the USA is dominant. This asymmetric linking coupled with the absence of any foreseeable regional political union as in the European case, opens the space for the USA to pursue its specific vision of democracy and the market for the entire region. Moreover, different business groups play a superordinate role in pushing forward a programme of market liberalization in the context of increased global competitiveness. This represents a rupture with traditional Mexican practices that although engaged in a modernization project, coupled such modernization with a strong nationalism and state control of the economy.[23] On the other hand, the Mexican technocratic élite made NAFTA a new project of modernization for Mexico, the only possible course and one that did not entail an equally radical project of political modernization in the sense understood in Europe with the incorporation of the southern members of the continent at the end of the 1970s to mid-1980s.

In other words, this agreement, formally for trade liberalization, is really aimed at the consolidation of the neoliberal model for the region as a whole. Whereas the USA and Canada want to guarantee a better competitive position for their products, Mexico wants a regular inflow of foreign (especially American) investment to Mexico.

The trickle-down effect is supposed to benefit everybody. However, this can hardly take place without any mechanisms for an homogenization of the members' standards, and a radical political democratization for the weakest of the partners.

PROCESS OF HOMOGENIZATION

In Europe, political homogenization was a precondition for economic cooperation. In the case of North America, such homogenization (regarding Mexico) is supposed to be a consequence of economic cooperation. However, neither political traditions nor economic indicators show any signs of homogenization, quite on the contrary, especially after the social and economic deterioration provoked by the 1994 crisis.[24] The homogenization that is taking place regards the rules of the game (liberalization, and radical reduction of the state's involvement in the economy) but not economic potential and living standards. The Mexican government presented NAFTA (with its injection of American and Canadian investment in Mexico) as the magic solution that would raise Mexican standards, but differences are so great that it would take at least 50 years for Mexico to reach US levels of income. This could call for a parallel agreement regarding compensation for the costs of the integration and a social chapter.[25] Even the US Congress asked President Bush to 'address issues like transition measures, wage disparity, environmental protection and worker rights' in order to grant him the authority to negotiate NAFTA on a 'fast track' (Pastor, 1992, p. 177).

The side agreements on environmental and labour cooperation, signed in September 1993, are a response to these concerns. However, even if they establish trinational commissions and councils to supervise their enforcement, they do not provide the necessary resources necessary to implement them.[26]

Homogenization by modernization was supposed to be limited to the economic sphere. In contrast to the Spanish and Portuguese integration experience, where the discourse of political and economical modernization 'went hand in hand' with EC membership (see chapter 9 this volume) political modernization regarding Mexico was far from being a goal. Neither the US government nor the Mexican technocratic élite had expected this project of integration to have any effects regarding a process of political transition towards a modern democratic system for Mexico. On the contrary, both the Mexican and the

US élites seemed satisfied with the Mexican authoritarian system and regarded it as a necessary guarantee that the neoliberal economic changes would not be upset by any social or political protest movements.

However, civil society has somehow reacted to this kind of regional institutionalization. Organizations within Canada, the USA and Mexico have been able to define common interests and development strategies regarding NAFTA's limitations and the kind of integration they would like to have, and it was due to their pressure that the environmental and labour side agreements were incorporated into NAFTA. They stress the negative consequence of neoliberalism for their countries and argue for an agreement that contains a social agenda to harmonize living standards and alleviate the social costs of integration.[27] A concrete example of these grassroots contacts is the cooperation taking place among environmental groups from both sides of the Mexican–American border (like the activities of the 'Tijuana-San Diego Environmental Committee') to stop the degradation of the environment that is taking place in this region as a result of the maquiladoras production.[28] Women organizations' cooperation across the border is also a good example in this sense,[29] and a third example is trade union coordination strategies across the three countries. Although the latter is still limited, their contacts continue and seem to promise greater cooperation.[30]

On the other hand, certain protest movements have a trend to jump borders. For the first time in history, the 12 October celebration (the day of the discovery of America by Columbus) gathered broad Hispano-American masses from the whole USA in Washington, protesting at the discrimination they were being subjected to: they carried many protest banners ('Ya Basta!') with the same slogans as the Zapatistas in Mexico.[31]

Culturally, although US predominance is unquestionable, there is not one American culture. Each of the groups described above have their own culture – some with a Latin and even a Mexican character. Even though the Mexican middle class is highly influenced by an American pattern of consumption – what we used to call an 'American way of life' – the premises for the fulfilment of such a model have changed and its influence may have diminished. On the other hand, several developments question the hegemony of a single American culture: post-modern trends, the appearance (or reappearance?) of multiculturalism in the US, Quebec's strong attachment to its French-Canadian culture, and the Chiapas Indian rebellion. Thus, a North

American regional identity may be as problematic to attain as a European one. Even more, when the modernization and welfare model offered by the US (as it was offered by the Northern European countries) is no longer so desirable or viable to obtain, what is the use of striving towards a regional identity that matches an institutionalization lacking in popular legitimacy?

But if regionalization is a process that breaks with the present state-buildings and gives way to a sort of federation in which small regions grow stronger and gain a greater autonomy, where local cultures and ethnic identities may have a chance to survive, then multiculturalism may be the basis for a regional identity. Should, for example, Indian groups be listened to and perhaps join forces all through North America, there may be a chance that the evil circle of a centralized and authoritarian state could be neutralized by a regional counterbalance.

CONCLUSION: IS NORTH AMERICA BECOMING A REGION?

It is very difficult to give a realistic assessment of NAFTA after only three years. All three countries have become somehow disappointed or worried by problems they had not foreseen, such as the Mexican economic crisis at the end of 1994. Other problems foreseen from the beginning, like Mexican illegal migration to the US, are still there, growing and waiting for NAFTA (or the US) to address them. This problem is part of the asymmetry we noticed above and is increasing in direct relation with Mexican unemployment.

In the US, criticism of the treaty has also increased, mostly from conservative sectors but even from progressive ones who question this form of regional institutionalization. Part of the problem seems to be the US's (both at the people and government level) reluctance to learn more and get involved with their nearest neighbours' culture and problems. Mexico is still regarded with contempt and ignorance frequently associated to illegal illiterate workers and attractive tourist resorts. Very little of its culture, attitudes and problems is known or acknowledged. Even political modernization involving a break with the old authoritarian patterns was not seen as a necessary or even desirable goal of regional institutionalization by the US power élites. For these élites, Mexico's importance is related to US security concerns that in this era have to do with control of natural resources (oil) and the struggle against drugs traffic and corruption linked to it. Not much on which to build a regional institutional agreement.

For its part, the Mexican government continues to believe in the desirability of this US institutionalization framework as the only alternative for Mexico's modernization project. On the other hand, the Mexican population has become more sceptical of the benefits of such a model and above all of the convenience of such a close dependence of the United States symbolized by NAFTA, spurring new feelings of nationalism that are becoming increasingly anti-American.[32] Moreover, the recent political changes with the victory of the left opposition candidate in Mexico City, in July 1997, showed that the old forms of an authoritarian political system are on their way out and that the integration effort will have to acknowledge this. However, integration as such is considered necessary by both the governments and the civil society. Moreover, if NAFTA were to be cancelled it is possible that Mexico would undergo an even longer recovery period, and the possibility of social revolts beyond Chiapas could become a real threat.

The Canadian government is also critical of NAFTA and may press for some modifications even if trade liberalization has benefited Canadian exports.[33] Canada also shares with Mexico certain problems regarding wheat exports and, as we have seen, the irritation caused by the Helms–Burton Law that both countries are trying to negotiate within NAFTA.

On the whole, regional integration from above is seriously being questioned from below. NAFTA is still, basically, a 'negative' form of integration, removing obstacles for the free movement of goods and capital, even though the agreements on labour and environmental cooperation may be the first sign of a 'positive' form of integration. Nevertheless, NAFTA is still far away from a common market or customs union which would imply among other things the free movement of labour, something the US government is far from accepting.

The diversity of attitudes and values within the region is enormous: individualism against corporatism, liberalism against authoritarianism, respect for human rights against repression and lack of respect for the law, free market against monopolies, and so on. Compared to Europe, North America presents far more economic and social contrasts. None of the countries in question is free from internal political, ethnic or socio-economical cleavages. The French–British cleavage in Canada may well result in the division of Canada. National/ethnic ruptures are something difficult to see in the near future in the USA but its racial and socio-economic problems may well provoke new waves of instability in certain states of the union. Mexico is being ravaged by social/ethnic and political problems that will certainly affect the US.

The forces that have pushed for a regional institutionalization are the modern, industrial and business sectors, to consolidate a model of economic performance (the neoliberal model). Political modernization in the form of democratization was never contemplated. The people at large were absent in this project. However, civil society or some sectors of it have found forms to participate and even to have some influence – through the agreements on labour and environment cooperation – on the process of integration. The question is how to try to solve the internal conflicts and problems in the three countries within a regional perspective that, taking into account the demands from below, is not neutralized from above. That is how to link the institutionalization of the region both to global changes and to internal transformations and needs. In fact the two cannot be separated.

Notes

1. This resentment only grew with the urbanization of the Quebecois society (by 1931 it had become 63 per cent urban), the loss of influence of the church and the rise of a new class of nationalist and radical intellectuals and trade unionists. *World Directory of Minorities*, 1990.
2. *Ibid.*, p. 17. A Royal Commission on Bilingualism and Biculturalism established by the federal government in 1963, showed disparities in income, education and employment between French and English speakers in Quebec with the French-speakers greatly disadvantaged. French-speaking Canadians have also populated other provinces.
3. The option 'sovereignty-association' (seen as a step towards full separation) was rejected in the referendum organized that year. In 1985, the PQ dropped its long-term goal of independence and also lost office in the Quebec elections.
4. The 'Meech Lake Accord', in June 1987; the 'Charlottetown agreement' in 1992.
5. They were defeated by only one percentage point and blamed 'the ethnic vote' (immigrants vote) for this defeat.
6. *World Directory of Minorities op. cit.*, p. 3. By 1880, in California alone, the Indian population fell from an estimated pre-European level of 350 000 to 20 000 (p. 6). In 1985 half of the Indian population was unemployed and 55 per cent of their homes were sub-standard, with suicides and accidents the most usual causes of Indian death (*ibid.*).
7. *The Europa World Yearbook 1993*, statistical survey.
8. This gave way to a certain sense of identity and to a radicalization (like Malcom X). The Black Power movement was part of this wave of the 1960s, and even the Black Panther party. In 1964 the Civil Rights Act was passed.
9. The black middle class has made notable advances: in 1990 of those blacks who worked 40 per cent were 'white collars'. They were only 10 per cent in 1950. However, racial marginalization coincides with serious

social problems. Approximately one-third of the Black American population live at or below the poverty level. See *Dagens Nyheter*, 15 November 1993. Mexican-Americans are 5 per cent of the total US population
(12.1 million) and represent 60 per cent of all the Spanish-speaking
people in the US (together with other Hispanic Americans: 7.3 million)
becoming the second minority of the US, after the blacks and they are
expected to become the dominant minority by the turn of the century.
Robert Pastor, 'NAFTA as the Center of an Integration Process: the
Nontrade Issues' in N. Lustig, B.P. Boswath and R.Z. Lawrence, *Assessing the Impact of the North American Free Trade*, Washington, DC, The
Brookings Institution. 1992, p. 178. It has been calculated that Mexico
has lost about 1 million persons to the USA every 10 years (*World
Directory of Minorities*).

10.   In 1980, Asian-American families had a median income of $23 660
compared to $20 800 for white families. Also they had higher levels of
education and professional qualifications and higher household participation rates than other groups, *World Directory of Minorities, op.cit.* p. 10.

11.   A showcase is the Los Angeles riots in 1992. The wave of ethnic violence
confronted mainly Hispanic-Americans against Koreans. Pierre Brian-
con, *ibid.*, p. 20.

12.   For the overall figures see *The Economist*, 4–10 May 1996, p. 102 and 13
April 1996.

13.   As the Perot phenomenom showed in 1993.

14.   Public expenditures on social welfare such as health, education, subsidies and so on decreased from 7.3 per cent of the GDP in 1981 to 3.2
per cent in 1988. The poor increased from 32.1 millions in 1981 to nearly
50 millions in 1988, that is more than 60 per cent of the population.

15.   From 1987 to 1990 infant malnutrition increased by 65 per cent. In the
countryside, at the beginning of the 1990s it was calculated that about 4
million children were undernourished. See Domínguez, 1995.

16.   In 1965 the 'Programa de Industrialización Fronteriza' (PIF) was
launched. This was done to create new jobs for those workers that had
to return to Mexico from the USA because of the termination of the
'guest-workers' programme put in place since the Second World War.
This was also a way to attract foreign investment. The PIF meant that
American industries established plants that could perform part of the
production process in Mexico and then return the product to the USA to
be sold or exported from there. In the beginning of 1996, maquiladoras
accounted for 40 per cent of all manufactured exports, employed more
than 600 000 workers (mostly women) and pay on average US $5 per
day, that is 30 per cent more than the minimum salary in Mexico
(INEGI, Mexico, by Internet, 2 February 1996.)

17.   The Indians can be considered marginalized among the marginalized:
malnutrition among them has increased from 66 per cent to 71 per cent
between 1987 and 1990 (Domínguez, 1993).

18.   To have an idea of Chiapas socio-economic unbalances see Suarez
Guevara, 1995.

19.   Mexico was consistent with this position during all these years although
relations between Cuba and Mexico were only maintained at the

diplomatic level; there was nearly no trade or other economic relations until the 1980s and 1990s. At present these relations have become rather significant for Cuba as Mexican private enterprises have made considerable investments in the island. The recent re-enforcement of economic sanctions by the USA has provoked a lot of protests internationally starting with Mexico.

20. See *La Jornada* (Mexico), 25 May 1996.

21. See Mexico, NAFTA report 31 October 96 and *La Jornada* (Mexico), 8 November 96.

22. *Mexico and NAFTA Report*, London 28 October 1993. For a discussion of Canada and the FTA see Jean Revel Mouroz, 'Integration-désintegration à echelle des continents: L'ALENA vu du Mexique', Seminaire GEMDEV-EADI 13–14 May 1993, Berlin. Also, *The European World Yearbook 1992*, ed. Europa Publications, pp. 660. For NAFTA's limitations on non-economic issues see Gustavo Vega's comments to Pastor's article in Robert Pastor, 'NAFTA as the Center of an Integration Process: the Nontrade Issues', *op. cit.* p. 200.

23. For example, the theme of privatization, especially regarding national resources and in particular the oil sector, has created an enormous debate in Mexico where most political parties and the majority of the population are opposed to such privatization.

24. In the mid-1990s Mexico still has some of the lowest salaries in the world, on average 10 times lower than American salaries. In the United States the GNP in 1990 was over US $5000 billion, in Canada about US $550 billion and in Mexico about US $200 billion (*The Europa World Yearbook, 1992*). Mexico's per capita GNP in 1991 was US $3030, that of Canada US $20 440 and that of the USA US $22 240 (World Banks's figures for 1991). Regarding unemployment it is estimated at 30 per cent (*Mexico and NAFTA Report*, no. 1, 1996), compared to 5 per cent in the US and 11 per cent in Canada, and it is calculated that Mexico needs to create 800 000 new jobs every year (Appendini, 1992, p. 1).

25. For a discussion of this alternative see Castaneda, 1993, pp. 21–41.

26. See: North American Agreement on Environmental Cooperation and North American Agreement on Labor Cooperation between the government of the United States of America, the government of Canada and the government of Mexico (13 September 1993). Regarding the environmental agreement a report by Public Citizen and Mexican RMALC (Red Mexicana de Acción Frente al Libre Comercio) claims that the promises for a cleaner environment have not been fulfilled, on the contrary, things have deteriorated. See Dominguez, 'Regional Integration in Uneven terms: the case of Mexico within NAFTA' (forthcoming). Labour cooperation is also disappointing even if there are some exceptions like the Sony case: *Mexico and NAFTA Report*, 1995, no. 5, p. 1.

27. See 'NAFTA' in *South Letter*, Winter 1992–93, p. 12. Also, interview with Bertha Lujan of the Mexican 'Red de Acción' against NAFTA. Apart from the social agenda these groups press for an ecological chapter and supranational bodies to supervise its fulfillment. It is important to notice that these groups are not against the process of integration in itself, but for a better form of integration than the one contained in NAFTA.

28.   Elisabeth Karlsson, 'Maquiladora, Miljö and Hälsa', 7p uppsats i Latin-amerikakunskap (paper presented at the end of the Latin American specialisation course), Vt. 1993, p. 39. See also the investigation carried out by the Commission for Environmental Cooperation of NAFTA in Puerto Maya, Cozumel in August 1996, *Mexpaz #84*, información, 1996.

29.   This cooperation enabled several members of the Mexican women's organization 'Comite fronterizo de Obreras' in the border, to attend the Women World Conference in Peking (Huairou) in September 1995. See Edmé Domínguez, 'NAFTA and Women Workers in Mexico: the case of the border Maquiladoras and of Agro-exports', paper presented at the ISA Conference in San Diego, US, April 1996.

30.   See the latest meeting of trade unions organized by RMALC (Red Mexicana de Accion contra el Libre Comercio), and the American AFL-CIO in July 1996. Boletin *Mexpaz #80*, informacion, 1996.

31.   See *Mexpaz # 94*, informacion, 1996.

32.   According to recent opinion polls 77 per cent of the inhabitants of Mexico City blamed NAFTA for the increase in poverty (such a belief was shared by 58 per cent of the same population in 1992). Also, 68 per cent of this same population thought that NAFTA would damage traditional Mexican culture and 55 per cent thought the treaty would make Mexico lose control of its oil (*Mexico and NAFTA Report*, 1996, no. 1, p. 4).

33.   In 1995, the United States trade deficit with Canada was $18.2 billion, $3.5 billion greater than in 1994, *National Trade Report*, Canada, on the Internet, Richard Martin. Also, 'El impacto negativo del ALC para los trabajadores Canadienses: perspectivas del TLC', in *Canada en Transición*, ed. Teresa Gutierrez and Monica Verea, CIAN, 1994. p. 337

References

Anderson, B. (1983) *Imagined Communities. Reflections on the Origin and Spread of Nationalism* (London: Verso).

Appendini, K. (1992) 'From Crises to Restructuring: The Debate on the Mexican Economy During the 1980s', Copenhagen, project paper 92.2, Centre for Development Research.

Bull, H. and Watson, A. (1984) *The Expansion of International Society* (Oxford: Clarendon Press).

Castaneda, J. (1993) *La casa por la ventana*, edit. Cal y Arena, México.

Deutsch, K.W. *et al.* (1957) *Political Community and the North Atlantic Area* (Princeton: Princeton University Press).

Domínguez, R.E. (1995) 'From Model to Catastrophe: Mexico Beyond NAFTA', *European Journal of Development Research*, vol. 7, no. 2, December.

Domínguez, R.E. and Hettne, B. (1996) 'In the European Footsteps: NAFTA as a case of Regionalism', in W. Karlsson and A. Malaki (eds), *Growth, Trade and Integration in Latin America*, Institute of Latin American Studies, Stockholm University, Sweden.

Domínguez, R.E. (1993) 'Neo-liberalisms in Mexico Today: Its Social Consequences and the Workers Movement', *Anales*, no. 3–4, Instituto Iberoamericano, University of Göteborg.

Domínguez, R.E. 'Regional Integration in Uneven terms: The Case of Mexico within NAFTA', in A. Inotai (ed.), *National Perspectives on the New Regionalism in the North*, vol. 2, forthcoming (Macmillan).

Edwards, G. and Regelsberger, E. (eds) (1990) *Europe's Global Links. The European Community and Inter-Regional Cooperation* (London: Pinter).

Grinspun, R. and Cameron, A.M. (1993) *The Political Economy of North American Free Trade* (New York: St Martin's Press).

Gutierrez, T. and Verea, M. (eds) (1993) *Canada en Transición*, CIAN, UNAM, Mexico.

Huntington, S. (1993) 'The Clash of Civilizations', *Foreign Affairs*, Summer, pp. 22–49.

Lustig, N. (1992) 'Mexico's Integration Strategy with North America', in C.I. Bradford (ed.), *Strategic Options for Latin America in the 1990s* (OECD).

Mouroz, J.R. (1993) 'Integration-désintegration à echelle des continents: L'ALENA vu du Mexique', *Seminaire GEMDEV-EADI*, 13–14 May, Berlin.

Pastor R. (1992) 'NAFTA as the Center of an Integration Process: The Non-trade Issues', in N. Lustig, B.P. Boswath and R.Z. Lawrence (eds) *Assessing the Impact of the North American Free Trade* (Washington, DC: The Brookings Institution).

Suarez Guevara S. (1995) 'Pobreza y Riqueza el antagonismo que exploto en Chiapas', IIE, UNAM.

11 The Challenges of Regionalism: Unbalanced Integration in the Americas

Pekka Valtonen

INTRODUCTION

The heyday of the discussions on a hemispheric free trade area embracing all of the Americas now seems to be behind us. The excitement created by the Enterprise for the Americas Initiative in 1990 ran high through to the Miami Summit in December 1994; since the Summit, very little actual progress has been achieved towards such a free trade regime, despite sporadic declarations to keep the idea alive. Both Latin America and the United States seem to have entered an era of realpolitik in their economic relations. The vision of a free trade area from Alaska to Tierra del Fuego still survives and has support, but the terms of the discussion have shifted from emotional sentiments stressing the geographic and historical unity of the Americas (imagined or true) to a greater acknowledgement of more global currents and circumstances, be it the emergence of Asia–Pacific cooperation or the triadic economic world order (US–EU–Japan). Present trends towards regionalization will by no means automatically lead to a single free trade area of the Americas (FTAA).

In Latin America this realpolitik is a function of the widespread public feeling of disillusionment with reforms, both economic and political. The peso crisis in Mexico just after the Miami Summit exposed the vulnerability of an open economy to international markets, and the lack of genuine social progress has frustrated the peoples of the region. The so called trickle-down effect of economic growth has not in reality occurred, and the sustainability of growth is dubious in many countries. Instead of the optimism of the early 1990s, it is now possible to talk about a backlash in Latin America.[1] While most Latin Americans are still broadly in favour of regional integration, in the case of Mexico integration has been counterproductive: 49 per cent of Mexicans think that NAFTA has brought them little or no benefit at all, and 39 per cent are opposed to any further integration within Latin America.[2]

It is obvious from the results of opinion polls that neoliberal reforms are no longer seen as a panacea for the economic, political and social ills of Latin America.[3] The euphoria over free markets has faded and the issue of integration is now looked at in a more pragmatic light. In this respect one of the most serious problems from a Latin American (and Canadian) perspective is the overwhelmingly predominant role of the United States in shaping the course of regionalism in the Americas. This is not just a corollary of the sheer size of the US economy, but a function of a deliberate US policy. A weakly institutionalized free trade regime, which enables the US to resort to protectionism when needed, and a preference for bilateral rather than multilateral integration schemes, are the two main elements of US policy that help to maintain the imbalance. In this chapter these factors are examined from the point of view of the impact on the other two NAFTA partners (Canada and Mexico) and Latin America. The perspective adopted is strategic and policy-oriented.

For the United States the importance of Latin America, with the exception of Mexico, is surpassed by a wide margin by the Asian-Pacific countries. Thus, the US feels little obliged to make concessions to its Latin American trading partners; instead Washington exercises a free hand in pursuing economic policies that are seen as appropriate to its interests at any given time, regardless of whether this contradicts international commitments it has signed or promoted. In either of the two most likely scenarios – that the US will continue to promote free trade but only through bilateral agreements, or that it will increasingly resort to protectionism (this being justified by national trade remedy laws[4]) – the consequences for Latin America are not favourable unless US–Latin American relations become based on a solid institutional foundation. This, however, is unlikely, given US policy preferences. As the United States hovers between free trade and protectionism, it is important for the rest of the American nations to enhance their economic and political relations with other regions. In balancing US dominance in the western hemisphere, the role of the European Union (EU) may thereby be of major significance. Increasing intra-Latin American trade is also a vehicle for achieving the same ends.

These strategies should be seen against a background of it being unlikely that any concrete multilateral steps towards a free trade system for all the Americas will be taken in the near future. The date set by the Miami Summit for an FTAA, the year 2005, is distant enough to allow the issue to be delayed and transferred to future governments. Presently the most (or only) feasible route towards greater hemispheric free trade seems to be through bilateral agreements with the United States, the route pursued by the US itself; although even this route has stumbling blocks as Chile's attempts to enter NAFTA have shown. In any event, the bilateral route has serious pitfalls for Latin America as such a system with the United States as the hub (it being the only country with free access to the markets of almost all Latin American countries) would only enhance US dominance and hamper the development of intra-Latin American trade.

NAFTA, THE UNITED STATES AND THE EUROPEAN UNION

Canadians, with their economy as intertwined with the United States as is the Mexican economy, have been in little doubt since the Canada–US Free Trade Agreement (CUFTA) that bilateral trade relations with the United States cannot be equal: despite the agreement Canadian exporters have been subjected to arbitrary protectionist actions on the part of US companies and authorities, based on US national trade laws.[5] An important motive for Canada in joining the Mexico–US negotiations for NAFTA was to seek the support of Mexico for a joint platform of economic policy to counterbalance US dominance and protectionism. A joint platform, however, has not emerged, partly because the institutional instruments provided by the final NAFTA agreement were as weak as those of the CUFTA, upon which NAFTA was mainly modelled. The weakness of Mexico since the peso crisis has also contributed to the absence of a joint policy. The discontent in Canada against the present regional trade arrangement and the need for a broader, multilateral basis have formed the background to Canadian support for a hemispheric free trade system, perhaps even more than the hope of increasing exports to the region.

Seen in this light, it is little wonder that Canada has also actively promoted the idea of a NAFTA–EU trade agreement. While the rationale for such an initiative are of course manifold (ranging from historic transatlantic connections to concrete trade issues), 'it also took much of its nourishment from the notion that a structure embracing many members and possessing a strong sense of procedure and regulation could do much to mould and configure the behaviour' of the United States, as observed by Allan Smith.[6] In other words, it was perceived in Canada that stronger institutional and multilateral monitoring, if not governance, of trade policies would help to alleviate problems arising from the loose structure of NAFTA. However, the course of events in this respect was disappointing for Canada. Although Canada was the first to suggest closer relations between NAFTA and the EU, the talks that evolved during 1995 were soon transformed to cover only US–EU relations, despite explicit efforts to get Canada to the negotiation table by the Canadian Minister of International Trade, Roy McLaren. The talks led to the New Transatlantic Agenda, signed in December 1995, between the United States and the EU.

The Agenda, lacking in substance as regards concrete trade issues, can be interpreted as a framework agreement for a further trade agreement between the two parties. As such, it resembles the framework agreements the United States has negotiated with almost all Latin American countries. It also reinforces the US preference for bilateralism, as the United States was negotiating on its own behalf rather than on behalf of NAFTA, even though the other party was also a bloc. NAFTA is not seen by the United States as a single actor or *global player* in its own right,[7] which reflects the US stance that national trade legislation generally takes precedence over international commitments.

Although in formal terms NAFTA is almost exclusively a trade and investment agreement with no political integration or institution-building, it is so extensive that it brings with it 'many elements of an economic community without an explicit common external tariff', as observed by Peter Morici.[8] It would be quite natural for such an entity to act as a single actor, or at least for the members to share a common platform when acting individually. This seems not to be the case with NAFTA. However, it is in the interests of the US to keep NAFTA as little institutionalized as possible, as it allows free access to the markets of its neighbours with a minimum of political pressure to harmonize or revoke often contradictory national trade laws, and allows more freedom to operate globally without having to take into account the considerations of the other two NAFTA members. True, the US strategy to negotiate bilaterally with the EU is rational precisely because NAFTA is not as unified as the EU, which in turn is due to NAFTA being a purely commercial agreement and to the disproportionate role of the US in it. Had negotiations between the EU and NAFTA as a bloc got underway, one might suspect that on many issues the interests of Mexico and Canada might have been closer to those of the EU than to those of the US (for example, in the fields of cultural products like books and films, in agriculture, in public sector services, and in dispute settlements, to name but a few).

Under these circumstances Mexico has unilaterally sought a free trade agreement with the EU. From the Mexican perspective, increasing trade with the EU is important both economically and politically. It would go some way towards balancing US dominance of the Mexican economy, it would enhance the feeling of sovereignty of Mexicans over their economic and foreign policy, and it would provide some indirect support in cases of dispute arising from the use of national trade laws in a protectionist manner by the US.[9] Commercially, the EU offers similar kinds of markets to those of the US, to which the Mexican export sector has already adjusted itself; that is to say markets with similar consumption patterns and purchasing power. For the EU, Mexico is of interest both as a market in its own right (offering trade potential) and as a member of NAFTA (offering investment potential).

The worst scenario for both Canada and Mexico, as well as for the rest of Latin America, would be a situation in which US–EU cooperation were consolidated in the form of an exclusive free trade agreement outside the framework of NAFTA or any regional integration system in the hemisphere that the United States might participate in. Such an agreement would add more judicial weaponry to the US arsenal, which could be used against other nations in a discriminatory or protectionist manner. It would also undermine the development of Latin American–EU relations, as any subsequent Latin America–EU agreement would be designed so as not to contradict it. Under a US–EU agreement, one can imagine that unilateral discriminatory acts by the US against any other American nation (such as the use of the Helms–Burton Act against Cuba and its trading partners; embargoes on Mexican tuna or Chilean timber and so on) would be less likely to arouse criticism in the EU than is currently the case. A more optimistic view would be that such an agreement would help to constrain the US from resorting to such acts, but on the other hand it seems unlikely that the US would concede (in the form of a US–EU agreement) any more binding power over national legislation than it has done with NAFTA or GATT.

LATIN AMERICA, THE UNITED STATES AND THE EUROPEAN UNION

The direct economic involvement of the United States in Latin America has been on the increase in recent years. The slump of the 1980s has passed and Latin America has again 'achieved' the relative economic importance it had for the US before the debt crisis: in 1994 exports to Latin America reached 18 per cent of total US exports – up from 13 per cent in 1986 and comparable to the figure of 18 per cent back in 1981.[10] But the circumstances are totally different now. The size of US exports to Latin America in 1994 reflects at least two elements: the rapid growth of exports to Mexico during the first year of NAFTA, and the relative ease with which the more or less liberated markets of Latin America can now be penetrated by US companies.

However, the overall growth of US exports in the 1990s has lagged behind that of most its competitors and trading partners. Though still the biggest exporter globally (in terms of total value), the United States has continued to lose its relative share in the global economy. Considering this, the peculiar mixture of free market dogmatism and inherent protectionism in US economic policy seems perfectly logical: with the former it can attempt to win back the position in global markets it once had, while with the latter it can try to contain the penetration of the more successful exporters of its domestic markets, the most affluent and consumer-oriented in the world.

For Latin America, the US policy combination of protectionism and free market advocacy is potentially dangerous. Although in relative terms Latin America is not as dependent on the US economy today as it was before and during the debt crisis: the extra-regional trade of Latin America is now more varied than ever and intra-regional trade has risen continuously; it is however still the single most important trading partner of most Latin American countries and continues to exercise strong political power in the region. The neoliberal orientation prevalent in the region is also a vehicle for the pursuit of US policy goals: investments and financial flows, strongly influenced by US-dominated financial institutions, are dependent on the continuity of present economic policies. In sum, the relative unimportance of any single Latin American country to the US economy (with the possible exception of Mexico) means that the US is not inclined to act in a genuinely reciprocal way in its bilateral trade relations.

The danger lies in the not so remote possibility that the United States may turn itself into a more protectionist 'fortress America', with markets which appear to be open in principle but in fact are made inaccessible by a plethora of national legislation; while the fortress itself continues to have a free reign over the more 'bucolic' economies in the hemisphere (that is, those of Latin America). Nominally reciprocal bilateral agreements (to which the US seems to have committed itself) may prove to be of little value in such a situation: under-institutionalized as they would remain, they would be no bastions of juridical and contractual equity against US economic interests. In addition, the US could block countervailing protective measures by Latin American countries by means of selective embargoes and restrictions (of which examples abound) and through pressure in the IMF, WTO and other such organizations.

Therefore, it is for their greater economic security that Latin American nations should seek a stronger multilateral and institutional basis for their extra-regional relations. This is all the more important because it is far from certain that a Free Trade Area of the Americas will materialize. Currently the situation works in the interests of the United States, as it can more freely exercise an *ad hoc* policy in its bilateral trade relations with Latin American countries, with little fear of larger political ramifications. This is, moreover, compatible with the US interest in keeping NAFTA from becoming a more institutionalized actor.

For the purpose of broadening and institutionalizing the extra-regional relations of Latin America, the EU offers probably the most willing and balancing partnership considering that, in particular, the ambitious proposals made at APEC meetings are as yet merely unfulfilled promises and, if APEC ever does become a fully fledged FTA, is likely to be dominated by the United States, Japan, China and the 'Asian Tigers'. In its Basic Document for EU–Latin American relations (31 October 1994), the EU advocates 'a dynamic increase in the economic exchanges between Europe and the emerging markets in Latin America, especially through rapid implementation of tariff reductions and the abolition of trade impediments'.[11] This, according to the Basic Document, could be realized through agreements with regional and sub-regional groupings as well as with individual countries. The groupings specifically mentioned here are the Rio Group, Central America (the San José Group) and Mercosur.[12] Clearly there is a great deal of intellectual consensus between the EU and Latin America on the principles of how international economic relations and disputes should be handled (reflected, say, in the unanimous condemnation of the Helms–Burton Act).

Since the Basic Document, a framework agreement between the EU and Mercosur has been negotiated, signed on 15 December 1995. This agreement on economic and commercial cooperation proposes the establishment of free trade between the two blocs through the elimination of trade barriers over the next 10 years. The agreement was signed within less than two weeks of the signing of the New Transatlantic Agenda, and both were signed within less than a month of the APEC meeting in Manila that laid the foundations for free trade between 18 countries of the Pacific Rim (of which four were American: the three NAFTA members and Chile). The timing is not just a mere coincidence, but reflects to an extent the concern of the EU that it would be left out of the integration schemes taking place in the Americas and in the Pacific. There is no denying that the EU is the most inward-looking of the main trade blocs, with two-thirds of the combined foreign trade of its members being intraregional, and with its common agricultural and external tariff policies. Nonetheless the EU cannot afford to ignore proposals involving the rest of the industrialized and semi-industrialized world to integrate and form units that would rival and exceed its own economic capacities. Seen in this light, the significance of closer and formalized trading relations between the EU and Latin America can be better appreciated from a European perspective too.

Although Mercosur is an area where the relative orientation of economies towards the EU is at its highest level in Latin America (not counting certain Caribbean islands), which makes a more recognized partnership quite natural, the Mercosur–EU agreement could well serve as a basic model for similar agreements with the rest of Latin America. The enlargement of Mercosur may also bring new countries into enhanced trade relations with the EU.

An important factor that strengthens the case for a deeper institutionalization of economic relations between the EU and Latin America is the fact that the EU is by far the most important donor of official development assistance (ODA) to Latin America. The EU accounted for over 60 per cent of the total assistance to the region in 1993, and even close to a half of the aggregated assistance in the period 1980–93 (see Table 11.1). Moreover, of the aggregated ODA of the United States in the period in question, over 53 per cent was directed to only three recipients: El Salvador, Honduras and Costa Rica (28.0, 13.5 and 11.8 per cent respectively), which is simply a reflection of their strategic importance to the US government in the Central American crisis of the 1980s. The EU assistance has been geographically more evenly distributed.[13]

Table 11.1   Official development assistance to Latin America, 1993 and 1980–93 (millions of dollars and percentages of total ODA by region)

	1993		1980–93	
	Value	*%*	*Value*	*%*
EU	2 323	61.6	16 443	46.6
US	528	14.0	11 343	32.2
Japan	727	19.3	5 495	15.6

Source: based on statistics in 'The Wider European Union: New Priorities for Latin America', *IRELA Conference Report*, no. 5, 1995. The EU figures include the disbursements of individual countries and that of the European Commission. Note also that the disbursements of Austria, Finland and Sweden – not Union members in those years – have been added (contributing 3.9 per cent of the 1993 share of the EU and 3.0 per cent of total ODA to Latin America).

Politically, development assistance is more important than simply the money involved, as it entails direct contacts between governments and authorities. The EU's assistance has been less subject to political and military considerations than that of the United States, making it less controversial and perhaps more efficient in pursuing economic and social progress. In order to support more directly the basic objective of its assistance policy, sustained growth and development in the recipient countries, the EU should steer its trade policy towards a more profound institutionalization of mutual trade with Latin America as a whole, in addition to the agreement with Mercosur. Latin American countries themselves could perhaps press a little harder on the issue, preferably as a single unified group, or alternatively as smaller groups. If such a trade policy were to enhance growth in Latin America, a part of the ODA could then be withdrawn and used to alleviate the problems of adversely affected sectors in the Union (for example the textile industry in Portugal, or the fishing industry in France). If an all-at-once solution is not viable, the EU could start with Central America, as the EU commitment to the San José process has been particularly strong.

On the other hand, however, for Latin America to continue unilateral economic liberalization, as it is exhorted to by the IMF, the WTO and the industrialized countries, without simultaneous guarantees for open access to the markets of the major blocs and superpowers, is a foolhardy path to follow. The industrialized countries have maintained their protectionist instruments despite their rhetoric in the WTO (such as the national trade laws of the United States, the common external tariff of the EU, or the non-tariff barriers of Japan), and should protectionism in the First World rise again (for example due to a severe recession) Latin American countries would find themselves in a more disadvantageous position than before: their exports impeded but their domestic markets still an open battlefield for the 'survival of the fittest'. Moreover, they would find that they have surrendered their main weapon before the battle has begun: they would not have tariff policy or the regulation of financial flows left to use as a bargaining chip at the negotiation table. As stated by Guerra-Borges, '*es poco convincente el argumento de que la política de liberalización unilateral no discriminatoria constituye un medio para preservar los mercados latino americanos frente a economías desarrolladas proteccionistas de gran agresividad comercial*'.[14]

Such 'open regionalism' in Latin America, with unilateral liberalization and weak institutionalization, would create a situation oddly resembling late colonial times of the eighteenth century, when the Spanish American markets were liberated but the strings on the economy of the region were still being pulled from outside, at the 'transnational' London banks and merchant houses using the Sevillan companies as their bulvanes. The liberalized economies of Latin America, with no corresponding 'liberties' abroad, would suffer from the extreme concentration of capital, production and markets in the hands of foreign companies, especially transnationals. The long-term benefits of unilateral liberalization are therefore doubtful, be it in terms of sustainable development, dependency, or consumer choice and prices.

If Latin American countries are to proceed with policies of liberalization, they should only do so on the basis of fully reciprocal commitments from their main external trading partners. The best way to secure this is probably through bloc-to-bloc agreements. In any case, economic growth does not require total liberalization. It is worth remembering that the South East Asian countries with extraordinary growth figures over an extended period of time: Japan, South Korea, Singapore and Taiwan, have not been open economies with a minimum of state intervention, especially in the earlier phases of economic expansion. Instead, as noted by Simón Teitel, those countries have exercised an economic policy of careful planning and elaborated state intervention, including elements of protectionism.[15]

Against the background described above, another means of strengthening Latin America both economically and politically is the idea of a Latin American Free Trade Area (LAFTA – not to be confused with the defunct Latin American Free Trade Association with the same acronym). Thus far the discussion on integration in the Americas has paid too little attention to this possibility, perhaps due to the failure of earlier attempts in that direction. Discussion has centred either upon smaller sub-regional schemes or on the hemi-spheric-wide scheme proposed by the United States. Both econom-ically and politically it could prove a rewarding strategy to unify the now separate integration processes of the region into a single process that would seek to establish such an area, or better still, a Latin American Common Market with a more institutionalized structure. The current process of liberalizing intraregional trade in Latin Amer-ica is based on several simultaneous 'integration clusters' and on bilateral agreements between single members of these clusters and outsiders; the result being a 'somewhat confusing overlap of agree-ments that has not yet been sorted out'.[16] It is obvious that such a situation weakens the abilities of Latin American economies to cope with the more or less triadic world economic order.

The still existing sentiments in favour of further integration in Latin America (despite disappointment with reforms at national levels), as recorded by Latinobarometro, make a policy of Latin American-wide integration politically fertile ground for governments to build on. If hemispheric free trade is repeatedly discussed at summits, then why not the quite natural idea of an economically united *Patria Grande*?[17] At least there is an urgent need for a common Latin American in-tegration strategy within the overall plan for an FTAA. This need is now beginning to be recognized: for example, the leader of the Chilean industrialists' organization, Felipe Lamarca, said recently that Latin American integration should be prioritized in order to negotiate an FTAA on an equal footing with the United States.[18] A Latin Amer-ican-wide regional integration arrangement would also help in turning what will most likely be a bilaterally negotiated FTAA into a more truly multilateral system by forming an institutional 'rim' that would connect the 'spokes' (that is Latin American countries) with each other as well as with the 'hub' (that is the United States), to use Wonnacott's well-known metaphor.

In spite of the fact that the US generally favours integration, it is possible that it would oppose a Latin American-wide integration initiative, and especially if it was designed to be more institutionalized than a purely commercial agreement. US strategic interests, especially north of the Panama Canal, could be too important to allow such a process to take place. However, for the remaining countries a South

American Common Market could be a viable option, as noted by Mario Pastore.[19]

Considering that of the six South American nations (excluding the Guyanas) presently outside of Mercosur, Chile and Bolivia are likely to become full members, while the others are taking part in the Andean integration scheme (overlapping in the case of Bolivia), an integrated South America seems not too distant a prospect.

In any case intraregional trade in Latin America, despite its rapid growth in recent years, is still at a relatively low level – around 20 per cent of total Latin American foreign trade (compared to 50 per cent in NAFTA and 60 per cent in the EU). Thus, a broader process of regional integration would offer significant growth potential without hampering extraregional trade. The potential is greater in non-traditional, manufactured products, of which a great proportion are imported from outside the region, than in traditional ones (like coffee, fruit, textiles), for which the main markets are and would remain extraregional. The current commercial profile of the Latin American economies, whereby they are more or less competitors in extraregional markets, should be transformed into one in which they complement one another in their regional markets.

CONCLUSION

Extraregional economic relations are important to all American nations that are to a greater or lesser extent inside the sphere of influence of the US economy. Such relations would balance this influence economically and politically, and they would give some leverage in the event that the United States resorts to a more protectionist policy by giving priority to its national trade laws over international commitments. The possibility of increased US protectionism is not excluded by international free trade agreements, considering the experience of Canada. Purely commercial agreements like NAFTA lack an institutional structure capable of establishing a truly reciprocal trading system based on equal terms, and of minimizing arbitrary protectionism used against competitors. Neither do bilateral trade agreements offer guarantees in this respect.

Therefore, both the other two NAFTA countries (Canada and Mexico) and the other Latin American countries need a stronger multi-lateral and institutional basis for their international economic relations. So far the most promising partnership for the purpose is offered by the EU. Such a partnership would have the potential for increased trade, reducing the dependency of many countries in the Americas on US markets, and it would provide some indirect support against the whims of US economic policy (like the Helms–Burton Act). However, it is to be noted that the EU has not been completely willing to cooperate in this respect, letting the agreement with Mexico become blocked owing to internal quarrels. As a policy recommendation, the EU should rapidly and decisively respond to the needs of Latin America and not let the process stop at the framework agreement with Mercosur.

Currently the progress towards a Free Trade Area of the Americas seems unsure. Under these circumstances Latin American countries should avoid excessive unilateral liberalization of their economies, as it reduces their bargaining power in later integration schemes and makes them more vulnerable to policy shifts in the industrialized world. Furthermore, they should seek to establish a broader and deeper process of regional integration between themselves: an institutional basis for a common Latin American agenda would enhance the position of the region *vis-à-vis* other regions and increase the potential for intraregional trade. Such institutionalization would be hard to establish at a later date, when an FTAA system, based on bilateral agreements and modelled on NAFTA, could have become a reality.

Notes

1. See *Economist*, 30 November 1996, pp. 23–6.
2. *Economist*, 26 October 1996, p. 59.
3. Another thing is that there is relatively little room left for manoeuvre for the governments to seek alternative policies, as most countries are deeply committed to neoliberal policies under the tutelage of the IMF, World Bank and WTO. Furthermore, countries with binding free trade agreements, Mexico in particular, have subjected themselves to the lock-in effects of these 'conditioning frameworks', as coined by Ricardo Grinspun and Robert Kreklewich ('Consolidating Neoliberal Reforms: Free Trade as a Conditioning Framework', *Studies in Political Economy*, no. 43, Spring 1994, pp. 33–61). The political and economic price of abandoning the neoliberal formula is very high. Therefore, strategic discussions in this paper are based on the premise that the overall neoliberal orientation in the region will prevail.
4. The most important of these laws are the Section 301 in the 1974 Trade Act and the 1988 US Omnibus Trade and Competitiveness Act ('Super 301'). Special laws like the Helms–Burton Act (concerning Cuba) or D'Amato Act (concerning Iran and Libya) are also national trade laws with international ramifications.

5. See, for example, Daniel Drache, 'Assessing the Benefits of Free Trade', in Ricardo Grinspun and Maxwell A. Cameron, *The Political Economy of North American Free Trade*, New York: St Martin's Press, 1994, pp. 73–87.

6. Allan Smith, 'Resisting Hegemony: Canada's Proposal to Link NAFTA and the European Union', unpublished paper presented for the Annual Convention of International Studies Association, San Diego, 16–20 April 1996.

7. For example, in the APEC meetings the three NAFTA members have been representing themselves distinctively as individual countries.

8. Peter Morici, 'An Architecture for Free Trade in the Americas', *Current History*, vol. 95, no. 598, February 1996, pp. 59–64.

9. This strategic aspect for Mexico has been stated expressly enough by the Minister of Foreign Affairs of Mexico, Ángel Gurría: '*La diversificación es una estrategia indispensable para México, en particular, por la intensidad de sus nexos con el norte del continente Americano. Al diversificar nuestros contactos, reafirmamos nuestra condición como un país de multiples pertenencias y reducimos la vulnerabilidad que podría derivarse de la concentración excesiva de nuestras relaciones con un solo país o región. Bajo esta perspectiva, las relaciones con Europa se advierten como una fuente de oportunidades para expandir nuestros nexos internacionales, al mismo tiempo que representan un factor de equilibrio en la vinculación externa de México.*' (From a speech given in Portugal in July 1995; 'Discursos del Secretario de Relaciones Exteriores', *Textos de Política Exterior*, July–August 1995, pp. 7–14.)

10. Peter Morici, *op. cit.*, p. 61.

11. Paragraph 9 in the 'Basic Document on the Relations of the European Union with Latin America and the Caribbean', in *Europe and Latin America: A Partnership for Action*, European Commission and IRELA, n.a. & n.d. paragraph 8.

12. *Ibid.*, paragraph 8. The case of the Caribbean (other than Cuba, Haiti and the Dominican Republic) is somewhat different, as the basis for the EU–Caribbean relations has been established by the series of Lomé Conventions and the subsequent, unified Union policy towards ACP countries (African, Caribbean, Pacific).

13. See table 9, in 'The Wider European Union: New Priorities for Latin America', *IRELA Conference Report*, Nr. 5, 1995.

14. Alfredo Guerra-Borges, 'Globalización de la regionalización en América Latina: un punto de vista alternativo', *Comercio Exterior*, vol. 46 (7), June 1996, pp. 436–42 (p. 437).

15. Simón Teitel, 'Qué estrategia de desarrollo debe adoptar América Latina?', *Comercio Exterior*, vol. 45 (9), September 1995, pp. 681–94 (p. 691).

16. Francoise Simon and Susan Kaufman Purcell, 'The Impact of Regional Integration on European–Latin American Relations', in Susan Kaufman Purcell and Francoise Simon (eds), *Europe and Latin America in the World Economy*, Boulder: Lynne Rienner Publishers 1995, pp. 39–84 (p. 50).

17. To be sure, the idea has been touched upon at some instances, like in the ALADI meeting in Montevideo, in December 1995.

18. See an IPS news feature by Gustavo Gonzalez ('US Protectionism Undermines FTAA') from Chile, 15 July 1997.
19. Mario Pastore, 'Democracy, Defense, Integration, and Development: A Long Run View of Latin America', *LASA Forum*, vol. *XXVII* (3), Fall 1996, pp. 4–7.

12 Trade Agreements between Unequal Partners: Does NAFTA Deal with these Inequalities?

Maria Elena Cardero

Mexico, as so many underdeveloped countries, has been engaged in an uphill struggle in order to surmount this condition. In past decades, the government implemented an 'import substitution' policy to create the conditions which would allow economic development and maintain a growth rate in accordance with population growth. At the beginning of the 1980s this model was changed, and the country initiated a transition period from a closed economy with a strong government – in terms of its presence in the economic structure – to one of the most open economies in the world and an ongoing privatization of those state structures that were built over the past decades.

During the transition, many of the institutions and economic and social policies of previous years disappeared. In addition to the dismantling of that trade protection apparatus which was undoubtedly one of the most important tools to explain the industrialization of previous decades, industrial promotion programmes, fiscal and credit subsidies for priority activities, external investment regulation, direct state production of certain goods and price control of some of those goods, as well as government procurement aimed to support the development of certain industries, in particular capital goods, also disappeared. For example, in agricultural policies for rural support, such as import controls, support prices, subsidies for fertilizers, electricity, agricultural insurance, rates of interest, and fiscal transfer to the rural banks – these all diminished or disappeared.

Amongst other purposes, NAFTA was negotiated to ensure the permanence of structural changes implemented in Mexico during the 1980s. Acting as a 'no return insurance', NAFTA guarantees that the economic policy implemented in Mexico during past decades as well as the institutions created formerly, will never reappear, leaving problems of growth and distribution of the benefits derived from it to be solved by the market. Thus Mexico seeks to solve the problems of under-development through an open market integrated to the US economy, brought about by the harmonization of economic policies among the three NAFTA countries, placing the solution of the distortions on the local and regional market. Such a premise assumes that the three economies have a similar institutional capacity to solve the problems of growth. In particular, the market itself will solve problems related to pricing, resource allocation, and distribution of the benefits derived from growth. The synergy generated by the Agreement will allow Mexico to grow within a new model, founded on a dynamic external sector. In sum, it is considered that with the change in economic policy, growth and the reduction of inequalities between Mexico and its two trade partners will be achieved. Under these premises the question remains whether the institutions and conditions necessary for this end were created, and if Mexico, the underdeveloped country, was granted the necessary benefits within the Treaty to outgrow this situation.

The purpose of this chapter is to analyze some aspects of what was negotiated by Mexico under NAFTA, and to evaluate if institutions or mechanisms favouring the disappearance of inequalities were created along with its implementation, or if the terms negotiated reinforce these inequalities. In several places, it will be relevant to compare NAFTA's treatment of Mexico with the conditions granted developing countries adhering to other international trade agreements, such as the World Trade Agreement.

Since NAFTA is a very broad agreement covering practically all areas of the economy and other national issues, only those aspects considered most relevant to the inequality issue are analyzed here: NAFTA's political and legal coverage, trade liberalization, investment rules, intellectual property, financial operation, government procurement and competition and monopoly policies.

POLITICAL AND LEGAL COVERAGE

It is interesting to note that NAFTA was approved as a Treaty by the Mexican Senate, while in the US it was considered an Agreement regulated by an Implementing Legislation. Under Mexican law, a Treaty is supreme law and has a level of obligation superior to ordinary

laws passed by Congress, and even above state constitutions. This
means that what is agreed to by a Treaty is applied equally at federal
and state level. This is not the case in the other two countries; in
matters such as government procurement or national treatment,
agreements at federal level may or may not be applicable at state
or provincial level. This highlights a substantial difference regarding
coverage and legal implications for the three countries, by which
Mexico is compelled at all levels of government, while the other two
countries only assume a federal obligation which other authorities may
or may not comply with according to their own state or provincial
legislation.

TRADE OF GOODS

Within 15 years the three economies will be, for all practical purposes,
totally open for trade among themselves. The only acknowledgment
within the Treaty towards Mexico as a developing country, was the
maintenance of concessions which it had already earned within
the Generalized System of Preferences of the other two countries. Of
the 7300 tariff categories the United States liberalized for Mexico on 1
January 1994, 4200 corresponded to the consolidation of free entry to
the GSP. The main stages of tariff elimination were: immediate, in 5,
10 and 15 years[1] (Tables 12.1 and 12.2).

Table 12.1   Tariff elimination granted to Mexico as a proportion of trade

	Immediate	5 years	10 years	15 years
USA	84%	8%	7%	1%
Canada	79%	8%	12%	1%

Note: 1991 trade figures – oil not included.

Table 12.2   Tariff elimination granted by Mexico as a proportion of trade

	Immediate	5 years	10 years	15 years
USA	43%	18%	38%	1%
Canada	41%	19%	38%	1%

Note: 1991 trade figures – oil not included.

Even though, proportionately, the US and Canada offered a considerable elimination of tariffs the results of this should be weighted adequately. Nearly 80 per cent of Mexico's trade is with the US, implying in real terms an almost total immediate opening of more than 32 per cent of its total imports.[2] This is not the case for either the US or Canada to which imports from Mexico represent a significantly lower proportion. For the US, the opening represents only 5.8 per cent of its total imports.[3]

In addition, as noted above, more than half of these tariff reductions had already been granted to Mexico as an underdeveloped country in the GATT through the US's Generalized System of Preferences (GSP),[4] and Canada's General Preferential Tariff (GPT). However it may occur that, because of measures taken in other chapters of NAFTA – for instance, rules of origin – the final result will not be as profitable for Mexico. In fact, to be favoured by GSP, the US requires a 35 per cent of local or regional content in goods. Under NAFTA, Mexico must fulfill at least, on average, 50 per cent of regional content, implying for example that goods from Caribbean countries will have lower entry requirements than those applying to Mexico.

Insofar as each country's tariff relief is concerned, it is clear that the reduction is unequal. While in the other two countries these have been undertaken over almost 40 years – considering their initial tariff levels when GATT was established in 1947 – Mexico will have to grant its main supplier total liberalization for some sensitive products in only 15 years. For the rest of the commodities, it will have to do it immediately or in 5 or 10 years, starting from an average weighted tariff higher than the one currently existing in the other two countries.

Among the questions related to market access, policies favouring foreign investment or production aimed to promote exports will disappear. Thus, regarding tax rebate, Mexico was permitted to maintain programmes for re-exporting commodities for seven years, while the US and Canada maintained theirs until January 1996 (two years longer than what was agreed upon under the Free Trade Agreement), and until the year 2001 in their exports to Mexico. Restrictions were fixed, however, on duties rebate: these were limited to the lower of the taxes charged in either the importing or the processing country.[5] By these means, the US safeguarded that Mexico and Canada will not be able to employ these programmes to attract enterprises from outside the region in order to then export to the US. In the long term this will result in the equalization of tariffs of the three countries towards the lowest level maintained by any of the three.

In general terms, the few employment-generating policies existing in Mexico will be affected, such as the in-bond industry and tax-exemption programmes. The national tax structure will also be affected insofar as fiscal income generated by imports will disappear in a rather short period. Investment opportunities among the three countries will converge, without permitting the establishment of any extraordinary incentive, nor of specific policies favouring the least developed country through the attraction of investment by specific mechanisms or policies, in detriment of the supposedly profitable status as 'trade partner' of the world's principal consumer.

This trade liberalization is set in a complex framework of rules of origin (many of which are of a protectionist nature) in order to prevent the benefits derived from it being extended to third nations by means of trade triangulation. Thus, special restrictions were designed for the industries considered vulnerable, as in the case of some dairy products, sugar, peanuts, fruits, vegetables, shoes, textiles and clothes, auto-parts and some electric components. A rule of origin was implemented for each product, which in fact is a means of defining different degrees of protection for the manufacturing sectors. Thus, rules of origin not only seek to define and limit goods originating in the region, but also become instruments of industrial policy which, as is the case of the automobile sector, are particularly favourable to the US since, on increasing the regional content to a higher percentage (between 62.5 and 60 per cent in this case) than the average, the regional market of the automobile industry of that country becomes particularly protected.

In general the demands imposed by rules of origin will probably result in cost and price distortion within the different links in the production chain, which may make such industries inefficient in addition to seriously affecting the country with the least integrated production chain as is the case of Mexico.

In the case of the agricultural sector, which is protected by all three countries, the differences in production, geographical and institutional factors between Mexico the US and Canada are overwhelming. The value of US farming production is more than $80 000 million per annum, which is equivalent to 40 per cent of Mexico's GDP. Almost one-fourth of Mexico's working population (23 per cent) is dedicated to farming activities, while in the US only 2.8 per cent are. Subsidies as a percentage of the value of farming production in the US is 30 per cent, while in Mexico it is only 2.9 per cent.

Mexico and the US agreed upon eliminating all their non-tariff barriers immediately by integrating them into the tariff structure.

Zero-tariff access quotas were established for a list of basic products; once these quotas are exceeded, the tariff is applied. These tariffs decrease each year so that imports of sensitive goods will be totally liberated by year 15 of the Agreement.

It is worth mentioning that with two products, sugar and citrus, for which the terms first negotiated had benefited Mexico, last minute understandings were signed in order to achieve the American congress's acceptance of NAFTA, thus limiting Mexico's export capabilities. In the case of sugar, the understanding limits Mexico's exports of sugar to the US for the next 15 years. The understanding concerning citrus stated that export volumes of frozen and concentrated orange juice were limited, thereby making Mexico lose any benefits accomplished in prior negotiations.

Mexico was not able to attain recognition as a developing country and thereby obtain special terms in agricultural matters. It was not accepted, as is the case of developing countries within the World Trade Organization, that 30 per cent of Mexican exports be exempted from tariffs or compensatory measures; this provision was limited to 5 per cent, as in the case of developed countries. Nor was it accepted that subsidies be granted to producers of illicit narcotics in an effort to encourage the planting of other crops, nor were subsidies for agricultural inputs for the poorest farmers accepted. Support subsidies for marketing or transportation for export products were also rejected.

INVESTMENT

The chapter on investment is the most important advance in investment liberalization among participant countries of a trade agreement. It is the true core of the Agreement. What was decided here was aimed at liberalizing and protecting investment and investors of the three countries. While for the US and Canada it meant no change with respect to what they had already agreed to in their Free Trade Agreement (FTA), for Mexico it implied a radical change regarding foreign investment legislation.

Investment within NAFTA covers any transfer of resources to the territory of the other partners, i.e. it includes, among others, company property, stock participation, loans between headquarters and subsidiaries, the company's debt instruments, company shares that permit the owner to participate in income or profits, property over real estate, shares that come about from carrying out contracts, and so on. It is important to point out that investors from the other countries that have 'substantial or substantive trade activities' in the territory of any of the partners can, from there, undertake investments in the territory of the other partner and be covered under chapter XI. The concept of 'substantive' is subject to the interpretation of each country. The intention is to avoid the Agreement being used to benefit investors from countries outside the Agreement, by the use of an apparent presence, such as a postal registry.

Foreign investment will be subject to national treatment, most favoured nation treatment, best level of treatment (which assumes national treatment or most favoured nation treatment, whichever is better), or minimum level of treatment (treatment of foreign investment at least in accordance with what is established by international law). The three countries are not allowed to demand from investors any performance requirements in order to establish themselves, operate or expand their operations. Issues concerned with the elimination of performance requirements in NAFTA are important and go beyond the FTA, and even those stipulated by the new World Trade Organization (WTO). In the WTO agreement, developing countries are granted up to five years in order for these type of measures to be eliminated, and they are permitted to set aside these dispositions for balance-of-payments reasons, granting them longer transition periods in order to terminate certain programmes so as not to leave new similar investments, or those that enjoy these dispositions, at a disadvantage.

Under NAFTA, Mexico was not granted any of these specific exceptions. The three countries agreed that they could consider granting incentives to the export of a certain level or percentage of goods and services, to technology transfer, or by acting as a supplier in a specific market. They also allowed for conditions to grant subsidies according to: (a) the place that production is undertaken; (b) where the service is rendered; (c) if there is employee training or creation of employment; (d) if particular facilities are constructed or enlarged; and (e) if research and development work is undertaken in their own territory.

Measures for the protection of investment also go beyond those established in the Codes on Liberalization of Capital Movements and the Operation of Invisible Currents of the OECD (which prohibits restrictions on fund transfers but have not yet developed instruments that guarantee protection). In NAFTA no restrictions exist for investors transferring profits or physical assets abroad. Also, if physical or financial assets are confiscated for any legitimate reason agreed upon by the three partners, investors must receive prompt, adequate and just payment. Investors must also have means of defending against arbitrary actions and measures imposed by the government of the country in question.

Therefore, all modalities for investment are the same for the three partners basically as they currently exist in the US – as for example the support given in that country for research and development – but no special treatment is admitted benefiting productive investment in a country which most needs it due to its lower level of relative development.

INTELLECTUAL PROPERTY

Concerning research and development which is linked to the agreements on intellectual property in NAFTA, one finds another sector where the institutional and economic disparities among the three economies are very noticeable. According to the data of the OECD (OECD Structural Indicators, 1996), the United States assigned 2.76 per cent and Canada 1.49 per cent of their GNP for research and development between 1990 and 1994, while Mexico assigned only 0.32 per cent. In the first two countries a significant part of this amount is covered by private enterprise, due to fiscal and incentive policies which the government grants them, while in the case of Mexico more than half of the amount assigned to research and development is covered by the government.

One of the issues considered beneficial to the participating countries in integration and trade agreements is the possibility of strengthening research areas of interest to the different partners, creating a synergy of cooperation and research which optimizes the use of resources. However, instead of handling these inequalities in such a way that the three countries benefit from the technological development and knowledge, in the Agreement no institution is foreseen to promote the development of research among the three economies, neither at the global nor in any specific sector. This limits the possibilities for the least developed country to utilize, learn, adapt and benefit from research and development, as many of today's developed countries do.

As compared to the Uruguay Round (now WTO) NAFTA goes beyond the measures which limit access to knowledge for developing countries, but grants them a five-year period to comply. Among the most important differences are the following:

- NAFTA gives protection to television broadcasting via satellite (coded satellite signals).
- It protects the acquisition of new plant varieties in a stricter way since the parties adhere to the UPOV (International Agreement for the Protection Against the Acquisition of Vegetables, 1978, or the International Convention for the Protection of New Plant Varieties, 1991, which is a Protocol of Reforms to the UPOV Agreement).
- NAFTA is the first international treaty that protects industrial secrets.
- Mandatory licenses regarding registry of integrated circuits or for reverse engineering for research or training purposes are not permitted. That is to say, after the license expires it cannot be made of public domain as it happens in the majority of countries.
- Canada excludes the industry of culture from national treatment (such as phonograms, publishing houses, radio and television broadcasts and the movie industry).
- NAFTA establishes cooperation and technical aid mechanisms in order to eliminate trade in products that infringe intellectual property rights.

For some obligations that were non-existent under Mexican law, for example national treatment or the reversal of the charge in the proof for procedure patents (when there is suspicion of theft of knowledge or patent, it is for the suspect to prove his innocence), Mexico did not have a transition period nor a period of grace as was provided for developing countries in the Uruguay Round.

Essentially, intellectual property protection within NAFTA mainly benefits United States entrepreneurs. It allows their entrance to the Mexican market without any loss of profit due to violation of rights while assuring the monopoly of their use. The Agreement limits the possibility of following a pattern of 'imitative technological development' – which was followed by the majority of developed nations – based on reverse engineering and adaptation and improvement of an existing innovation.

In the words of J. Bhagwati (1994), policies followed in matters of intellectual property rights in the US arise from multinational corporations' predatory practices, which then petition governmental agencies through intensive lobbying with lawmakers to formulate policies that allow them to meet their objectives. The most evident case is that of intellectual property protection. Greater protection means greater profits. But these rules are not necessarily optimum in social terms. Given that the maximizing principle is extremely weak, the 'defenders' of this protection have emphasized the problem as one of 'theft'. The Ministry of Commerce and the Secretary of USTR, talk of 'piracy' and 'theft' when they demand protection of intellectual property, instead of emphasizing options that could produce the most beneficial impacts on the economy. The attitude of the World Bank, intellectuals and scholars on the subject are equally disappointing.

FINANCIAL SECTOR

The agreements in this sector apply to financial intermediaries, investors and investments in financial institutions, but leave out activities related to public retirement plans and social security systems.

While Canada and Mexico permit universal banking, in the United States there exist local and state regulations that make it extremely complex to undertake financial negotiations since doing so implies dealing with many parties. There is an enormous asymmetry in the size and financial structure in the three countries where, for example, if total 1990 banking assets of the three trade partners were added up, Mexican assets would come to around 4.8 per cent of the total, Canada's to 27.1 per cent and the US' to 68.1 per cent.

Among the most important aspects negotiated for the Mexican banking sector were:

- A transition period until the year 2000, up to when net capital from foreign banks cannot, on an individual basis, have more than 1.5 per cent of total net capital of the system nor 15 per cent of aggregate net capital.
- After four years, by 2004, a total opening of the sector will occur, but restrictions may be imposed for up to three years if aggregate capital of foreign banks exceeds 25 per cent of total capital. Should this level be reached, Mexico will be permitted to consult with its partners regarding potential adverse effects and the possibility of introducing temporary limits to correct the adverse effects of this increase in foreign participation.
- Acquisition of a national bank whose size exceeds 4 per cent of net capital of all established banks, will not be permitted.
- Different types of intermediaries will be permitted as long as they are considered financial institutions within the host country. In

other words, in Mexico there are many services that are not offered, so that only those that are legally established as such will be permitted. Permission was granted, however, for the presence of the so-called *non-bank banks*, that is, intermediaries with limited objectives such as those that finance certain types of consumption, grant credit through credit cards, and so forth.

- Due to the fact that in the US associations between banks and stock brokers are prohibited, Canada and Mexico face limitations when these type of financial groups wish to operate in the US on a joint basis.[6] On the other hand, in the case of Canada and the US there is a powerful link between banks and industrial and trade groups, with a high degree of power concentration that in principle is prohibited in Mexican legislation. In this sense Mexico accepted that when a trade presence already exists of a trade affiliate, such as the case of Sears, Mexico reserves the right to grant the banking license of an affiliated bank if the relationship is not substantial or harmful. A similar case is with the partner's stock brokerages which also have strong links with non-strictly financial sectors, where their presence will depend on the discretion of the Mexican financial authorities who must consider if such a presence will have an adverse effect on Mexico.

- In order to avoid a peso market outside Mexico, cross-border services cannot be expressed in pesos. In the case of Mexico, the open lending of cross-border financial services is permitted when they arise from consumers' mobility. Insurance coverage is permitted when the potential policyholder moves physically to the other country, and this is valid only with life, sickness and travel insurance. Certain types of re-insurance are also permitted.

Diverse opinions have arisen regarding negotiations in matters of finance. While for some experts, economic and financial integration implies giving up national sovereignty in exchange for a vaguer concept of shared sovereignty, for others the absence of financial integration such as with trade and investment implies an asymmetry in which the existence of segmented capital markets bring about differentiated prices of capital for firms that operate in different markets. In other words, market segmentation produces distortions as those caused by quotas and tariffs in the commodity market. It skews the yield relationship among assets and gives certain companies implicit subsidies to their profits over those of competitors.

Each country's capital returns in some way reflect its national industries and the existing risks, so that assets have differentiated prices even for the same level of risk, and the unbalance of capital markets affect real markets. The asymmetry in the case of Mexico and in that of the other two countries arises from the fact that, using Errunza and Losq's concept (1985), the capital market of the NAFTA countries is divided into very well integrated 'central' markets and a 'peripheral' market that maintains subordinated ties, particularly with the US market. This imbalance affects real markets, the distribution of resources and the price of economic factors, greatly increasing the cost of financing in the Mexican market and becoming a very real entrance barrier for capital intensive industries, thus distorting the natural advantages that Mexico country could have in other aspects like the abundance of labour.

In a market such as Mexico, where transactions are not carried out in a sole currency (Castaingts, 1995), but rather in two, a dominant dollar and a subordinate peso, and where two large subsystems can be differentiated (the monetary circuit of commodities and the monetary circuit of finances and the stock market), the result is that the system of expectations on risks and returns operates within a system with two currencies. Thus in order to maintain savings in pesos it becomes necessary to maintain lingering expectations of devaluation and high interest rates, so that the real interest rates in dollars becomes the 'floor' rates in the market. The growth of the monetary mass responds to this financial 'reward', which does not correspond to an increase in the production of goods and services but creates a 'wealth' effect that encourages and stimulates the importation of goods, particularly consumer goods within an open market environment.

The existence of monetary financial circuits, open for some time now and not subject to any type of limitation (such as, for example, restricting the entrance of speculative capital through systems that demand a minimum temporary permanence or that penalize accelerated transfers through taxation), were left intact. Eventually the financial opening will tend to expand, favouring an even more widely segmented market. The recent crisis in which the US Federal Reserve had to support the Mexican financial system revealed the existence of an enormous amount of US financial resources invested in the Mexican stock market, and the need to 'rescue' these resources on the part of the US monetary authorities.

GOVERNMENT PROCUREMENT

In the case of government purchases, an open and defined policy exists in the US and Canada to use such purchases as support mechanisms for certain productive sectors. The US has the *Buy American Act* and the *Small Business Set Aside* and Canada has several regional and provincial support policies for private corporations that guarantee their access to public markets. There are no such clearly defined mechanisms in Mexico, although existing law up to the moment of the negotiation of the Agreement stated that, for public purchases, products made in the country had preference over imported ones.

The United States exempted Mexico and Canada from the Buy American Act but not from the one corresponding to small businesses and minorities. Canada, in turn, exempted its partners from complying with certain laws, but not all. Since Mexico has no equivalent legislation it was permitted a permanent market reserve of $1000 million up to the year 2002 and $1200 million starting in 2003. The Mexican oil company (PEMEX) and the electricity company (CFE) are permitted a reserve of $300 million as of 2003.

With the opening of trade, Mexico loses any possibility of providing support to its industry through government purchases, aside from those related to small business and companies which the country, similarly to what happens in the US, deems necessary to support. Also in the case of 'turn-key' investments for the construction of a plant or purchase of equipment, Mexico established a 40 per cent reserve of national content when it is labour intensive, and 25 per cent when it is intensive in capital goods.[7]

It is interesting to point out that in the case of government procurement, the Agreement not only applies to goods purchased, as is the case in other international trade agreements, but also to services and public works. Purchases by the public sector were also included, since in the case of Mexico these entities are the main buyers. However, as the state, provincial and local governments of Canada and the US are exempt from the obligations of this chapter, 70 per cent of the purchases by the US are excluded. In the case of Canada, the percentage is probably higher due to the level of provincial autonomy.

SECOFI (Secretaria de Comercio y Fomento Industrial) estimates that the Mexican market for government purchases was opened for the equivalent of $8.3 billion, while the equivalent figure for the US is $58 billion. Yet, figures provided by US negotiators point out that the US carries out around $191 billion of purchases by the federal government, of which $169 billion are subject to exclusion by legislation. Of the remaining $22 billion, $17 billion are products not saleable by Mexico, such as space vehicles, lunar rockets and so on. Thus $5 billion remain, or 2.7 per cent of total purchases, which compared to what Mexico opened, translates into a greater market opening in Mexico than in the US. In addition, the coverage of corporations in the three countries is completely asymmetric. Mexican oil, electricity, railroad, road construction and telecommunication public companies, are subject to rules and regulations that the other partner's equivalent private companies will not have to abide by. In other words, Mexico accepted an asymmetrical treatment which the European community members rejected, based on the principle that some private US companies have monopoly over the relevant market, so they should be subject to the same regulations as public companies. One example is the Mexican State constructing company for roads and bridges, CAPUFE, which is subject to NAFTA principles, while the public builders of the other partners are not only not subject to the Agreement, but in addition are required to buy US steel and cement when their purchases are financed by federal funds.

This chapter, as recognized by the Implementing Legislation of the United States, 'includes several regulations related to the behavior of corporations [Mexican], which will help meet the objectives of market opening, specially those associated to the energy sector'. In other words, in Mexico, PEMEX and CFE, for example, will not be able to provide subsidized energy in favour of other sectors, since crossed subsidies are prohibited. If these corporations discriminate against the goods, investments or services from Canadian or US companies, they will be subject to the dispute mechanisms, including arbitration between an investor and the state.

POLICIES REGARDING COMPETITION, MONOPOLIES AND STATE CORPORATIONS

An important restriction for the applicability of certain economic promotional policies is included in the chapter on Competition Policies, but it does not state the harmonizing of such policies, nor does it establish the link between antidumping and the same policies in order to limit the arbitrary use of antidumping measures by the more powerful nation. It only establishes a commitment to adopt or maintain provisions to prohibit non-competitive business practices but it does not provide mechanisms to ensure compliance beyond the cooperation among national authorities. Neither is there any regulation to prevent extra-territorial application of US antimonopoly laws to the other parties.

In this chapter, the United States succeeded in maintaining total discretionality on the monopoly of knowledge since, under NAFTA, the agreement was not to consider as monopoly the only supplier of patented goods, if exclusivity derives from being the sole rights-holder to the patent. Therefore, NAFTA is conceived as an instrument that serves mainly for 'market administration', to strengthen changes previously initiated in Mexico and to go deeper into them with new requirements particularly in the knowledge and investment areas.

CONCLUSION

The Treaty not only did not create institutions that in some way *may* benefit the least developed country or the region as a whole, allowing Mexico and the entire region to reach sustained growth in the long term, but caused the disappearance of many of the institutions and economic policies which existed in Mexico that *had* favoured economic development and which *had* empowered the state in the regulation and control of transnational corporation onslaughts.

In the new framework created by NAFTA concerning the main factors of production: capital *is* granted unconditional liberty and *'knowledge' is limited* while the *most* abundant factor for Mexico, labour, receives only a discretional regulatory frame.

If social inequalities deepened with the opening of previous years, with the new limitations framing the economic policy oriented almost exclusively to a 'market administration' which favours large companies, it is evident that NAFTA not only did not create institutions favouring an integral development of the region, but that it has opened the way for an increasingly unequal development of the three partners, propagating heterogeneous structural differences and social fragmentation between those sectors of the Mexican population which are competitive and those which are not, favouring at the same time dependency on external capital and knowledge, while limiting the development of knowledge either through imitation or resource association.

If many of the terms negotiated are not modified and the creation of institutions that allow the synergy created by integration to promote the region's growth are not promoted, as for instance joint investments in research and development to empower and protect the use of regional resources, the development of supporting programmes for marginalized or less-developed regions in order to assure resources for a healthy growth of the common borders, and so on, the asymmetries with Mexico will be accentuated and this will undoubtedly have repercussions in the medium term on its nearest neighbour.

Notes

1. A few goods were liberated through 18 different stages, some of which were non-linear.
2. Under the assumption that to 43% of tariffs liberated by Mexico we apply a percentage of 80%, that represents Mexico's trade with the US.
3. Assuming that to the immediate tariff liberalization of 84%, we apply 6.9%, which is the approximate percentage of the imports that this country received from Mexico in 1991.
4. Of the $19 000 million of effective coverage offered by the US in 1991, $7493 million corresponded to Mexico. Mexico only took advantage of 52% of this total. See UNCTAD, GSP, 1992.
5. If Mexico imports a Japanese good and that good pays US $30 dollars in taxes, whereas the same good pays US $6 dollars in the US, the Mexican importer will only be eligible to receive a tax refund of $6 dollars.
6. In this regard Mexico received dispensation for an additional five-year period for some Mexican banks that were already operating in the US, starting from their date of establishment which had to be previous to January 1992.
7. These 'turn-key' figures have arisen in Mexico as a result of the limits, imposed for reasons of public deficit control, that state productive firms are subject to in matters of investment. So long as they have surpluses in current expenses they ask other investors to undertake the building of a new plant (new plant and equipment) with their own resources, and later a mechanism is created where the state utility becomes owner of the assets of the company.

References

Bhagwati, J. (1994) 'Which Way? Free Trade or Protection?', *Challenges*, vol. 37, no. 1, January–February, New York.
Castaingts, T.J. (1995) 'Un modelo de interpretación de la bolsa mexicana de valores', in A. Girón, Ortiz and Correa (eds), *Integración Financiera y TLC: Retos y Perspectivas*, siglo XXI and IIE, UNAM, Mexico, pp. 403–20.
Errunza, Vihang y and Losq, Etienne (1985) 'International Asset Pricing under Mild Segmentation: Theory and Test', *Journal of Finance*, vol. 40, pp. 105–24.

13 Successful Integration and Economic Distress: The New Dual Economy – the Case of Mexico in NAFTA

Sima Motamen-Samadian and
Etelberto Ortiz Cruz

INTRODUCTION

1994 was the first year of Mexican integration in the North American Free Trade Agreement (NAFTA), and the start of a period when Mexico was supposed to benefit from the further opening up of its economy. It turned out, however, to be one of the most turbulent years in the recent history of the Mexican economy. The substantial outflow of capital which began in the second quarter of 1994, ultimately led to a significant loss of foreign exchange reserves, abandonment of the pegged exchange rate regime, and a 71 per cent real depreciation of the peso. The question frequently raised was, what went wrong with the Mexican economy? After all, it appeared that the programmes for stabilization and structural change that were implemented by the Mexican authorities from the mid-1980s were rather successful in reducing the rate of inflation and improving the efficiency of Mexican producers. Above all, the core of the new programmes was from the begining oriented towards creating a new structural relationship with the rest of the world: essentially a new pattern of integration.

The core of the policies for 'structural change' rested essentially on two programmes: a re-orientation of trade policies, and a complete abandonment of massive government subsidies and direct intervention. The first steps early in 1984 started a continuous process of trade liberalization. By 1985 Mexico had joined GATT and started a unilateral process of tariff reductions. The economy went from an average tariff rate of over 100 per cent and a long list of direct controls in 1982, to a common tariff with a maximum of 20 per cent in early 1988. The main results of this period were the achievement of a relatively homogeneous tariff structure and the elimination of direct controls, except for a few branches such as the motor car industry.

The period from 1988 up to the inception of NAFTA saw further reductions in protectionist measures combined with a slight fall in the real exchange rate. By the time the negotiations on NAFTA started in 1989, the Mexican economy was almost completely open to foreign trade. The sole exceptions were the motor car industry, telecommunications and a few other industries where direct controls continued to prevail. Nevertheless, the aim of economic integration in NAFTA was the most ambitious means of developing the Mexican economy. Gaining access to the 'biggest market in the world', it was thought, would provide a powerful impulse for investment and trade, and leading advocates of this policy claimed that Mexico was on the verge of becoming part of the 'First World'. There were also other important aims in joining NAFTA, which included the need to establish a legal framework on trade with the US economy. It was believed that this would help to eliminate the vast discretionary powers that American enterprises were exercising prior to NAFTA on the basis of their own domestic legal system.

The objectives of this chapter are twofold. First, it intends to show that the experience of trade liberalization observed during the 1980s and early 1990s fairly accurately reflects the true capabilities of the Mexican economy to respond to conditions of free trade. Secondly, it will show that the pattern of growth that resulted from integration, with the US economy in particular, has resulted in the creation of a new 'structural duality'. This notion describes a dual pattern of linkages and production, one basically integrated in the world (US) economy, and another that is oriented towards domestic markets. The first requires a huge flow of imported inputs, which therefore relies on policies to ensure cheap foreign exchange; while the second depends crucially on low wages. In view of this, we consider that the crisis which emerged in 1994, although appearing to have been instigated by the sudden outflow of portfolio capital, in fact had its roots in problems which were related to the pattern of structural change that had been under way since the early 1980s.

The approach to structural change adopted in Mexico rested heavily on the notion that an entirely new economic environment was necessary, one in which market efficiency would act as the main engine of growth. The construction of such a model necessitated the adoption of 'market friendly' policies, with a set of new institutions based upon an 'open economy'.

But the idea that the whole model of structural change should rest on trade policies, and particularly on economic integration into NAFTA, is questionable. As pointed out by Bairoch (1996), the idea that free trade and integration should lead to growth in exports and faster improvements in income and employment is not necessarily valid. For example, the trade liberalization programme adopted in 1988, although it did lead to some change in the pattern of trade and a rise in exports, resulted in an even greater rise in imports, and a process of internal marginalization that is inconsistent with the presumption of either internal or external 'convergence'. It is also necessary to identify the actual policy objectives of NAFTA. Of particular importance is the fact that the NAFTA project was not exclusively conceived of in terms of trade targets, and the arguments for NAFTA cannot be sustained solely on the grounds of a windfall profit from trade. This was evident in 1988–89 when the rate of growth of manufacturing exports started to slow down in the absence of sufficient production capacity to create an export surplus. It was clear even then that once the domestic market started to grow, the export surplus would diminish. Therefore, the basic view of the potential gains from NAFTA was the possibility of attracting an important flow of investments that could provide the necessary push for new, competitive technologies associated with a new position in world markets. In a way this was a recognition of the fact that Mexican enterprises were not able to move ahead on their own. Strategic alliances were considered helpful in giving them a stronger bargaining position *vis-à-vis* transnational corporations.

To address the above issues, this chapter is organized as follows: first we discuss the pattern of trade liberalization policies implemented in Mexico from the beginning of 1983, followed by an analysis of the relationship between trade conditions and actual changes in the structure of production from 1988. This includes an assessment of the effects of trade liberalization programmes on trade patterns. We then discuss the effects of financial liberalization on the mobilization of domestic and international capital in Mexico, and finally offer a conclusion and a reflection on some policy issues.

TRADE LIBERALIZATION, OBJECTIVES AND PROCESS OF IMPLEMENTATION

In the early 1980s, Mexico had a very sheltered economy. Tariffs were very high and direct controls were widely exercised within some important sectors covering up to 100 per cent of activities. But it was also an inefficient structure of protection, since in some sectors as far back as the late 1960s and early 1970s the effective rate of protection was negative.[1]

The initial moves in the direction of attaining a more efficient structure of protection began in 1983. This was achieved via a unilateral reduction of tariffs, by becoming a member of GATT and by the reduction of controls. The next step comprised trade liberalization measures early in 1989 and the move towards NAFTA. Bearing in mind that over 70 per cent of Mexico's total trade is with the United States, by 1994 tariffs and direct controls on about 43 per cent of imported items from the US were almost eliminated. These mostly consisted of capital goods. However, the schedule for the removal of tariffs within NAFTA allows for a five-year period of adjustment for 18 per cent of industries, such as textiles, and ten years for another 38 per cent of industries. The latter group includes industries such as automobiles for which adjustment may be more difficult.

Thus, in the absence of other distortions such as exchange rate overvaluation, the NAFTA agreement enables the above industries to benefit from a positive rate of effective protection for the next five to ten years. This is because while they continue to enjoy the shelter afforded by tariffs on the import of rival North American products, their imported capital inputs are not subject to a tariff. However, it is important to point out that between 1993–94 the exchange rate based on 1988 prices was estimated to be about 38 per cent overvalued. This implies that by the time the NAFTA agreement came into effect in 1994, the combination of tariff reductions and an overvalued peso made the Mexican economy extremely vulnerable to imports.

STRUCTURAL CHANGE IN MEXICO

The first period of economic boom after the crisis of the 1980s and the process of structural change was 1989–91. In the years that followed, that is from 1992 to 1994, the economy was affected by the negotiations and inception of NAFTA. Not only was the growth rate in this period considerably lower – and decreasing – than the rate of growth in the former period, it was also characterized by an uneven rate of growth across various sectors. That is, while some sectors such as motor cars, electronics, cement, beer and chemicals showed an increased rate of growth between 1988 and 1995 after the opening up

Table 13.1   Rate of growth and net exports, 1970–95

	Sectoral indexes				
	Rate of growth[1]			*Rate of net exports*[2]	
	1982–87	*1988–93*	*1988–95*	*1982–87*	*1988–93*[3]
Total	−0.07	3.15	2.54		
Primary	1.4	0.97	1.68	−4.78	−15.67
Extractive	0.43	1.11	1.0	149.43	199.1
Food industry	0.85	3.97	3.72	12.49	0.063
Light industrial	−1.29	0.14	1.34	−6.04	−42.52
Chemical and petrochemical	2.54	3.37	2.42	−10.63	−54.61
Metal industry	1.62	3.32	2.42	−2.38	−4.81
Motor cars and others	−0.97	6.88	3.6	−38.07	−204.2
Non-tradables	−0.03	3.22	2.66	−0.02	−0.43

Notes:
[1] NIPA, 1970–93; 1980=100 INEGI
[2] Average share of the trade balance (export–import) to the total balance, for all sectors (72 sectors, NIPA).
[3] Average growth rate per year; 1993=100 GDP, NIPA, 1988–95.
Source: NIPA, 1970–93; INEGI.

of the economy, older sectors such as textiles, light industries and primary industries exhibited a reduction in their rate of growth (see Table 13.1).

Table 13.1 shows that motor cars, metal industries, and chemical and petrochemicals can be considered the leading growth sectors. But this is due not only to the rate of export growth, but also because their share of total exports was higher than that of other sectors. This applies particularly to the motor car industry, which of the above sectors was the only one that continued to benefit from protection. Moreover, these industries were the primary recipients of foreign investment by big concerns as far back as the early 1980s. Therefore, the advance of their exports can not be attributed to an improvement in their comparative advantage in international markets, or to technological advantages, but to a particular linkage of transnational corporations with the Mexican economy that rests primarily on intra-firm trade. The table also shows that once the NIPA accounts were adjusted for overvaluation of the exchange rate in the 1988–95 series, the rate of growth of the presumed leading growth sectors turns out to be lower than was previously believed.

It is also important to point out that the leading growth sectors were the main recipients of imported intermediate and capital goods. This explains why a sectoral analysis of *net* exports reveals that the only sectors which showed a surplus were the food industry and extractive industries, dominated by the oil industry. Consequently, all the so-called leading growth sectors in fact showed a growing deficit. In particular, as can be seen from Table 13.1, both the motor car and the chemical and petrochemical sectors experienced a growing trade deficit following the opening up of the economy, thereby contributing to the rise in trade deficits between 1990–94.

Table 13.1 therefore also indicates that the figures for net exports should be assessed more carefully, as the contribution of various sectors to total net exports varied significantly. Considering that the manufacturing sectors in Mexico are highly dependent on imported intermediate and capital goods, any assessment of the effects of trade liberalization should take into account the changes in both the export and import requirements of a sector. Indeed, a closer examination of the data reveals that while exports of the leading sectors appeared to grow by 20 per cent in nominal terms between 1988 and 1994, in real terms they grew only by an average of 8 per cent per annum. However, this was at a time when the imports of leading sectors grew at the considerably faster rate of 17 per cent per annum in real terms. With

Table 13.2   Trade structure, exports and imports as shares of GDP (%)

	1976	1981	1988	1994	1995
Exports					
Total	100	100	100	100	100
Oil	15.4	72.5	32.5	12.2	10.6
Primary sector	32.1	7.4	8.1	4.4	5.0
Oil extractive	5.7	3.4	3.2	0.6	0.7
Manufacturing	46.7	16.7	56.2	39.6	44.6
Maquila (net)	10.0	4.9	11.3	9.5	6.2
Maquila (gross)				43.1	39.1
Imports					
Total	100	100	100	100	100
Consumption	8.9	11.7	10.2	12.0	7.4
Intermediate	60.4	56.6	68.5	45.4	44.5
Capital	30.6	32.5	21.3	16.8	12.0
Maquila			25.8	36.1	

Source: Indicadores Económicos, Banco de México, June 1996.

that in mind, the share of intermediate goods of total imports did not in fact decrease throughout the transition period between 1981–87, nor afterwards when the economy was more open to trade. This is evident from Table 13.2 which shows that the sum of imports of intermediate goods, including maquila temporary imports, totalled 71.2 per cent in 1994, and 80.5 per cent in 1995. Thus, it is apparent that despite all the criticisms which were attached to the Import Substitution Industrialization (ISI) strategy for its role in increasing the dependency of the manufacturing sector on imported intermediate goods, the new strategy did not do much to change this pattern.

In this respect, the data on the leading tradable goods sectors (motor cars, communications and chemical industries) reveal that they have managed to grow mostly on the basis of a massive inflow of imports, the growth of which far exceeded the rate of growth of exports in leading sectors. Moreover, their growth did not contribute much to the growth of real GDP. This is particularly so from 1990 to 1993, when real exports were growing at an average rate of 8 per cent per annum, but real GDP grew at a much slower pace of 2.27 per cent per annum. More importantly, despite the growth of exports, according to the INEGI data the rate of growth of real GDP steadily slowed down, and dropped from 4.5 per cent in 1990 to 0.4 per cent in 1993. A more careful study of GDP composition reveals that whereas between 1982 and 1987, when the economy was fairly closed, total exports as a proportion of real GDP increased from 13.5 per cent to 17.9 per cent, by 1994 with the full opening of the economy the share of exports of real GDP had only gone up to 19.5 per cent. Overall, whereas total exports of goods increased by 98.3 per cent between 1988 and 1994, imports of goods increased by 182.2 per cent, causing the trade deficit to increase from $-2.4 billion in 1988 to $-28.8 billion in 1994.

Despite this deterioration in the trade balance it is fair to say that trade liberalization has led to some gains in efficiency. However, the rises in productivity have been mostly achieved at the expense of employment, as is evident from Table 13.3. This data allows us to address the issue of changes in productivity in order to pose the following question: Has NAFTA, so far, made any difference to the pattern of trade? Table 13.3 shows that this is not very evident yet. Once the NIPA figures are revised after the crash of 1994 (due to exchange rate overvaluation), gains in productivity cannot be attributed to the leading growth sectors, as shown in column three, because the other sectors, that is primary, extractive and food industries, show increases that are by and large bigger than the former. Moreover, the

Table 13.3   Productivity and employment, 1970–95

| | Sectoral indexes | | | | | |
| | Productivity (1980=100) | | | Employment (1980=100) | | |
	1982–87	1988–93	1988–95[1]	1982–87	1988–93	1988–95[1]
Total	98.10	111.74	126.64	105.7	111.6	110.2
Primary	104.31	104.73	122.71	104.44	105.01	99.3
Extractive	103.91	101.0	145.83	120.25	129.9	84.5
Food industry	102.25	113.46	139.01	108.45	113.3	106.7
Light industrial	103.87	109.53	123.93	94.44	91.9	103.6
Chemical and petrochemical	104.58	124.15	126.45	113.79	119.25	102.9
Metal industry	99.34	125.59	137.84	99.62	94.9	95.0
Motor cars and others	102.76	136.35	123.92	1.0	96.9	112.9
Non-tradables	100.06	104.64	114.97	109.0	115.7	114.0

Notes:
[1]GDP per worker and employment index, 1988=100, NIPA 1988–95.
Source: NIPA, 1970–95.

difference between the two right-hand columns suggests that productivity increases have been obtained at the expense of employment.

To what extent is this result to be attributed to exchange rate policies, or to the very conditions under which economic integration was undertaken? To approach this question it is necessary to discuss the behaviour of imports. The current hypothesis is that imports grew very rapidly due to the overvaluation of the domestic currency. The alternative hypothesis is that imports would have grown to such an extent anyway as a result of the removal of trade barriers under the NAFTA agreement, and even as a result simply of the expectation of NAFTA. There is evidence to support both hypotheses. The real exchange rate estimates made by the Banco de Mexico, the central bank, show that based on the 1988 level the exchange rate was 38 per cent overvalued by 1993. The rates of 1987 or 1988 could be considered as the equilibrium rates given the fact that those were the rates at which external trade was in balance. Under the same index the extent of overvaluation for 1994 is calculated to be 39.49 per cent. On the other hand, public officials argued that the pressures to obtain imported intermediate inputs were very high at any dollar valuation. Consequently, they preferred to stick to the pegged exchange rate under the pretext of controlling inflation. Nevertheless, the real impact of that policy was to introduce a violent distortion in prices which created particularly profitable conditions for sectors whose productive conditions rested heavily on imports. This is the case with the leading export and growth sectors mentioned before.

Another means of showing the essential characteristics of actual structural change is to observe the transformation in linkage coefficients. Considering total linkage coefficients for the Mexican economy, a large trend towards smaller and reducing linkages can be observed, particularly once the economy was open to free trade, as shown in Table 13.4.

Nevertheless, Table 13.4 also shows that the main drop in linkage coefficients is observed in the leading growth sectors, while they have increased in some inward-oriented sectors like agriculture. The question is: would those leading sectors have been able to grow as fast as they did had the exchange rate not been overvalued, or would a different pattern of integration between domestic producers and international suppliers have occurred? To answer this question, two factors have to be taken into account. The first is that throughout the period of

Table 13.4   Linkage coefficients totals, Mexican economy 1950–95

Sector	1950	1960	1970	1980	1985	1988	1990	1995[1]
Agriculture	1.48	1.56	1.85	1.82	1.77	2.29	1.99	1.99
Oil and gas	1.29	1.92	2.62	1.68	1.67	2.79	1.58	1.58
Food industry	1.2	1.33	1.29	1.27	1.13	1.76	1.16	1.16
Beer			1.13	1.10	1.046	1.056	1.06	1.05
Glass			1.91	1.85	1.77	1.77	1.62	1.49
Cement			2.12	1.98	1.92	2.08	1.82	1.81
Petrochemicals			3.28	2.936	4.45	4.057	2.66	2.61
Motor cars		1.18	1.12	1.12	1.075	1.064	1.038	1.016
Motor parts			2.23	2.17	1.603	1.367	1.44	1.283
Electricity	1.107	2.02	2.24	2.385	2.49	2.86	2.49	2.63
Transport, communications	1.17	1.51	1.52	1.44	1.49	1.20	1.406	1.404
Hotels, restaurants	1.00	1.15	1.21	1.22	1.218	1.17	1.22	1.25
Services	1.22	1.35	1.37	1.32	1.33	1.51	1.44	1.46
Retail	1.17	1.34	1.47	1.31	1.34	1.45	1.32	1.35
Average	2.308	1.69	1.80	1.745	1.711	1.84	1.627	1.61
Standard deviation	1.74	0.47	0.648	0.613	0.671	0.797	0.565	0.571

Note:
[1] Preliminary estimates on input–output matrices for 1990 and 1995, STATMAT, México 1990.
Source: Ortiz Etelberto, Competencia y crisis en la economía mexicana, ed., siglo XXI, México 1994, p. 139.

exchange rate overvaluation the economy suffered a loss caused by the total quantity and thereby the costs of imports. Evidence of this is also provided by the fact that import prices were increasing a lot faster than export prices. For certain industries, such as automobile parts, this was a rather strange situation because they were continually cutting their links with domestic Mexican producers and increasing their imports from their own suppliers. This was in fact done on the basis that the quality of goods produced by domestic producers was unsuitable for international standards necessary for export.[2] Second, these industries were able to make larger profits than otherwise, just by increasing their import of inputs. Therefore, those excess profits were associated with the external deficit.

FINANCIAL LIBERALIZATION AND ITS IMPACT ON THE ECONOMY

To improve the availability of funds for investment purposes, a programme of financial liberalization was introduced in 1988. This was mostly implemented through the privatization of the banking sector, the elimination of selective credit controls and changes in bank reserve requirements. The former was in line with the view that the private sector should be the main engine of growth and should be encouraged to take a more active role in economic activities. In addition, the government authorized the formation of financial groups whose members included large private business corporations, banks, insurance companies, stock exchange agencies and other intermediaries.

The sale of public banks at a price higher than the market value of banks not only increased the government's revenue, but also reduced its expenditures and helped to reduce the budget deficit. As can be seen from Table 13.5, from 1988 to 1992 the ratio of the public sector deficit to GDP steadily declined, and in 1992 the deficit turned into a

Table 13.5   Public finances as shares of GDP

End of period	Public sector balance	Total net debt of the public sector	Domestic debt	External debt
1988	−9.3	66	17	48.9
1993	0.7	24.4	5.5	18.9
1994	−0.3	24.8	4.3	20.5

Table 13.6   Gross national savings (GNS) and investment, GDP 1980–96

Year	Gross fixed investment	GNS saving[1]	External saving (functional)[2]	External saving (net)[3]	Public saving[3]	Private saving[4]
1980	24.75	23.01	1.74	1.17	−0.69	23.7
1981	26.85	24.88	1.97	4.91	−6.35	31.23
1988	18.5	21.3	−2.8	−7.7	−7.3	28.6
1989	17.2	18.3	−1.0	−5.8	−4.3	22.6
1990	17.9	17.8	0.01	−0.3	−1.0	18.8
1991	18.7	16.6	2.	3.3	0.5	16.2
1992	19.6	15.2	4.4	2.5	2.1	13.0
1993	18.6	15.3	3.3	6.1	1.2	14.1
1994	19.4	15.2	4.1	−2.9	0.87	14.4
1995	16.1	19.8	−3.6	−9.0	0.3	19.5
1996	18.6	24.8	−6.2	−5.2	−2.11	26.91

Notes:
[1] NIPA, 1980–96.
[2] Functional rate: trade deficit + net non-factor income interest received by domestic residents. Net rate: net debt + foreign investment − foreign debt service. Balance of Payments, 1980–96, El Banco de México.
[3] Estimated as public balance + inflation tax; SHCP and El Banco de México.
[4] Is obtained as a residual.

surplus. Over the same period, the ratio of both the domestic and external debt of the public sector to GDP declined, and the ratio of the total net debt of the public sector to GDP declined from 66 per cent in 1988 to 24.8 per cent in 1994.

Financial liberalization led to some rise in domestic bank savings, and an improvement in the bank savings ratio. The rise in bank deposits, however, was not sufficient to meet the domestic demand for investments, in spite of the fact that the rate of Gross Fixed Investment to GDP has been kept 5 to 7 points below its 1980–81 level. In fact a curious movement in the behaviour of savings can be observed, as can be seen in Table 13.6.

It is remarkable that throughout the period, both after the initial adjustments from 1983 and after the process of financial liberalization, the economy has been unable to increase its rate of investment to the levels attained before 1981, nor has it been possible to increase the rate of domestic savings. The rate of gross domestic savings and of private savings shows a consistent decline up to 1992. Thereafter, the flow induced by the huge payments of external debt increased the rate of domestic savings but not the rate of capital formation. Hence, overall it can be observed that the outcome of the model on the productive side resulted in the generation of a trade deficit, which evidently enforced a savings deficit. The trouble was that the financing of the model through external savings meant a decline in private savings, a very risky process leading to the over-exposure of the financial sector through a process of over-lending and excessive pressure on domestic interest rates. This in turn led to a very dangerous growth of bad debt.

In the early 1990s, economic recession in the USA and other industrialized countries forced US and other international interest rates below the Mexican market rate. The relaxation of capital controls in 1991 thus opened a window of opportunity for private banks to borrow at a cheaper rate on the international markets and use the funds for lending at a higher rate in the domestic market. Large private non-financial institutions also found it cheaper to borrow from the international markets. Thus, between 1991 and 1994 the external debt of both commercial banks and the private non-financial sector increased by 42.1 and 131.4 per cent respectively. Overall, as mentioned earlier, from 1988 to 1994, while the external debt of the public sector increased by 5.4 per cent, that of the commercial banks and private non-bank sector increased by 246.6 and 221.8 per cent respectively.

Between 1988 and 1994, while interest payments on external debt by the Bank of Mexico declined from $0.4 billion to $0.2 billion, that of the non-financial private sector increased from $0.9 billion in 1988 to $2.2 billion in 1994, which is an increase of 144 per cent. The increase in interest payments on the external debt of commercial banks was even higher, rising from $0.5 billion in 1988 to $1.6 billion in 1994, which amounts to an increase of 220 per cent. The relaxation of capital controls also led to a significant rise in portfolio investment. From 1990 to 1991, while direct investment increased from $2.6 billion in 1990 to $4.8 billion in 1991, portfolio investment increased from $3.4 billion to $12.8 billion. The increase in portfolio investment continued in the following years and increased to $18.0 billion in 1992 and $28.9 billion in 1993. The rise in portfolio investment also contributed to the significant rise in the total amount of funds traded on the stock market, increasing from $5.2 billion in 1991 to $14.4 billion in 1993.

At the time when economic growth in Mexico came to a halt the trade deficit was still growing, and yet the government was reluctant to abandon the flotation band exchange rate regime. In 1993, while the trade deficit amounted to $13.5 billion, interest payments on foreign debt were $7.9 billion, and portfolio investment denominated in pesos amounted to $18.1 billion. This critical situation further deteriorated in 1994, when on the one hand uncertainty about the political climate increased the risks of investment in Mexico, and on the other hand the rise in US interest rates provided international investors with a new investment opportunity at a lower risk. The rise in US interest rates not only increased the cost of debt repayments for Mexican commercial banks and the private sector, but also reduced the price of Brady bonds, which was inversely related to yields on very-long-term bonds in the United States. These bonds were mostly bought by US investment funds which had invested in Mexico. As reported by the Bank of Mexico, the fall in the price of the above bonds compelled the investment funds to sell their most liquid assets, which were CETES. These factors increased the expectation of a forthcoming devaluation, and led to a growing capital outflow from mid 1994 that put an unbearable pressure on foreign exchange reserves. From the beginning of January 1994 to 20 December 1994, international reserves dropped by $19.124 billion (US dollars), and the real exchange rate, based on consumer prices, depreciated by 15.9 per cent. The extent of this fall was most significant during November and December 1994 when international reserves dropped by $4.758 billion and $6.630 billion respectively. All of this led to a 54.35 per cent depreciation of the nominal market exchange rate between November and December 1994, and an 83.33 per cent depreciation for the whole year between January 1994 to January 1995.

Thus, it can be seen that though financial liberalization was intended to improve the domestic mobilization of funds and improve investment opportunities, it was of little help in raising overall savings and investment ratios. Moreover, it mostly led to an increase in the private sector's foreign borrowing, and erratic short-term capital flows. Thus, once again the economy was exposed to risks associated with the fluctuation of interest rates and foreign exchange rates in the international financial markets.

CONCLUSION

The main conclusion of this chapter is that the whole package of policies, although leading to a degree of progress in certain areas, not only failed to achieve its principal goals but in some respects actually undermined them.

There is no doubt that the new model has been successful in creating a new linkage with the world economy, particularly with the US, but the whole approach has not resulted in the creation of a self-sufficient model of growth. Undoubtedly Mexico now has a considerably greater capacity to export manufactured goods than before, particularly within NAFTA. The problem is that the quantity of imports has increased to such an extent that the net gains from trade are not evident. This is particularly the case given that, taking the economy as a whole, the so-called leading sectors have had very little impact on growth and structural transformation. The winners from this model have been but a few sectors, in which productivity gains can by and large be explained in terms of changes in relative prices and job losses. The key determinant of their success is a stable exchange rate rather than rising incomes in the economy.

The rest of the economy has achieved low rates of growth, except for the food industry, which can partly be explained by exports of beer. Characteristically, such sectors rest their competitive strategies on low wages, but are nevertheless the main source of employment in manufacturing, just as in the old days of import substituting industrialization.

The new economic model demanded the creation of a rather comprehensive set of institutional arrangements, which can not be reduced to NAFTA. In fact it was well backed by the deregulation of economic activities, labour markets and the central bank, as well as by programmes of privatization and financial liberalization. It is thus essential to observe that from an orthodox perspective the Mexican experience was conceived as a coherent project, particularly in terms of the construction of a new institutional framework for the model. Therefore, the current crisis cannot be explained in terms of *'insufficient'* institutional support. The answer lies instead in the incoherence of the 'new' institutional framework relative to the needs of the actual economic model, given that the priority is to generate self-sustaining growth. Therefore, the problem is in the *nature* of the new institutionality, as a framework unable to accommodate a model of growth that is coherent in its own terms.

Our remarks point to the limitations of the actual results, particularly as regards the characteristics of the structural transformation so far achieved: the leading growth sectors, which are seen as the engines of growth, have established strong linkages with the international economy but rather weak linkages within the Mexican economy. The result is a new 'dual economy' within the 'modern' sector: one part with a strong impact in the balance of trade but a weak impact on employment; another loosely related to the world economy, with a high impact on employment but extremely sensitive to low wages. This characteristic has consequences on two levels:

1. *Social*: the model, even in periods of growth, does not respond to the needs for employment and social development in a society with a strong expectation of social integration.
2. *Financial*: the model is not viable in spite of growing exports, because the profitability of the leading sectors rests on the need to create external deficits, both on current account and as regards savings.

It is unsurprising that the discussion concerning the recent crisis followed two conflicting lines of argument:

1. The core of the recent crisis, the central bank and the Ministry of Finance argue, is a short-run financial problem, solely attributable to mistakes in the management of the exchange rate. The presumption here is that the basic model of growth is working properly.
2. For the objective of long-term growth, the core of the model is essentially contradictory, since recurrent balance of payments and financial crises have turned out to be a common feature. Moreover, this model necessarily rests on the creation of a new dual economy.

Nevertheless, some of those who adhere to the first position put the blame for the recent crisis on the failure to accelerate further institutional changes, for example pushing for more 'flexibility' in labour markets. In this view the problem derives not from the inadequacy of ongoing institutional changes, but the failure to implement more of the same thing. However, it is also necessary to pursue a new and different line of thought, not alien to mainstream economists, by posing the question: is it possible to conceive of an institutional framework that is more attractive for investment than the one already constructed?[3] According to this analysis there are a host of elements comprising the kind of institutional framework that is essential to the stability of a fully-fledged neoclassical model, such as labour contracts, social welfare provision and so forth. Therefore, a case can be made for a more well-conceived institutional framework to enhance capital accumulation, which is reduced neither to 'liberalization' nor 'deregulation'.

But in our view, new institutions for a more stable growth model should include a prohibition on increasing public debt for the purpose of financing balance of payments deficits, which as seen are essential for the generation of profits in a few productive sectors, but at the expense of the rest of the country. New economic institutions should take into account the need for internal integration as well as external, competitive integration. A truly positive international framework for economic development demands the recognition of a community of interests, such that the means exist to confront balance of payments crises and structural disequilibria which erode the stability of trade and overall development. A realistic and complete institutional framework should have built-in institutional arrangements to ease the social costs of adjustment, particularly in respect to labour.

Nevertheless, there is not a single instrument within NAFTA offering a solution to any of these problems. The recent crisis showed just how fragile the payments system is, as well as the lack of systematic, reliable instruments for adjustment purposes. Needless to say the intervention by the Clinton administration in response to the crisis cannot be considered a solid mechanism to solve future problems of payments within NAFTA.

Therefore, the emphasis in this chapter has been on the failure of economic policies to address fundamental weaknesses in the Mexican economy, and their inadequacy in providing a fully coherent approach to the already accepted strategy.

Notes

1. A negative effective rate of protection occurs when the nominal rate of protection on inputs is so high that protection on inputs is higher than on the final product. It means a negative real value added.
2. But there is also another argument, that they might have been over-invoicing their intra-firm trade.
3. See Hahn and Solow (1996).

References

Bairoch, P. (1996) 'Globalization Myths and Realities: One Century of External Trade and Foreign Investment', in R. Boyer and D. Drache (eds), *States Against Markets* (New York: Routledge).

Bueno, G. (1960) 'La estructura de proteccion en Mexico', mimeo.

Garrido, C. (1995) 'The Mexican Financial System in the Nineties', UAM working paper.

Hahn, F. and Solow, R. (1995) *A Critical Essay on Modern Macroeconomic Theory* (London: Blackwell).

Tybout, J.R. and Westbrook, M.D. (1995) 'Trade Liberalization and the Dimensions of Efficiency Change in Mexican Manufacturing Industries', *Journal of International Economics*, vol. 39, pp. 53–78.

Official Publications

Cuentas Nacionales, INEGI, 1970–95.
International Financial Statistics, published by the IMF (1985–95).
Mexican Bulletin of Statistical Information, no. 13, July–September 1994.
The Mexican Economy, 1995, El Banco De Mexico.
Indicadores Economicos, El Banco de Mexico. Junio 1996.

Index

Note: 'n.' after a page reference indicates the number of a note on that page.

227